BUDA'S WAGON

BUDA'S WAGON

A Brief History of the Car Bomb

MIKE DAVIS

VERSO

London • New York

First published by Verso 2007
© Mike Davis 2007
All rights reserved

The moral right of the author has been asserted

1 3 5 7 9 10 8 6 4 2

Verso
UK: 6 Meard Street, London W1F 0EG
USA: 180 Varick Street, New York, NY 10014–4606
www.versobooks.com

Verso is the imprint of New Left Books

ISBN-13: 978-1-84467-132-8

British Library Cataloguing in Publication Data
A catalogue record for this book is available from the British Library

Library of Congress Cataloging-in-Publication Data
A catalog record for this book is available from the Library of Congress

Typeset in Bembo by Hewer Text UK Ltd, Edinburgh
Printed and bound in Germany by GGP Media GmbH

To Tom Engelhardt, friend extraordinaire

Contents

List of Illustrations

How can you sleep with death just around the corner?

Chechen warning

Figure 1   Mario Buda's Wall Street bombing, September 1920.

1

Wall Street 1920

> You have shown no pity to us! We will do likewise.
> *We will dynamite you!*
>
> Anarchist warning (1919) [1]

On a warm September day in 1920, a few months after the arrest of his comrades Nicola Sacco and Bartolomeo Vanzetti ("the best friends I have in America"), a vengeful Italian immigrant anarchist named Mario Buda parked his horse-drawn wagon near the corner of Wall and Broad streets, next to the new federal Assay Office and directly across from J.P. Morgan and Company. The Morgan partners, including the great Thomas Lamont and Dwight Morrow (Charles Lindbergh's future father-in-law), were discussing weighty financial matters in a lower-floor conference room. Perhaps Buda tipped his cap in the direction of the unsuspecting robber barons before he nonchalantly climbed down and disappeared unnoticed into the lunchtime crowd. A few blocks away, a startled letter-carrier found strange, crudely printed leaflets warning: "Free the Political Prisoners or it Will Be Sure Death for All of You!" They were signed: "American Anarchist Fighters."

Buda, aka "Mike Boda," was a veteran supporter of Luigi Galleani, anarchist theorist and editor of *Cronaca Sovversiva* ("Sub-versive Chronicle") which the Department of Justice in 1918 had condemned as "the most dangerous newspaper in this country." The Galleanisti (probably never more than 50 or 60 hardcore activists) were chief suspects in various dynamite plots, including the notorious Preparedness Day bombing in San Francisco in 1916 (for which union organizers Tom Mooney and Warren Billings were framed) and the letter bombs sent to prominent members of the Wilson administration as well as J.P. Morgan and John D. Rockefeller in June 1919. The *Cronaca Sovversiva* reading circles that met in the shadows of Paterson silk factories and Youngstown steel mills – not unlike certain contemporary Quran study groups in gritty neighborhoods of Brooklyn and south London – were lightning rods for immigrant alienation; an alienation that grew into rage in the face of wartime anti-foreign hysteria, which resulted in the so-called Palmer Raids in 1919 against radicals of all denominations. When Attorney General A. Mitchell Palmer signed Galleani's deportation order in February 1919, anonymous flyers appeared in New England factories promising to "annihilate" the deporters "in blood and fire."

As Buda, who had appointed himself the avenging angel of the imprisoned and deported anarchists, made his escape from Wall Street, the bells of nearby Trinity Church began to toll noon. Before they had stopped, the wagon packed with high explosive (probably blasting gelatin stolen from a tunnel construction site) and iron slugs erupted in a huge ball of fire, leaving a large crater in Wall Street. Windows exploded in the faces of office workers, pedestrians were mowed down by metal shrapnel or scythed by shards of glass, building awnings and parked cars caught fire, and a suffocating cloud of smoke and debris enshrouded Wall Street. Skyscrapers quickly emptied. Panicked crowds fled past crumpled bodies on the sidewalks, some of them writhing in agony. On the treeless street, green leaves bearing presidents' portraits – some of the estimated $80,000 in cash abandoned by terrified or wounded bank messengers – fluttered with each choking gust of wind and ash. No one knew whether more explosions would follow, and frightened authorities suspended trading at the Stock Exchange for the first time in history.

An attack on Wall Street, of course, was immediately construed as a national emergency. One hundred regular soldiers, rifles loaded and bayonets fixed, were sent quickly from Governor's Island to guard the badly damaged Assay Office and adjacent Subtreasury, while America's chief sleuth, William Flynn, the head of the (federal) Bureau of Investigation, was dispatched from Washington on the first available train. Over the next few days, the NYPD's Detective Bureau assembled the grotesque remains of an "infernal machine": a horse's head, some severed hoofs, and the twisted metal of a wagon axle. Anarchists, the IWW, and the new-fangled Bolsheviki all automatically became suspect and the *New York Times* soon screamed "Red Plot Seen in Blast." While police and federal investigators focused on 'celebrity' Reds such as labor-organizer Carlo Tresca, Buda quietly made his way home to Italy. (It is unknown whether other Galleanisti participated in the organization of the bombing or whether Buda was an astonishing one-man show.)

Meanwhile, the coroner was counting 40 dead (some mangled beyond recognition), with more than 200 injured including Equitable Trust's president Alvin Krech and J. P. Morgan Jr's son Junius. Joseph P. Kennedy, walking in the street, was badly shaken but unharmed. Buda was undoubtedly disappointed when he learned that "Jack" Morgan himself was away in Scotland at his hunting lodge, and that his partners Lamont and Morrow were unscathed. Nonetheless, a poor immigrant with some stolen dynamite, a pile of scrap metal, and an old horse had managed to bring unprecedented terror to the inner sanctum of American capitalism.

2

Poor Man's Air Force

A complex weapon makes the strong stronger, while a simple
weapon – so as long as there is no answer to it – gives claws to the
weak.

George Orwell[1]

Buda's Wall Street bomb (perhaps inspired by the infamous horse-
cart device that almost killed Napoleon in the Rue Saint Nicaise in
Paris in 1800)[2] was the culmination of a half-century of anarchist
fantasies about blowing up kings and plutocrats. But it was also an
invention, like Charles Babbage's Difference Engine, far ahead of
the imagination of its time. The truly radical potential of the
"infernal machine" would be fully realized only after the barbarism
of strategic bombing had become commonplace, and after air forces
routinely pursued insurgents into the labyrinths of poor cities.
Buda's wagon, in essence, was the prototype car bomb: the first
modern use of an inconspicuous vehicle, anonymous in almost any
urban setting, to transport large quantities of high explosive into
precise range of a high-value target.

Despite some improvisations (mostly failed) in the 1920s and
1930s, the car bomb was not fully conceptualized as a weapon of
urban warfare until January 12, 1947, when rightwing Zionist
guerrillas, the Stern Gang, drove a truckload of explosives into a
British police station in Haifa, Palestine, killing 4 and injuring 140.
The Stern Gang, soon joined by the paramilitaries of the Irgun from

whom they had split back in 1940, would subsequently use truck and car bombs to kill Palestinians as well: a creative atrocity that was immediately reciprocated by British deserters fighting on the Arab side. (Fifty years later, *jihadis* training in Al Qaeda camps in Afghanistan would study Menachem Begin's *Revolt*, a memoir of the Irgun, as a classic handbook of successful terrorism.)[3]

Vehicle bombs thereafter were employed sporadically: producing notable massacres in Saigon (1952), Algiers and Oran (1962), Palermo (1963), and again in Saigon (1964–66). But the gates of hell were not truly opened until four undergraduates, protesting campus collaboration with the Vietnam War, exploded the first ammonium nitrate-fuel oil (ANFO) car bomb in front of the University of Wisconsin's Army Mathematics Research Center in August 1970. Two years later ("Bloody Friday," July 21, 1972) the Provisional IRA devastated the business center of Belfast with a series of such devices. These new-generation bombs, requiring only ordinary industrial ingredients and synthetic fertilizer, were cheap to fabricate and astonishingly powerful: they elevated urban terrorism from the artisan to the industrial level and made possible sustained blitzes against entire city centers as well as causing the complete destruction of ferro-concrete skyscrapers and residential blocks.

The car bomb, in other words, suddenly became a semi-strategic weapon that under certain circumstances was comparable to airpower in its ability to knock out critical urban nodes and headquarters as well as terrorize populations of entire cities. Indeed, the suicide truck bombs that devastated the US embassy and Marine barracks in Beirut in 1983 prevailed over the combined firepower of the fighter-bombers and battleships of the US Sixth Fleet and forced the Reagan administration to undertake a humiliating retreat from Lebanon. Other suicide car-bombings played a crucial role in dislodging the supposedly all-powerful Israeli Defense Forces from the Shiite-majority region of southern Lebanon.

Hezbollah's ruthless and brilliant use of car bombs in Lebanon in the 1980s to counter the advanced military technology of the United States and Israel soon emboldened a dozen other groups to bring their insurgencies and *jihads* home to the metropolis. Many of the new-generation car bombers were graduates of the sabotage and explosives courses set up by the CIA and Pakistani Inter-Services Intelligence (ISI), with Saudi financing, in the mid-1980s to train *mujahedin* to terrorize the Russians then occupying Kabul. Others learned their skills at training camps sponsored by other governments (India and Iran, especially), or simply cribbed the requisite formulas from explosives manuals in widespread circulation in the United States.

The result has been the irreversible globalization of car-bombing know-how. Like an implacable virus, once vehicle bombs have entered the DNA of a host society and its contradictions, their use tends to reproduce indefinitely. Between 1992 and 1999, 25 major vehicle bomb attacks in 22 different cities killed 1337 people and wounded nearly 12,000. More importantly from a geopolitical standpoint, the Provisional IRA and a Brooklyn cell of the Egyptian Islamist group, al-Gama'a al-Islamiyya, inflicted billions of dollars of damage on the two leading control-centers of the world economy – the City of London (1992, 1993, and 1996) and lower Manhattan (1993), respectively – and forced a reorganization of the global reinsurance industry.[4]

In the new millennium, almost 90 years after that first massacre on Wall Street, car bombs have become as generically global as i-Pods and HIV/AIDS, cratering the streets of cities from Bogotá to Mumbai and frightening tourists away from many of the world's most famous islands and resorts. Car bombers are currently or recently active in at least 23 countries, while another 35 nations have suffered at least one fatal car-bombing during the last quarter-century.[5] In sheer number, the historical total of all car-bombings in Western Europe is probably neck and neck with that of the Middle East, followed at some distance by South Asia, then South America, North Africa, sub-Saharan Africa, and North America. (East Asia, uniquely, has been so far immune to exploding Toyotas and booby-trapped Datsuns.) Suicide truck bombs, once the exclusive signature of Hezbollah, now have been franchised to Sri Lanka, Chechnya/Russia, Saudi Arabia, Turkey, Egypt, Kuwait, Palestine, Indonesia, and Afghanistan. On any graph of urban terrorism, the curve representing car bombs is rising steeply, almost exponentially.

US-occupied Iraq, of course, has become the global epicenter: a savage inferno with more than 9000 casualties – mainly civilian – attributed to vehicle bombs in the two-year period between July 2003 and June 2005. Since then, the frequency of car-bomb attacks has dramatically increased: there were 140 per month in fall 2005 and 13 in Baghdad on New Year's Day 2006 alone.[6] If roadside mines remain the most effective device against American armored vehicles, car bombs are the weapon of choice for slaughtering Shiite civilians in front of mosques and markets and thus instigating an endless cycle of sectarian warfare. Although the car-bomb factories of Baghdad and Fallujah will undoubtedly sustain their record outputs for some time to come, the most rapid increase in the incidence of car-bombings has occurred in Afghanistan since early 2006. In country where the *mujahedin* formerly eschewed such suicide tactics, *kamikaze* car-bomb attacks on NATO convoys or police loyal to the regime of President Hamid Karzai are now almost daily events.

Under siege from weapons indistinguishable from ordinary traffic, the core apparatuses of administration and finance are retreating inside "rings of steel" and "Green Zones," but the larger challenge of the car bomb remains patently intractable. Stolen nukes, sarin gas, and anthrax may be the sum of our fears, just as malevolent "net-wars" and "swarming" are the abstract icons of postmodern strategic theory,[7] but vehicle bombs are the brutal hardware and quotidian workhorses of urban terrorism. It is the car bombers' incessant blasting-away at the moral and physical shell of the city, not the more apocalyptic threats of nuclear or bioterrorism, that is producing the most significant mutations in city form and urban lifestyle.

The car bomb, therefore, like any triumphant modern technology, deserves its proper history, with particular attention paid to key technical and tactical innovations. Table 1 is a roadmap of the brief history that will follow, enumerating some of the critical thresholds in the car bomb's evolution toward lethal universality. Before considering its genealogy however, it may be helpful to

Table 1   Car Bombs: Lethal Thresholds

Innovation	Date	Place	Group
1. modern prototype	1920	Manhattan	Italian anarchist
2. truck bomb	1947	Haifa	Stern Gang
3. multiple car bombs	1948	Jerusalem	Palestinians
4. hybrid: car bomb plus other explosives	1964	Saigon	Viet Cong
5. used against embassy	1965	Saigon	Viet Cong
6. ammonium nitrate/fuel oil (ANFO) bomb	1970	Madison	"New Year's Gang"
7. economic warfare	1972	Belfast	IRA
8. deaths in excess of 100	1981	Damascus	Moslem Brotherhood
9. *kamikaze* truck bomb	1981	Beirut (Iraqi embassy)	Syria?
11. attack video-recorded	1982	Beirut	Hezbollah
10. 1-ton TNT equivalent	1983	Beirut (US embassy)	Hezbollah?
12. major geopolitical impact[8]	1983	Beirut (Marines)	Hezbollah
13. female suicide car bomber	1985	Lebanon	SSNP
14. used in regular military attack	1985	Sri Lanka	Tamil Tigers
15. mass technology transfer	1985 onward	Pakistan	CIA/Pakistani ISI
16. targeting tourism	late 1980s	Corsica	FLNC
17. entire neighborhood	1992	Lima	Sendero Luminoso
18. cultural heritage	1993	Italy	Mafia
19. more than $1 billion damage	1993	London	IRA
20. against voters	1995	Johannesburg	white supremacists
21. 5-ton TNT equivalent	1996	Dhahran	Hezbollah/Iran?
22. simultaneous, several cities	1998	E. Africa	Al Qaeda
23. "with wings"	2001	Manhattan	Al Qaeda
24. nearly starts nuclear war	2001	New Delhi	Pakistani ISI?
25. more than 500 fatal bombings	2003–06	Iraq	various

summarize those salient characteristics that make Buda's wagon the "poor man's air force" *par excellence.*

First, vehicle bombs are stealth weapons of surprising power and destructive efficiency. Trucks and vans can easily deliver the explosive equivalent of the bomb load of a B-24 (the workhorse heavy bomber of the Army Air Forces in World War Two) to the doorstep of a prime target.[9] Even the average family SUV with 10 cubic feet of cargo space can transport a 1000-pound bomb.[10] Moreover, the destructive power of such weapons is still evolving, thanks to the constant tinkering of ingenious bombmakers, and we have yet to face the full horror of semi-trailer-size explosions equivalent to 60 tons of TNT with a lethal blast range of 200 yards or dirty bombs sheathed in enough nuclear waste to render mid-Manhattan radioactive for generations. In addition, the entire range of transport technology, from bicycles and rickshaws to containers, ships, and airliners, offers customized variations on the same fundamental principle: the September 11 attacks were conceived by their chief planner, Khalid Sheikh Mohammed, as a scaled-up version of his nephew Ramzi Yousef's 1993 van-bombing of the World Trade Center.[11]

Second, car bombs are "loud" in every sense. In addition to their specific operational functions (killing enemies, disrupting daily life, generating unsustainable economic costs, and so on), such explosions are usually advertisements for a cause, leader or abstract principle (including Terror itself). To borrow a striking phrase from Régis Debray, they are "manifestos written in the blood of others."[12] In contrast to other forms of political propaganda, from graffiti on walls to individual assassinations, their occurrence is almost impossible to deny or censor. This certainty of being heard by the world, even in a highly authoritarian or isolated setting, is a major attraction to potential bombers.

Third, car bombs are extraordinarily cheap: 40 or 50 people can be massacred with a stolen car and approximately $500 of fertilizer and bootlegged electronics. Ramzi Yousef, the mastermind of the 1993 attack that caused an estimated $1 billion damage to Manhattan's World Trade Center, bragged that his most expensive outlays were long-distance phone calls: the explosive itself (one half ton of urea) cost $3615 plus the $59 per day rental for a ten-foot-long Ryder van. Timothy McVeigh, likewise, spent less than $5000 on fertilizer, racing fuel, and van rental fees to blast the front wall off the Alfred P. Murrah Federal Building and kill 168 people in Oklahoma City in 1995. In contrast, the cruise missiles that have become the classic American riposte to overseas terrorist attacks cost nearly $1 million each.[13]

Fourth, car-bombings are operationally simple to organize. Although some still refuse to believe that the pair didn't have secret assistance from some government or dark entity, two men in the proverbial phone booth – that is to say, Timothy McVeigh, a security guard, and Terry Nichols, a farmer – successfully planned and executed the Oklahoma City atrocity with bombmaking manuals and word–of–mouth know–how acquired from the gun–show circuit. In response to this atrocity, Congress in 1996 passed anti–terrorist legislation that mandated the Justice Department "to determine just how easy it was for terrorists and others to find bomb–making instructions." The investigators were horrified when "a cursory search of the holdings of the Library of Congress located at least 50 publications [such as *Advanced Techniques for Making Explosives and Time-delay Bombs*] substantially devoted to such information, all readily available to any member of the public interested in reading them and copying their contents."[14] The esoteric knowledge once imparted in Afghan *madrasas* or CIA-sponsored training camps is also available on–line from *jihadi* websites (the notorious "Irhabi 007," now arrested, offered a how–to–make–a–car–bomb Powerpoint presentation on his site) and even via Amazon.com.[15]

Fifth, like even the "smartest" of aerial bombs, car bombs are inherently indiscriminate: "collateral damage" is virtually inevitable. If the logic of an attack is to slaughter civilians and sow panic in the widest circle, to operate a "strategy of tension" or just demoralize a society, car bombs are ideal. But they are equally effective at destroying the moral credibility of a cause and alienating its mass base of support, as both the IRA in Northern Ireland and ETA in Spain have independently discovered. As we shall see later, the imprisoned Nelson Mandela was perspicacious indeed when he polemicized against the employment of such weapons by the South African freedom movement. The car bomb, when all is said and done, is an inherently fascist weapon guaranteed to leave its perpetrators awash in the blood of innocents. (This categorical censure, of course, applies even more forcefully to the mass terror against civilian populations routinely inflicted by the air forces and armies of so–called "democracies" like the United States, the United Kingdom, France, and Israel.)

Sixth, car bombs are highly anonymous and leave minimal forensic evidence. Buda basked unmolested in the sunshine of his native Romagna (where he supposedly switched camps and become a spy for Mussolini), leaving William Flynn, J. Edgar Hoover, and the Bureau of Investigation (which later became the FBI) to make fools of themselves as they chased one false lead after another for more than a decade. Most of Buda's descendants have also escaped identification and arrest. Anonymity, in addition, greatly recommends car bombs to those who like to disguise their handiwork, including the CIA, the British SAS, the Soviet KGB, the Israeli Mossad, the Syrian GSD, the Lebanese Army's "Foreign Work and Analysis Unit," the Iranian Pasdaran, and the Pakistani ISI – all of whom have caused unspeakable carnage with such devices. Ironically the classical "weapon of the weak" is also the most popular clandestine instrument of terror employed by strong governments and superpowers.

Yet – point *seven* – the most dramatic impact of the car bomb has been precisely its enfranchisement of marginal actors in modern history. Vehicle bombs offer extraordinary socio-political leverage to small, even ad hoc groups without significant constituencies or mass political legitimacy. Poorly equipped and unpopular conspiracies that otherwise would ferment in darkness or blow up in the faces of their organizers now possess a simple and reliable DIY arsenal for wreaking spectacular destruction. Car bombs also give sharper "claws" (in the Orwellian sense) to resistance groups with genuine popular support, like Hezbollah or the Provisional IRA. Whatever the case, no other weapon in the history of warfare has proven to be such a promiscuous equalizer of combat between elephants and fleas.

Car bombs, in other words, increasingly define what Pentagon pundits call "fourth-generation" or "open-source" warfare. Indeed some counter-terrorism theorists, notably John Robb and Martin Shubik, claim that globalization's technological "super-empowerment" of destructive individuals has produced an epochal revolution in the lethality of small groups and networks.[16] This revolution, moreover, takes the form of a seamless merger of technologies: the car bomb *plus* the cell phone *plus* the Internet together constitute a unique infrastructure for *global networked terrorism* that obviates any need for transnational command structures or vulnerable hierarchies of decision-making. Cells or clones can now synchronize car-bomb attacks across continents without any personal contact or obligatory commander-in-chief.

Likewise protagonists of the *Machine infernale* no longer have to wait for the enemy media to report their explosions and interpret their manifestos: "propagandists of the deed," thanks to video and Internet, have become exactly that. With the World Wide Web, car bombers are now hip *auteurs* who film, edit and then videostream images of their atrocities for maximum impact on target audiences. As Debray, a famed theorist of guerrilla warfare in the 1960s now turned into a guru of Médiologie, has argued, 'terrorism' and propaganda have always coevolved ("escalade concomitante de l'informatif and de l'explosif"): from the guillotine and the semaphore in the days of Robespierre to dynamite and the telegraph in the 1880s, and now to car bombs and their websites in the world of Bush and bin Laden.[17]

3

Preliminary Detonations

A great cloud of black smoke was rolling up. Under it, I saw the
tangled remains of a car. Part of a human body was caught in the
steering wheel. Three or four other bodies were lying on the
ground near by.

witness, Bath (Michigan), May 1927[1]

During the interwar years, exploding sedans, reduced to molten
metal by bombs hidden in their engine compartments or under-
neath their frames, became a sophisticated signature of professional
mob and political assassinations in the United States. A superficial
perusal of the *New York Times Index* shows the geographically-
concentrated popularity of such devices in the New York–New
Jersey region, although other "car bombs" were reported in Mary-
land, California, and Europe. Surprisingly less ingenuity was applied
to using vehicles as delivery systems to create deadly explosions in
public spaces. ("Car bomb" will be used throughout this book as a
synonym for what the Pentagon officially calls a VBIED: Vehicle
Borne Improvised Explosive Device. When used generically, "car
bomb" will include van and truck bombs as well, but not vehicles
booby-trapped exclusively to kill their occupants.) Nonetheless, car
bombs *sensu stricto* were spontaneously improvised on several
occasions by revolutionary groups in Catalonia and Cuba, as well
as by one of the most monstrous serial-killers in American history.
    The motorization of Buda's deadly wagon was first undertaken by

Catalan anarcho-syndicalists on April 24, 1921, just seven months after the Wall Street bombing. Barcelona, in fact, was the killing field of early postwar Europe, with an estimated 900 political murders in the city and its environs between 1918 and 1923.[2] Following the military repression of the 1919 general strike, mercenary gunmen organized by the reactionary Captain-General Jaime Milans del Bosch and paid by the Employers' Federation systematically eradicated the leadership of the stubbornly militant Confederacíon Nacional del Trabajo (CNT). In return, anarchist *pistoleros* such as the extraordinary Buenaventura Durruti and his comrade Francisco Ascaso replied with daring *atentados* against the bosses and generals. It was in the course of this grim spiral of assassination and revenge that some supporters of the CNT conceived of blowing up a military parade with a stolen taxi laden with high explosives.

According to Barcelona writer Marc Viaplana, who has researched the incident:

> On April 24, a sunny Sunday, three *camaradas* hijacked a cab, loaded it with a big pharmacy mortar or iron bell filled with explosives, and tried to deliver it C.O.D. to the officers on parade. There are two versions of what took place: In one account the driverless cab was sent careening toward the parade but instead struck a streetlamp; in the other telling, the conspirators parked the vehicle as close to the procession as possible and lit the fuse. In either event, the device failed to explode and the taxi was eventually towed away by an armored wagon to the official explosives' disposal area. (Barcelona didn't gain its nickname of "City of Bombs" for nothing!)[3]

The next iteration of the car bomb was unfortunately more successful. In contrast to the deeds of his infamous contemporaries, Leopold and Loeb, or to such modern disciples of the devil as Manson and McVeigh, the ghastly crime of Andrew Kehoe, a Michigan farmer and school-board official is curiously repressed in the national memory. Yet Kehoe, who blew up the Bath Consolidated School with dynamite and then car-bombed the survivors in May 1927, retains the macabre distinction of being the greatest mass murderer of children (38) in American history.

The core of Kehoe's rage was the obsession that his personal financial difficulties – which culminated in the bank foreclosure on his farm in 1927 – were the result of local taxes levied to build the modern school in Bath, a hamlet near the state capital of Lansing. After unsuccessfully opposing campus construction as elected school treasurer, in 1926 Kehoe connived to have the board appoint him as the new school's handyman.

According to historian Debra Pawlak,

> He used his new position to get revenge. For months, he traveled from store to store, in and around Lansing, purchasing small amounts of explosives, which he took to the school. There, he developed an intricate wiring system connecting the carefully laid dynamite beneath the floor and in the walls and rafters of the Bath Consolidated School. By May of the following year [1927], he had laid thousands of feet of wire linking over one thousand pounds of dynamite, which he planned to detonate with a clock. Not a man to leave loose ends, Kehoe also rigged the buildings on his farm.
>
> On May 17, 1927, Kehoe put his painstaking plan into action. First, he filled the back seat of his pickup truck with old tools, nails, shovels and any other metal materials he could find. On top of the junk, he placed a package of dynamite. Next, he laid a loaded rifle on the front seat. Then, he murdered his wife.[4]

The next morning, at about 8:45 a.m., Kehoe set off the explosives around his farm. Not quite an hour later, while frantic neighbors were still dousing flames and worrying about the fate of the Kehoes, the village was shaken by a terrifying explosion at the school. Despite Kehoe's meticulous planning, however, only half of the huge cache of dynamite actually detonated. The school's north wing, housing the third through sixth grades, collapsed, burying children and their teachers in the ruins, while the south wing, which included the first and second grades, was largely spared. "The villagers came running," reported the *New York Times*, "and at once started the work of rescue . . . The workers brought scores of the 90 trapped children, moaning and shrieking, out of the ruins in their arms. The piercing lamentations of mothers added to the heartrending cries of the sufferers and the terror-stricken screams of children."[5]

After about twenty minutes, Kehoe pulled up to the front of the school and got out to talk with the school superintendant. Suddenly, he took a rifle from the truck and fired into the back seat full of dynamite and metal scrap. "There was a flash and a roar," said the *Times* correspondent, "and Kehoe was hurled through the air, his body dismembered." Three other adults, including the superintendant, were also blown to bits as well as an 8-year-old survivor of the original carnage. In total, Kehoe had massacred 45 people, mainly children, and grievously injured another 45 or 50 more.[6] Eighty years later, the survivors and their descendants still recall the horror of that warm spring day on a memorial website.

Kehoe, of course, was a diabolical amateur, but the next essay in car-bombing enjoyed academic expertise. In the early 1930s Havana had replaced Barcelona as the city most frequently serenaded by concerts of dynamite: indeed the Catalan model of terrorism was greatly admired in Havana, although here the bombmakers were younger members of the bourgeoisie rather than starving proletarians. At the beginning of 1931 the dictator Gerardo Machado and his death squads had crushed the oppositional Student Directory at Havana University and driven professors and students into increasingly violent underground resistance. The radical but anti-Communist wing of the opposition, mainly middle-class students and older professionals, regrouped around a secret terrorist society known as the "ABC" because of its hierarchical structure (each member of an "A" cell organized a "B" cell, and so forth).[7]

By the summer of 1932, bombings had become a daily occurrence in the capital and the ABC had managed to kill Captain Calvo, chief of the so-called *expertos*, Machado's dread torturers. "No government official or sympathizer," wrote the wife of the *New York Times*'s Havana correspondent, "was safe from bombing and attacks. Armored cars were hurriedly imported and constructed as a mode of transportation. The Government killed students in revenge and the situation became generally complicated."[8]

In April 1933 the increasingly desperate regime cracked down hard on the social base of the ABC: murdering 6 student leaders (an application of the notorious *ley de fuga* in which fleeing suspects were shot in the back) and imprisoning 100 others. A few days later, on April 19, the police raided the home of engineering professor Antonio Chivas, who taught at the National University, and found "an infernal machine which was in reality an automobile made into a monster bomb." The technical ingenuity of the *autobomba*, supposedly built by Chivas's son and two other students, stunned contemporary investigators, and even today would presumably win accolades from *aficionados* in ETA or Hezbollah. More than 350 pounds of TNT were concealed in a cleverly designed compartment under the car's chassis with one wire connected to the magneto and the other to the handbrake. "The youths," claimed the police, "planned to abandon the car close to police headquarters so that when the handbrake was released to remove the car from the streets, the circuit would be closed, exploding the huge TNT charge, thus wrecking the headquarters building and killing the majority of police reserves quartered there."[9]

Word of the doomsday device was leaked to the police, who, in addition to arresting Chivas, his son, and two friends, also jailed several prominent doctors (one the relative of former President Alfredo Zayas) as accomplices or possibly ABC masterminds. The would-be car bombers, however, were spared execution under the *ley de fuga* by the indirect intervention of Franklin D. Roosevelt in August, whose emissary suggested that the unpopular Machado take a "leave of absence" for the mutual good of Cuba and the United States. The bombing campaign, however, resumed in October as ABC turned its wrath against the new, progressive military government of President Ramón Grau San Martín, whom it simultaneously accused of being a "counterrevolutionary" and "a stooge for the Communists." Although no more *autobombas* were constructed, explosions continued to echo in the streets of Havana until the eve of World War Two.[10]

4

Oranges for Jaffa

Neither Jewish morality nor Jewish tradition can negate the use
of terror as a means of battle.

Stern Gang, 1943[1]

Members of the Stern Gang were ardent students of violence; with
the Holocaust in the background, these messianic young Zionists
steeped themselves in the terrorist traditions of the pre-1917
Russian Socialist-Revolutionary Party, the Internal Macedonian
Revolutionary Organization, and the Irish Republican Army.
Although their founder, the handsome and charismatic Avram
Stern (who was murdered by British police in 1942), was an
admirer of Mussolini who had shocked the Jewish community
by proposing a military alliance with the Axis powers in 1941,
Lohamei Herut Israel (or LEHI) – as Stern's group was officially
known – was characterized less by uniformity of ideology (which
individually ranged from the extreme Right to the far Left) than by
a ferocious, almost suicidal dedication to driving the British, "the
main enemy," from Palestine. LEHI had splintered from the rightwing military group Irgun early in World War Two after Stern's
refusal to condone even a temporary truce with Churchill's government for the purpose of fighting Hitler.

As the most extreme wing of the Zionist movement in Palestine
– "fascists" to the Jewish Agency and "terrorists" to the British – the
Stern Gang was morally and tactically unfettered by considerations

of diplomacy or world opinion. They also seemed to have been simultaneously driven by apocalyptic despair and utopian hope. "There had never been a revolutionary-army organization quite like LEHI," writes one historian of Zionist violence. "A tiny group of strange men and women, desperate beyond measure, on the far edge of history, despised by their opponents, abhorred by the orthodox, denied by their own, hunted and shot down in the streets; they lived briefly, during those dark years of despair, on nerve rather than hope."[2] Although their repertoire of violence was impressively diverse, the LEHI leadership was particularly feared for its excellence at detonations of all kinds. When he split from the mainstream of the Irgun in 1940, Stern took with him much of the explosives expertise that had been deployed with deadly effect against Palestinian civilians in a series of notorious bombings of Arab markets, cinemas, and coffee houses during 1937–38.[3]

It is no surprise, then, that Stern's followers were the first to improvise vehicle bombs as a sustained tactic, initially against the British forces, then against the Palestinian population. In early winter 1946–47 when LEHI began to rig its first car bombs, the group was informally allied with the Irgun in a desperately unequal struggle against 80,000 British paratroopers and police. While trap bombs, suitcase bombs, and especially landmines (IEDs in current argot) wreaked havoc on police foot patrols and even troops in armored cars, LEHI wanted a weapon powerful enough to blow up police stations and breach the concrete walls of so-called "Tegart fortresses." Early experiments in 1946 with hijacked taxis recapitulated the misfortune of the Barcelona anarchists in 1921: "One such charge went off prematurely; already primed, it jogged and exploded, leaving the LEHI taxi a blackened, twisted wreck near the Damascus Gate in Jerusalem."[4]

On January 12, 1947, however, LEHI had better luck: three militants disguised as policemen parked a truck loaded with high explosives inside the Northern District police compound in Haifa. Soon after, a guard spotted the burning fuse but panicked and fled into the six-story police building, which was blown to rubble, killing 4 and injuring 142, including civilians in adjacent streets and buildings. "The entire city," wrote an American correspondent, "was shaken and streets for blocks around were littered with glass and splinters. The telephone exchange and post office near-by were badly damaged." Like other Stern operations, the goal of the bombing was to sabotage a truce between the British and the mainstream Zionists. Indeed, "the terror attack came just as Palestine received the news that General Alan Cunningham, high commissioner, reportedly had been successful in his fight in London to save the Holy Land from martial law." By bombing the station at the foot of Mount Carmel in a mixed Jewish/Arab quarter of the city, LEHI hoped to force the British Army back into the streets, thus strengthening their argument for all-out Zionist resistance. Their wish was punctually granted as the First Infantry Division was moved into city and its "95,000 residents were put under virtual house arrest."[5]

Several months later, on a warm Saturday afternoon (March 1), the *New York Times's* correspondent Clifton Daniel was at his hotel window watching the Jewish families promenading along King George Avenue in Jerusalem when "within three minutes I heard a stammering series of machine-gun and rifle shots, interspersed with light explosions, then there was a gigantic blast." An Irgun sabotage team had managed to navigate a truck loaded with explosives inside the barbed-wire compound of a British officers club, just down the street from the King David Hotel, which they had blown up (91 dead) the previous July. They brazenly unloaded suitcase bombs, shoved them through an open window in the club lounge, then escaped in a hail of gunfire. The powerful blast collapsed the club into rubble: the 16 dead included some young officers who were sunbathing on the roof. Martial law was immediately imposed on Jewish neighborhoods.[6] Two months later, in a "blood for blood" reprisal for the executions of several of their comrades, two Stern Gang guerrillas used a stolen postal truck filled with dynamite to wipe out another police barracks in Sarona, a suburb of Tel Aviv, killing 5 and wounding 6.[7]

LEHI's (and to some extent, the Irgun's) single-minded focus on beating the British led them to underestimate Arab resistance to the establishment of even a small Jewish state, much less the vast biblical empire imagined by Avram Stern. When the Palestinians did launch their own formidable counter-offensive, however, LEHI was ruthless in deploying their new-fangled car bombs as weapons of mass terror. Ground zero was Jaffa. In December 1947, following the UN vote to partition Palestine, full-scale fighting broke out between Jewish and Arab communities from Haifa to Gaza. The only exception was the singular "non-aggression pact" negotiated between members of the Arab Higher Committee in Jaffa and their Jewish Agency counterparts in Tel Aviv next door. In addition to safeguarding their families, both elites had an overriding interest in protecting the area's all-important citrus exports to Europe. But LEHI, the zealots of total war, sabotaged the truce with exemplary carnage.

After the failure of an initial attempt in December 1946 to blow up Jaffa's waterfront with a booby-trapped crate of oranges, the Stern Gang devised a clever plan – shades of Buda's wagon – to camouflage explosives in a truckload of oranges that would be left next to the Saraya, the city's Ottoman-era administrative center. (It is unclear whether LEHI knew that a soup kitchen for orphans was also housed in the municipal center.) A fluent Arab speaker, codenamed "Rigoletto," volunteered to drive the truck, but as Uri Milstein, one of Israel's foremost historians of the War of Independence, explains, he unexpectedly ran afoul of angry local cabbies:

> Rigoletto drove the truck as planned but discovered that a pair of iron posts now barred entrance to the alley where he was to park . . . Taxi drivers on the crowded thoroughfare shouted at him to get moving and stop blocking traffic. Having no choice, Rigoletto, followed by a suspicious driver, circled the plaza searching for a place to park. He found his path blocked by an Arab truck parked next to a café. As Rigoletto attempted to pass the truck, he went up on the sidewalk. One of the patrons angrily struck him with a stool. Rigoletto shot him with his pistol, got out of the traffic jam, and fled up King George Avenue

(now Jerusalem Boulevard) with a number of vehicles in pursuit. On the outskirts of Jaffa, Arab guards, mistaking the pursuing drivers for Jews chasing an Arab, held them up with threats to open fire. Rigoletto escaped to Tel Aviv.[8]

On January 4, 1948, "Rigoletto" with another comrade in Arab dress returned to the center of Jaffa in a truck again ostensibly loaded with oranges. This time it was raining, and there was no problem parking in front of the Saraya. Displaying the cool nerve for which the Stern Gang was renowned, they lingered for coffee in a nearby café, leaving just a few minutes before the detonation. "A thunderous explosion," writes historian Adam LeBor, "then shook the city. Broken glass and shattered masonry blew out across Clock Tower Square. The New Seray's [sic] centre and side walls collapsed

Figure 2   The *Palestine Post* Car-bombing,
February 1, 1948.

in a pile of rubble and twisted beams. Only the neo-classical façade survived. After a moment of silence, the screams began, 26 were killed, hundreds injured. Most were civilians, including many children eating at the charity kitchen." The bomb missed the local Palestinian leadership, who were in another building, but as LeBor emphasizes in his sorrowful history of Jaffa, the atrocity was a great success in breaking the truce, terrifying residents, and setting the stage for the eventual flight of most of the Arab population.[9]

The larger Zionist fighting organizations quickly emulated LEHI's example. On January 5, sappers from the Haganah – the mainstream Zionist national militia – bombed the Semiramis Hotel in Jerusalem, leaving 26 dead, including the Spanish consul.[10] Two days later the Irgun improvised its own unique version of a car bomb. Five Irgun men, disguised as Hebrew settlement police and driving a stolen armored car, managed to talk their way past British guards at the Jaffa Gate of Jerusalem. Once inside, surrounded by milling crowds of pedestrians, they pushed two huge drums of explosives out the back door, killing 15 civilians and wounding 33 others. Several weeks later, the Irgun tried to repeat the attack at the Jaffa gate, this time using "a car bomb camouflaged as a Shell fuel truck."

According to Milstein,

> The operation was assigned to Menachem Madmoni, a Kfar-Shiloah native who looked Arab. An Arab traffic officer at a roadblock, however, recognized and stopped Madmoni, who then was tortured to death by Arab guards. The bomb was dismantled and the car given to the Arab policeman as a prize for his vigilance. These events cast a pall over ETZEL's [the Irgun's] Jerusalem branch, which undertook no more operations until April 9 [the infamous massacre of 120 Palestinians at Deir Yassin].[11]

Although the national Haganah leadership recoiled from the implications of indiscriminate violence against the Palestinians, LEHI and the Irgun were coldly committed to a strategy of terror via car bombs and explosions in public spaces, knowing full well that Jewish settlements would soon receive cruel repayment in kind. Milstein quotes without dissent the comment of a contemporary Arab observer:

> The Jews were the first to use explosives for the purpose of killing Arabs indiscriminately, destroying houses, inflicting heavy material losses on the Arabs and instilling fear in their hearts . . . But it wasn't long before the Arabs struck back using the enemy's own weapons. Once they had learned how to use these arms, and became adept at detonating all types of mines and explosives, they carried out punitive actions.[12]

Milstein says that the Irgun types originally scoffed at the Palestinians' technical skills, but the Arab Higher Committee had its own secret weapon: blond-haired British deserters. Nine days after the Jaffa atrocity, some of these deserters – led by Eddie Brown, a former police corporal whose brother supposedly had been murdered by the Irgun – commandeered a postal delivery truck, which they packed with explosives and detonated in the center of Haifa's Jewish quarter, injuring 50 people.[13]

Two weeks later, Brown, driving a stolen car and followed by a five-ton truck driven by a Palestinian in a police uniform, successfully passed through British and Haganah checkpoints and entered Jerusalem's New City. The truck driver parked in front of the *Palestine Post* building, lit the fuse, and then escaped with Brown in his car. The newspaper headquarters (which also contained a Haganah post and arsenal) was devastated with 1 dead and 20 wounded. Abdel Kader al-Husseini, the military commander of the Arab Higher Committee, publicly claimed authorship of the attack, but the Haganah, who still discounted Palestinian competence, blamed the British police, while Ben-Gurion speculated that "German saboteurs encamped in Hebron" were responsible.[14]

After a few days, however, Zionists began to accept that the Stern Gang's hellish innovation had been franchised to the other side. Jewish Jerusalem was soon rife with rumors and intelligence reports about "convoys of car bombs" headed for the city. "The Arabs," warned a Haganah briefing on February 10, "are attempting to plan operations similar to those carried out by the Jews, daring penetration missions." Indeed, al-Husseini had again unleashed Brown and a team of five renegade Brits in a bold plan to bomb another of the Haganah's principal strongpoints in Jerusalem. A stolen British armored car, with a tall blond man in police uniform in the turret, led three trucks through the Haganah's Romema roadblock on the western side of the city. They transported hellish cargo.[15]

"Each of the trucks," write Larry Collins and Dominique Lapierre, "had been carefully packed with over a ton of TNT by Fawzi el Kutub, Abdul Khader's explosives expert. He had seeded each charge with a vicious addition of his own devising, a mixture of two hundred pounds of potassium and aluminum powder packed in a dozen oil cans. Their presence, he had calculated, would raise substantially the temperature of the explosion and send a spray of miniature Molotov cocktails through the damaged area. His fuses were fixed onto the dashboard of each truck. Kutub had passed them through a metal tube so that, once ignited, they could not be cut or ripped from their charges."[16]

The convoy drove to the Atlantic Hotel on Ben-Yehuda Street, the headquarters of the elite Haganah troops (known as "Furmans") who guarded the convoys carrying refugees, food, and arms between Tel Aviv and Jerusalem. A curious watchman was murdered when he confronted the gang, who then drove off in their armored car after setting charges in the three trucks. The explosion was huge: "the stone façade of the six-story Vilenchick Building bulged slowly outward, then tumbled into the street. The interior of Hotel Amdursky collapsed in slow, majestic movement. Across the street, two apartment buildings crumbled to the ground as if they had been clouted by some gigantic sledgehammer." Forty-six bodies were dug out of the rubble and 130 people were seriously injured.[17]

In the face of such slaughter, the Haganah remained disciplined, but LEHI and Irgun gunmen went berserk. Again blaming the British, they raged through Jewish Jerusalem, shooting every soldier or policeman they could find – 16 in all. Ben-Gurion, meanwhile, had arrived to console the survivors on Ben Yehuda Street. Later that night, he wrote in his diary: "I had never imagined such destruction. I didn't recognize the streets. Horror and hatred. But I couldn't forget that 'our' thugs and murderers had blazed this trail in Haifa, at the King David, the Goldshmidt House and elsewhere."[18]

Meanwhile, the Haganah's secret team of Arab or Arab-speaking Jews – the Mista'aravim – was searching for the garage used to outfit al-Husseini's deadly vehicles. They soon pinpointed the Abu Sha garage in downtown Haifa and decided to car-bomb the car bombers. According to a history of the Israeli intelligence services, the Haganah men battered the front end of a passenger car to make it appear that it had been in a collision, then concealed a huge charge – 300 kilograms of high explosives – in its trunk.

One of the Mista'aravim, Ya'akov ("Yakuba") Cohen, disguised as an Arab and speaking with the appropriate local accent, told the garage hand that the car had been in an accident and needed attention. "In these bad times we don't serve people we don't know," the worker replied. "How do I know you don't have a bomb inside?" Cohen remonstrated with the garage hand. He would give his name to the local national committee for "refusing to extend help to a fighter who had just driven through Jewish territory." The garage worker, partially convinced, told Cohen to wait for the owner. The Jewish agent surreptitiously triggered the bomb's delayed-action detonator and drove away with his partner "Yitzhak" in a back-up car towards the "Fortified Triangle," a nearby British military area. A minute or so later, the bomb exploded, killing thirty Arabs and wounding seventy others.[19]

If the Haganah thought the February 28 Haifa garage massacre would put the other side out of action, they were cruelly mistaken. Although the window of opportunity for car-bombings – the possibility of passing, even in disguise, from one zone to another – was rapidly closing as Palestinians and Jews braced for all-out conventional warfare, the chief Palestinian bombmaker Fawzi

Kutub would send the Haganah one more gift. On March 11 1948, the official limousine of the American consul general, flying the Stars and Stripes and driven by the usual chauffeur, was admitted to the courtyard of the heavily guarded compound in Jerusalem which housed the Jewish national institutions. Although the Haganah general staff had warning that an assault on the Jewish Agency offices was imminent, there was no inkling that the attacker would be a US citizen, much less a past collaborator with Zionist intelligence.

But the consul general's Armenian–American driver, Anton Da'ud Kamilyo, also known as Abu Yussef, was actually a Palestinian double agent. Hidden in the trunk of the green Ford were 220 pounds of TNT: this was more than enough, in the estimate of Kutub, to wipe out the entire general staff of the Haganah. Da'ud parked the consulate car in front of the Agency headquarters and fled in a taxi, but a security official named Chaim Gur-Arieh became suspicious of wires dangling from the trunk, and he moved the car. "As Gur-Arieh set the brake, the charge exploded. The wall outside the lower two stories was destroyed and part of the wing collapsed. Flames engulfed the building." The chairman of the Jewish National Fund, Leib Yaffe, and 6 colleagues were killed, and almost 100 were injured.[20] As Ben-Gurion had so rightly feared, the car bomb had been returned to sender – with interest.

5

Our Man in Saigon

A woman sat on the ground with what was left of her baby in her lap; with a kind of modesty she had covered it with her straw peasant hat.

Graham Greene, *The Quiet American*[1]

This brief but furious exchange of car bombs between Arabs and Jews would enter into the collective memory of their conflict, but it would not be resumed on a large scale until Israel and its Phalangist allies began to terrorize West Beirut with vehicle-bombings in 1981 – a provocation that would awaken a Shiite sleeping dragon. Meanwhile, the real sequel was being played out in Saigon during the last days of the French occupation: a series of motorcycle and car bomb atrocities in 1952–53 that British writer Graham Greene incorporated into the plot of his famed *roman à clef*, *The Quiet American*. In the novel, Greene, who had made four visits to Saigon as a journalist, portrays the bombings as secretly orchestrated by CIA operative Alden Pyle, who is conspiring to substitute a pro-American party for both the Viet Minh (upon whom the bombings were blamed) and the French (who are unable to guarantee public safety).[2]

Although Greene explicitly denied any connection, most critics have assumed that the real-life "Quiet American" was the legendary counter-insurgency expert Colonel Edward Lansdale, and indeed Lansdale himself boasted that he was the model for the idealistic but murderous Pyle. Fresh from victories against peasant Communist rebels in the Philippines, Lansdale became the patron and paymaster of General Trinh Minh Thé, a dissident leader of the Cao Dai religious sect (accurately portrayed by name in Greene's novel), who based his private army on the so-called Holy Mountain near the Cambodian border. There is no doubt, according to Thé's biographer, that the US-supported general "instigated many terrorist outrages in Saigon, using clockwork plastic charges loaded into vehicles, or hidden inside bicycle frames with charges. Notably, the Li An Minh [Thé's army] blew up cars in front of the Opera House in Saigon in January 1952. These 'time-bombs' were reportedly made of 50-kg ordnance, used by the French air force, unexploded and collected by the Li An Minh. These bombs were hidden inside two Dodge cars . . ."[3]

The Opera House atrocity, which was synchronized with another car-bomb blast in front of the Hotel de Ville, was hideously immortalized in a *Life* photographer's image of the upright corpse of a rickshaw driver with both legs blown off, as well as in a famous passage from *The Quiet American*:

> . . . what struck me most in the square was the silence. It was like a church I had once visited during Mass – the only sounds came from those who served, except where here and there the Europeans wept and implored and fell silent again as though shamed by the modesty, patience and propriety of the East. The legless torso at the edge of the garden still twitched, like a chicken which has lost its head. From the man's shirt, he had probably been a rickshaw driver.
>
> Pyle said, "It's awful." He looked at the wet on his shoes and said in a sick voice, "What's that?"
>
> "Blood," I said. "Haven't you ever seen it before?"
>
> He said, "I must get them cleaned before I see the Minister."

Was there truly an "Alden Pyle" on the sideline, as depicted by Greene, choreographing the atrocities and blaming them on Ho Chi Minh as part of a Machiavellian plot to establish a pro-

American "Third Force"? Lansdale was not yet on the scene, but there was a large US mission in Saigon that French military writer Jean Lartéguy claims was really a cover for the CIA's clandestine operations. According to Lartéguy, the French Sûreté had discovered in the course of its investigation of Thé's atrocities that the Li An Minh had been given military detonators and timers by a "young member of the United States Information Service (USIS)" following orders from a "Colonel Stubbs" in Bangkok.[4]

In an autobiographical memoir, Greene himself reflected on the "evidence of contacts between the American services and General Thé."

> A jeep with the bodies of two American women was found by a French rubber planter on the route to the Holy Mountain – presumably they had been killed by the Viet Minh, but what were they doing on the plantation? The bodies were promptly collected by the American Embassy, and nothing more was heard of the incident. Not a word appeared in the press. An American consul was arrested late at night on the bridge to Dakow (where Pyle in my novel lost his life) carrying plastic bombs in his car. Again the incident was hushed up for diplomatic reasons.[5]

The novelist's most authoritative biographer, Norman Sherry, emphasizes that "Greene never moved an inch from his conviction that the CIA were involved," and confirmed through interviews with US intelligence officials that at least one of Greene's assertions, about the mysterious dead American women, was true, and that the story about the American consul, although denied by the CIA, came directly from an "impeccable source," the French commander-in-chief in Indochina, General Salan (whom we will meet later as the leader of mutinous car bombers in Algiers in 1962).[6]

Whatever the truth of these allegations, there is no question that Lansdale, who arrived some months after the Opera House bombing, was well aware of General Thé's authorship of these sophisticated attacks (the explosives were hidden in false compartments next to the cars' gas tanks), Indeed, as the pro-French Minister of National Security, Nguyen Van Tam, explained to the foreign press a few weeks after the atrocities in front of the Opera and Hôtel de Ville, General Thé's radio station had openly bragged about the explosions and one of his lieutenants had been captured while setting off some bicycle bombs.[7] Yet Lansdale ignored these revelations to publicly champion the dissident Cao Dai warlord as a patriot in the mold of Washington and Jefferson. With American support, General Thé was invited to join the South Vietnamese delegation to the Bandung summit of Asian and African countries; in return, he supported the "Revolutionary Committee" that deposed the French puppet, Emperor Bao Dai, and sent his troops to help the Americans install Ngo Dinh Diem as the "Third Force" president of South Vietnam, in defiance of the Geneva accords.[8] After Thé was killed under enigmatic circumstances (the French, Viet Minh, and Binh Xuyen sectarian rebels were all immediate suspects) Lansdale eulogized the terrorist general to a journalist as "a good man. He was moderate, he was a pretty good general, he was on our side, and he cost twenty-five thousand dollars."[9]

6

Festivals de Plastique

Thus France's overseas imperial adventure ended: in flames, kidnappings, and bloody chaos.

Benjamin Stora[1]

After Jerusalem in 1948 and Saigon in 1952, the car bomb's logical destination should have been Nicosia in the mid-1950s during the Greek Cypriots' bloody campaign to evict the British. Colonel George Grivas, the military leader of the EOKA guerrillas, was a master of terror whose deadly deployment of homemade landmines against British armored cars prefigured today's battle of IEDs-versus-Humvees on the road from Baghdad. Curiously, however, Grivas showed no interest in emulating the Stern Gang's improvisation of vehicle bombs against barracks and police stations.[2] Perhaps he was sensitive to the inevitable "collateral damage" amongst Greek civilians. In any event, the car bomb instead found its next home in Algeria, in a colonial war where one camp ultimately embraced carnage as its very *raison d'être*.

According to Philippe Bourdrel's encyclopedia of atrocity (*Le livre noir de la guerre d'Algérie*), the first attempted vehicle-bombing in North Africa was organized by Youssef Zighout, the commander of the National Liberation Front (FLN) in North Constantine (the mountainous coastal region east of Algiers) during the movement's major offensive in August 1955. However the two trucks packed with explosives and fuel oil were intercepted by French troops before they reached their intended target, the police headquarters in Philippeville.[3] Three years later, after the famed Battle of Algiers, the FLN attacked France itself: fuel dumps were blown up, gendarmes were machine-gunned, a limpet mine was planted on a battleship in Toulon harbor, but there were no car bombs or public massacres on the mainland. Indeed, as Alistair Horne emphasizes in his celebrated history of the Algerian War, "there was not one act of promiscuous bombing against civilians."[4]

The Organisation de l'Armée Secrète (OAS) had no such scruples. With General Raoul Salan as its figurehead, this sinister alliance of diehard *pieds noirs* and mutinous *paras* and *légionnaires* turned to indiscriminate terrorism after the failure of its April 1961 uprising. With no real goal beyond the preservation of settler supremacy, its declared enemies included General de Gaulle himself, the security forces, Communists, peace activists (including Jean-Paul Sartre), and, especially, Algerian civilians. (Oddly enough, the OAS seldom confronted the FLN directly.)

In order to disrupt the Evian peace talks between de Gaulle's representatives and the Algerian leaders, the OAS launched a series of *festivals de plastique* (380 bombings throughout Algeria in July 1961 alone), using the 4132 kilos of plastic explosive and 1000 electric detonators that it boasted of having liberated from army arsenals.[5] Chief of the OAS's dreaded "Delta Commandos" was Roger Degueldre, a 36-year-old veteran of Dien Bien Phu who led 500 Légionnaire deserters and *Algérie française* ultras from his hiding place in the *petit blanc* district of Bab-el-Oued. In early 1962, as de Gaulle began to yield to FLN demands for complete independence, Salan declared "total war" and ordered Degueldre to unleash the Deltas against both Algeria and France.[6]

Alistair Horne poses the mystery of CIA involvement with the Deltas ("only partially explained to this day") and quotes Salan (whom he interviewed in the 1970s) on a meeting with two Americans, claiming to be CIA representatives, in Algiers in November 1961. "No, they were not *agents provocateurs*," explained Salan. "Why? Because they actually began delivering the goods; a shipment of some fifty machine-guns arrived from Spain, via a small port near Cherchel." According to other OAS veterans, the CIA expected that Salan would "cede military bases and preferential economic treatment (i.e., access to Saharan oil) in the event of his success in creating an independent, *pied-noir*-dominated state along the lines of Rhodesia."[7]

In any event, the Deltas were scarcely dependent upon clandestine American aid when they had so many willing collaborators inside the police and army eager to provide explosives and intelligence. Such liaisons were especially useful to the OAS terrorists organizing the *festival* inside France. In late January 1962, for example, Deltas managed to detonate a bomb inside a small van in front of the Quai d'Orsay (the French foreign ministry): a diplomatic courier was burned alive and a dozen other civil servants were seriously injured.[8] A month later, the OAS in Oran – Camus' hometown, the setting of *La Peste* – blew up a large car bomb in a major intersection next to the FLN-controlled Ville Nouvelle, killing 30 Moslem civilians. Five days later they detonated two trucks loaded with plastic explosive, gasoline and butane tanks next to the wing of the jail holding Moslem prisoners, inflicting 14 casualties.[9]

March began with "Operation Rock and Roll," 120 *plasticages* in two hours (on March 2), followed a week later in France by the explosion of a van in front of the municipal hall in Issy-les-Moulineaux outside Paris, where the Communist-led Peace Movement was holding its national congress (3 dead and 47 wounded, including 5 schoolgirls).[10] Although the OAS was effectively decapitated in April with the arrests of Salan (codename: "The Sun"), Degueldre and other key leaders, the at-large middle leadership – *les colonels* – was even more fanatically fixated than the generals on provoking an Algerian *Götterdämmerung*. Their almost insane strategy was to massacre so many ordinary Moslems that the otherwise highly disciplined FLN would be forced to break its truce with French forces and retaliate massively against the *pieds noirs*. The OAS "bunker," in other words, was deliberately fomenting a race war that they hoped might topple de Gaulle and lead to a "Rhodesian" or "Israeli" solution.

In late April the OAS unleashed its final and most massive murder campaign against targeted segments of the Moslem working class, from dock workers to cleaning women. On April 25, 1962, a car bomb exploded in front of Place du Gouvernement, one of the principal entrances to the Casbah, killing 2 Moslems on their way to work and wounding 22 others. On May 2, Deltas parked a sedan containing *plastique* and a large quantity of scrap metal in front of the hiring hall at the Port of Algiers, where every morning at dawn a large crowd of Moslem dockers lined up in desperate hope of finding some work in the depressed conditions of the economy. According to American journalist Henry Tanner:

> Between 100 and 200 men were standing in front of the hiring hall when the explosion occurred. Parts of the car and chunks of metal mowed down the victims, hurling them against a wall. Single torn shoes, shreds of clothing and remains of red fezzes, the traditional Moslem caps, were scattered everywhere. Witnesses said that panic broke out among the longshoremen in the building. Filling the width of the streets, the men rushed toward the nearby business section and from there to the nearest Moslem neighborhood. According to some reports, the fleeing men came under submachine fire from balconies in one of the European sections through which they had to pass.
>
> The rush of men wrought havoc with the European rush-hour traffic. Frightened drivers approaching the scene of the explosion stopped, tried to turn around and then were hemmed in by the cars following them. Many of the drivers abandoned their cars and fled on foot. One, a middle-aged oil worker, was swallowed for an instant by a maelstrom of crazed longshoremen. He vanished. A few moments later his body was seen in the gutter, his throat slit.[11]

This was the only spontaneous retaliation for the murder of at least 62 dockers, as FLN militants quickly took charge of the scene, evacuating the wounded and restoring order with the help of French troops. Two days later, the "colonels" again attempted to detonate all-out sectarian war, using the most apocalyptic device conceived in eight years of conflict. Deltas stole a 4000-gallon gasoline tanker, rigged it with plastic explosive, and then tried to push it off a mountain road above a poor Moslem *bidonville*; fortunately the vehicle's wheels were snagged by the raised shoulder of the road and it blew up prematurely. Although 2 people died in the ensuing conflagration as burning gasoline raced through sewers and gullies, *Le Monde* estimated that 2000 to 3000 residents might have been burned to death if the tanker had fallen on their homes.[12] (The *Times*'s Tanner was told by a French officer at the scene that three months earlier the Army had seized an OAS directive in which Salan himself outlined a plan for "setting fire to filling stations in the residential areas overlooking the city and having the burning gasoline flow down the streets on public buildings.")[13]

OAS car-bombings continued throughout May, along with hundreds of other bombings, assassinations, and lynchings. On a single day (May 10) 18 young Moslem women and girls were murdered; supposedly in revenge for the killing of a *pied-noir* woman. In fact, as Tanner explained to readers of the *Times*, having "succeeded in driving virtually all Moslem men from their jobs in the European quarters," the Deltas were now concentrating on terrorizing charwomen and shop girls.[14] Their goal remained nothing less than total apartheid. A few days earlier, Tanner had marveled at the "amazing restraint" of ordinary Moslems who were "bowing to orders from nationalist authorities to remain calm in the face of violent provocations,"[15] but by mid-May tit-for-tat killings were daily occurrences and just as their OAS masters had wished, ordinary *pieds noirs* were being slaughtered in increasing numbers. Far from undermining de Gaulle, however, the carnage in Algiers and Oran only rallied the majority of French voters around the Evian Treaty, while bolstering the FLN's resolve to make no concession whatsoever to the *pieds noirs* and their Nazi-like *colonels*. Thanks to the OAS, "suitcase or coffin" was the only choice remaining to more than one million *petits blancs*.

"In less than a year," observes Alistair Horne, "the OAS had killed 2,360 people in Algeria, and wounded another 5,418 . . . in the Algiers zone alone their activities over the last six months of the war had claimed *three times as many civilian victims* as had the FLN from the beginning of 1956 onwards; i.e. , including the Battle of Algiers."[16] Although the car-bomb explosions ceased in June, OAS operatives – whether underground in Paris, welcomed as heroes in Franco's Spain, or discreetly ensconced in new criminal occupations in Corsica, Lebanon, and Sicily – continued to practice their craft or, at least, transmit their skills to local apprentices. *Plastique*, as a result, would become almost as much a staple of the Mediterranean's violent ethnic politics as olives were of its cuisine.

7

Demon Seeds

The Ciaculli car bomb marked a historical point of no return.

John Dickie[1]

The car bomb – *avec plastique* or with dynamite stolen from the quarry – made its next Mediterranean appearance in Palermo, only a year after the *pied-noir* exodus from Algeria. The Sicilian Mafia, on the verge of a civil war between two upstart factions, had paid avid professional attention to the Algerian bombings and terror attacks. Indeed Angelo La Barbera, the Mafia *capo* of Palermo-Centre, probably leased some OAS expertise when he launched his devastating sneak attack on his Mafia rival, Salvatore "Little Bird" Greco, in February 1963. (The indelible signature of the OAS, the use of *plastique*, was already legible in some Mafia murders in 1962, spurring the Italian Senate to an urgent investigation of rising violence in Sicily.)[2] Few remember the original pretext (perhaps a drug deal gone sour), but the slaughter caused by this so-called "First Mafia War" was legendary.

Greco's bastion was the town of Ciaculli outside Palermo, where, protected by a large army of relatives and loyal henchmen, he was seemingly invulnerable. La Barbera surmounted this obstacle with the aid of the Alfa Romeo Giulietta. "This dainty four-door family saloon," writes John Dickie in his history of the Cosa Nostra, "was one of the symbols of Italy's economic miracle – 'svelte, practical, comfortable, safe and convenient,' as the adverts proclaimed." The first explosive-packed Giulietta destroyed Greco's house; the second, a few weeks later, killed one of his key allies. The Greco gunmen retaliated, wounding La Barbera in Milan in May; in response, La Barbera's ambitious lieutenants Pietro Torreta and Tommaso Buscetta (later to become the most famous of all Mafia *pentiti*) unleashed more deadly Giuliettas.[3]

On June 30, 1963, "the umpteenth Giulietta stuffed with TNT" was left in one of the tangerine groves that surround Ciaculli; a tank of butane with a fuse was clearly visible in the back seat. Another Giulietta had already exploded that morning in a nearby town, killing two people, so the *carabinieri* were cautious and summoned army engineers for assistance. "Two hours later two bomb disposal experts arrived, cut the fuse, and pronounced the vehicle safe to approach. But when Lt. Mario Malausa made to inspect the contents of the boot, he detonated the huge quantity of TNT it contained. He and six other men were blown to pieces by an explosion that scorched and stripped the tangerine trees for hundreds of metres around . . ." So little remained of the unfortunate *carabinieri* that their coffins were "virtually empty" when they were carried from Palermo Cathedral accompanied by a funeral procession of 100,000 Sicilians three days later.[4]

By the time the Cosa Nostra civil war ended in 1964, the Sicilian population had learned to tremble at the very sight of a Giulietta, and car bombs had become a permanent part of the Mafia repertoire. Indeed, deadly Fiats again terrorized Palermo during the early 1980s as part of the Mafia's *matanza* (slaughter) of Left activists and independent magistrates. Among the most "illustrious corpses" harvested by car bombs or planted mines were Communist leader Pio La Torre and General Carlo Alberto Dalla Chiese in separate attacks in 1982; Judge Rocco Chinnici and his bodyguards in 1983; and the companions of Judge Carlo Palermo (who was seriously injured) in 1985.[5] Even more famous judicial assassinations would follow the conviction of Cosa Nostra leaders in a series of sensational "maxi-trials" in the early 1990s, then – after the arrest of godfather Totò Riina in 1993 – explosives-packed Fiats were unleashed against some of Italy's most celebrated churches and museums. The most notorious of these blind-rage car-bombings – organized by Riina's successor, Bernardo "The Tractor" Provenzano and his notorious Corleonese gang – was the explosion in May 1993 that damaged the world-famous Uffizi Gallery in the heart of Florence (see Chapter 18).

The Algerian War also planted the seeds of violence on another Mediterranean island. Unlike Sicily with its fabled plains of wheat and terraces of lemons, Corsica is a poor, mountainous place with only 15 percent of its surface low-lying or flat enough for cultivation. The shortage of arable land was greatly exacerbated by the resettlement of wealthy *pied-noir* viniculturalists expelled from Algeria in 1962. Thanks to preferential treatment by Paris, by 1979 378 of these *colons* controlled 90 percent of the island's wine production, while nearly 4000 Corsican peasants accounted for a mere 10 percent. State-sponsored tourist development also ate away at scarce farm land, while island youth, lacking industrial jobs or access to higher education, were forced to emigrate to mainland France. The result was the ever-increasing marginalization of native Corsicans, their language, and traditional livelihoods. From a population of more than 300,000 in 1900, Corsican speakers were reduced to a mere 120,000 by 1970.[6]

Corsican grievances, in other words, were as legitimate and deeply rooted as those of Catholics in Northern Ireland or Basques in Spain, but they were – and are – almost invisible to the rest of the world (which tends to automatically equate "Corsican" with organized crime). To make themselves heard, Corsican nationalists were forced to borrow the verb *plastiquer* from the OAS, and as early as June 1965, they began small bombings of expatriate farms as well as the offices of SOMIVAC, the rural development agency believed to discriminate in favor of the former *pieds noirs*. During the distractions of May 1968, Corsican activists managed to steal several tons of high explosives and thousands of detonators which they subsequently used to blow up power pylons, *pied-noir* homes, and – most originally – ships carrying industrial waste from Italy.[7]

By 1973, the Fronte Paisanu Corsu di Liberazione (later, the FLNC), whose manifesto demanded the expulsion of the *colons* monopolizing former communal lands, was being taken seriously in Paris as an emergent Corsican IRA. In January 1974 the FLNC organized the first of its notorious "Nuits Bleues" (nine bombs exploding simultaneously in Ajaccio, Bastia, and Ghisonaccia), and in August 1975 it led a quasi-insurrection in Bastia with enthusiastic participation by local youth. Four years later the FLNC was blowing up tourist agencies in Paris, and in 1981 one of its bombs narrowly missed French President Giscard d'Estaing. In 1982 the group launched *le sommet du plasticage*, a veritable Corsican Tet Offensive of more than 800 bombings of government offices, restaurants, hotels, the Club Méditerranée, second homes, police stations, and so on.[8]

The car bomb (*voiture piègée*) came late to this festival of explosions: probably because the Corsican emphasis through the end of the 1970s was on the destruction of property rather than lives. The struggle hardened considerably during the 1980s as a result of the heightened repression associated with the draconian reign of Charles Pasqua as Interior Minister (his official slogan: *terroriser les terrorists*) and because of growing internal tensions within the movement. In response to the mass arrest of nationalists in April 1988, the first car bomb *à la libanaise* was set off near the Ajaccio international airport, injuring five passing gendarmes. By 1990 the FLNC, like the IRA and ETA before it, had split into two wings, the smaller of which – the FLNC Canal Habitual – favored car bombs as a fast-lane strategy to publicize their claims to leadership.

Fortunately, no one was wounded by the vehicle that the FLNC Canal Habitual blew up in front of the Conseil Général de Haute-Corse in May 1991, but three people were seriously injured during a bombing of a tax office in Nice in December 1992. As the group hoped, the bombings garnered hysterical headlines, but their opponents, the Canal Historique, countered with a press conference in January 1996 that left an even deeper impression upon the French media: "Between 500 and 600 heavily armed and hooded Corsican nationalists gathered near the village of Tralonca in Haute-Corse. They paraded past the press an arsenal of weapons both mind-boggling and terrifying: rocket launchers, grenade launchers,

Glock and Jericho automatics, Galil sniper rifles, UZIs, HKs, M-16s, Kalashnikovs – you name it."[9] But the Canal Historique made this show of strength in preparation for a ceasefire and negotiations with Paris.

Four years later (July 1, 1996), the Habituals used a car bomb to assassinate Petru Lorenzi, the Historique leader who advocated a political settlement along the lines of what Sinn Fein was negotiating in Belfast. The huge explosion at Bastia harbor that killed Lorenzi also wounded 14 other people and wrecked the island's 1996 tourist season.[10] Then, in February 1998, a dissident group of the Historique (soon to regroup with the Habituals in a new FLNC *union des combatants*) led by Yvan Colonna murdered the Prefect of Corsica, Claude Erignac, the highest-ranking victim in 30 years. Both assassinations reinforced a single message: "We will never give up the struggle." Or, as Cuncolta Naziunalista, the legal wing of the former Historique, lamented after the murder of Lorenzi: "It is incontestable that some individuals and factions are determined at any price – including the price of blood – to prevent conditions of constructive dialogue from being established and preparing the way for essential reforms."[11] In any event, nationalist intransigence has been reinforced by the arrogance of Paris, the structural malaise of the island's economy, and the continuing blight of vacation homes that makes housing unaffordable for locals. With the announcement in 2006 that the Basque revolutionaries of ETA were declaring a permanent ceasefire, the embittered shards of the FLNC maintain a lonely vigil over the last armed struggle in Western Europe.

8

Welcome to Bombsville

Communist terrorists have been sent into Saigon to blow up government and American military installations and kill American personnel.

AP wire, November 19, 1963[1]

The return of the car bomb to Saigon in 1963–66 was a remarkable if now largely forgotten chapter in the Second Indochina War. For 36 months, Viet Cong urban guerrillas bombed American billets and even the US Embassy almost at will, generating spectacular headlines across the world that dramatized the growing security crisis and undermined claims that Saigon government enjoyed broad support from its urban population. "In the cities there has been no end to the ingenuity employed in terroristic sabotage," complained one top-secret US Army report.[2] In this campaign, the Viet Cong were aided by growing anti-Americanism amongst the city's working classes, many of whom were victims of the callous urban renewal that accommodated the growing US presence.

Already before the fall of Dien Bien Phu, the Americans were establishing themselves in Saigon in imperial splendor: "Even their lavatories were air-conditioned," complained Graham Greene's alter ego, Thomas Fowler.[3] By the end of the 1950s, moreover, the Diem regime was aggressively displacing ordinary residents to make room for the hundreds, then thousands of American advisors and technicians. "In Saigon," writes former Viet Cong Justice

Minister Truong Nhu Tang, "the government pursued 'urban redevelopment' with a vengeance, dispossessing whole neighborhoods in favor of modern commercial buildings and expensive apartments, which could only be utilized by Americans and the native upper classes . . . The displaced moved onto sampans on the river or to poorer, even more distant districts. In the slums and shanty villages resentment against Americans mixed with a simmering anger toward the regime."[4]

This anger was soon translated into resistance. Although car-bombings ceased for some years after General Thé's death, throughout the late 1950s there were sporadic grenade and *plastique* attacks on Americans in Saigon, with both anti-Diem rebels (especially the Binh Xuyen and Hoa Hao sects) and the Viet Minh (later Viet Cong) as suspects. In October 1957, for example, time bombs blasted the United States Information Service office (which Larté-guy alleged was a "cover" for the CIA), as well as a military bus and an officer's billet in "a sudden outburst of anti-Americanism in Saigon." The next year, an American officers' mess was blown up in Cholon, with seven employees killed.[5]

By the early 1960s, the growing complex of US administrative buildings, officers' billets, bars, and sports facilities became an irresistible target for the insurgent Viet Cong. In May 1963 they launched a bicycle-bomb attack on the US military aid mission compound which was taken straight from General Thé's (or was it Allen Dulles'?) operational manual. As a later, top-secret American study of Viet Cong tactics explained, "Sometimes the bicycle itself is the instrument of death, its hollow tubular frame packed with plastic explosive and the timing devices located under the saddle. Terrorists ride the bicycle into the area, lean it up against the building to be destroyed, set the fuse, and walk off."[6] In this case, two bicycles were left alongside the compound walls, while a third was parked outside the US officers' quarters a few blocks away. "The bombs," reported the *Washington Post*, "obviously were aimed at the Americans, but it was the Vietnamese who suffered most as has happened in many previous terrorist incidents": 11 killed and 39 seriously injured, along with 3 wounded Americans.[7]

Open season on American military and embassy personnel followed in February 1964, with deadly bombings of the Playboy Bar, the Pershing Sports Field during a softball game, and the Kinh Do Cinema; altogether, 9 were killed and 112 wounded. Urban legends about a Macheath's army of terror quickly arose: "The Viet Cong," the *Chicago Tribune* claimed, "are known to be recruiting taxi drivers, hooligans, beggars, and others . . . these people are being taken into D Zone [north of Saigon] for three days of training in explosives handling and then sent back into Saigon."[8] In fact, the Viet Cong's local cadre were more likely to be students, dock-workers and teachers than lumpen-proletarians, and they soon made Saigon the world's foremost laboratory of urban guerrilla warfare.

The first Viet Cong car bomb was synchronized by accident or design to greet the arrival of Bob Hope in Saigon on Christmas Eve 1964. He had just disembarked from his plane at the airport when 200 pounds of *plastique* hidden in a van blew up in the parking garage of the Brink Hotel, a walled and heavily guarded compound for US officers just behind the old Opera that General Thé had bombed in 1952.

> The explosion occurred in the ground floor garage of the building, catching many men dressing for a big party to be held in the popular rooftop officers' club and mess . . . The U.S. Armed Forces Radio Station on the ground floor of the billet, which feeds programs to American servicemen throughout South Viet Nam was shattered . . . Nine military vehicles on the ground were destroyed and 15 damaged. Sidewalks were splattered with blood, and debris, including heavy truck tires, was hurled through the air.
>
> "I was in a printer's shop," an American sergeant related. "Just as the foreman pushed a button to signal the workers to go home we heard this crackling explosion. I rushed into the street and saw this mushroom cloud. It was pink." He laughed at the incongruity. "It was the same color as the sunset. Then the pink cloud became black."[9]

Officers fought their way through flames to rescue wounded comrades trapped in burning rooms. 'An entire wing of the L-shaped structure was wrecked, a lieutenant colonel and an American civilian were killed, and 107 Americans and Vietnamese were wounded. "The first sight that greeted Hope's troupe, looking across from their own hotel, was the wreckage of the Brink Hotel."[10]

In February 1965 the Viet Cong introduced a new battle slogan, "Two Americans a Day," with the car bombing of the four-story US enlisted-men's quarters in the coastal city of Qui Nhon, 267 miles north of Saigon. In an eerie repetition of the Brink Hotel bombing (100 pounds of *plastique* concealed in an auto parked in a basement garage), the Viet Cong killed almost a two-week quota of Americans (23).[11] In retaliation for Qui Nhon, as well as earlier guerrilla attacks on US barracks at Pleiku, the Johnson administration unleashed Operation Rolling Thunder, the sustained aerial bombardment of North Vietnam.[12] (How can we compare on the scales of morality the Viet Cong's mortar attacks, satchel charges, and car bombs against the almost *8 million tons* of high explosives – the destructive equivalent of more than 100 Hiroshimas – that American planes eventually dropped on Indochina?)[13]

After Qui Nhon, US security experts in Saigon braced for new attacks. Invisible to American and South Vietnamese intelligence, the Viet Cong in early 1965 had reorganized their three separate Saigon sapper platoons into what *Life* magazine would later describe as "one of the most lethal terrorist organizations in history: F-100."[14] As garnered from the torture interrogation of a senior cadre arrested in 1967, F-100 was a partisan organization of almost unprecedented sophistication, clearly overshadowing anything achieved by the *maquis* in Lyon in 1943 or the FLN in Algiers 1956. Perhaps only the Haganah in Jerusalem in 1947 had possessed such an elaborate organization chart. According to Nguyen Van Sam, the leader of a Viet Cong bomb team who was captured as he was trying to blow up another American dormitory, the mother network comprised:

sapper units of sizes and functions: "groves," groups, cells, inter-cells, and special action units . . . While it is commonly supposed that Vietcong terrorism is haphazard, or spur of the moment, F-100's operations are planned with an almost fanatical attention to detail, painstakingly rehearsed, carried out with split-second timing, and endlessly critiqued. F-100's table of organization includes mapmakers, photographers and demolition experts. It has its own finance section, its own communications section and a specialist who converts wristwatches into mechanisms for detonating time bombs. Its arsenal includes every weapon from a heavy mortar on down, and the unit has even issued instructions explaining how its men can make flame throwers from commonplace equipment easily found in Saigon . . . Throughout the city the organization maintains a vast system of safe houses − secret meeting places − purchased with an apparently inexhaustible treasury. Some of these safe houses are private dwellings. Others are small business establishments such as bicycle repair shops or food stores, and no trouble is spared to make the cover perfect.[15]

Led by the mysterious "Brother Hoang" and relying on the technical expertise of science graduates and engineers, F-100 was constantly infiltrating small quantities of explosives into Saigon by "the ant method": concealed in bicycle frames, shopping baskets, baby carriages, even women's brassieres.[16] In mid-March the Saigon police proudly announced that they had "thwarted a plot to bomb the embassy" with the confiscation of 35 pounds of *plastique* from a Viet Cong safe house. In fact, they had not derailed the plot at all. At 11 a.m. on March 30, the CIA station chief in Saigon, Peer de Silva, was talking on the phone and absentmindedly looking out of his second-story window in the Streamline Moderne embassy at the end of the Street of Flowers.

Gazing out casually, I noticed an old gray Peugeot sedan being pushed up to a position directly beneath my window . . . The driver raised the hood of the car, peered in at the engine, and began to argue with the policeman, who was armed with an M-1 carbine. Suddenly, I saw it. Looking from my window down into the Peugeot, I saw, jammed between the back of the driver's seat and the seat itself, what we in the trade call a time pencil. This is a detonating device, consisting of a brass tube, pencil size, filled with ignition powder . . . That is what I saw, the time pencil and the gray smoke emerging from the ports. My world turned to glue and slow motion as my mind told me this car was a bomb. With the phone still in my hand and without conscious thought, I began falling away from the window and turned as I fell, but I was only halfway to the floor when the car exploded with 350 pounds of C-4 plastic explosives packed into its frame.[17]

De Silva was permanently blinded in one eye, his secretary was killed, and 30 other Americans, including Deputy Ambassador U. Alexis Johnson, were injured. The office of Ambassador Maxwell Taylor, then visiting Washington, was almost completely destroyed. Out in the street, 15 Vietnamese pedestrians were dead along with the two Viet Cong and the policemen who were interrogating them.[18]

Beyond the damage to the embassy, the Viet Cong had succeeded in instilling fear in all levels of the American community. "Soon the Americans," wrote one local resident, "were described by Vietnamese children as 'Big Monkeys' because their lives were lived behind huge wire nettings, resembling cages."[19] "Saigon," adds Navy nurse Bobbi Hovis, "became an increasingly hazardous duty station. Eventually, it became known as *Bombsville* to those in the military stationed outside the city. Personnel on R and R preferred to visit other locations – anywhere but unstable Saigon. Some soldiers I met said they found it safer to be on duty in the Mekong Delta."[20] Such anxieties were hardly irrational. The dynamiting of the My Canh floating restaurant on June 25, which killed 12 Americans and 31 others, created another citywide scare and led to a redoubling of security.

In perhaps its most daring raid, F-100 struck in August where an attack was least expected. A special action team in a Ford sedan followed a police jeep to the entrance of the National Police compound, the headquarters of the campaign against urban terrorism, and then dashed into the courtyard right behind the cops. "Meanwhile two other terrorists in a smaller car followed closely and opened fire with submachine guns on the two police guards on duty outside the gates, killing both. The men in the Ford jumped from the moving vehicle, which contained a big load of explosive material, and raced back toward the street. One was hit by small-arms fire but was dragged along by his companions. Two more Viet Cong agents waiting at the nearest intersection in still another car, drove the four-man assault party away."[21] The police, who suffered 5 dead and 17 wounded, were humiliated.

Brother Hoang, of course, had not forgotten about the Americans. Although the Metropole, a downtown billet for enlisted men, was heavily guarded, two cells of F-100 had little trouble in blowing it up on December 4 with a large truck bomb. Charles Mohr of the *New York Times* reported the "boldest act of Vietcong terror against Americans in many months."

The attack was well coordinated. A gray panel truck pulled up in front of the Metropole at 5:29 AM and armed Vietcong terrorists leaped out. One had a submachine gun. An American guard emptied his shotgun and an automatic pistol at them, but was wounded in the shoulder and escaped into the building. As the terrorists fled, the bomb, in the truck, exploded, leaving a deep and gaping crater in the street, into which a taxicab toppled grotesquely. The explosion blew a hole three stories high on the west side of the multi-story hotel.[22]

Eight enlisted men were killed and 157 were wounded, but the toll might have been much higher: a Claymore mine had been hidden in the street, set to detonate in the faces of rescuers and fleeing hotel residents. "The stopwatch timing device on the mine," explained Mohr, "had made electrical contact with the detonator, but for some reason, it malfunctioned."[23] This diabolical tactic of using one bomb to drive panicked crowds into the path of another, even more deadly bomb would later be repeated in Belfast, Beirut, Baghdad, and Bali.

By 1966 the US population in Saigon had soared to an estimated 35,000 troops and civilian personnel, about 10,000 of whom were housed in 83 requisitioned hotels and apartment buildings scattered through the central city. To protect the Americans, a Combined Security Committee was established under the direction of national police chief Nguyen Ngoc Loan (later to become infamous for his public execution of a Viet Cong suspect during the 1968 Tet uprising). As hundreds of American MPs provided security for embassies, hotels and restaurants, and 12,000 regular police manned a "nightly cordon against infiltrators," the 700-strong Vietnamese Special Branch, notorious for torture and summary executions, stalked Viet Cong cadre and sympathizers in the urban labyrinth of Saigon–Cholon (population 2 million).[24]

Loan's aggressive policies won much applause from the US Embassy, especially after his police in January 1966 successfully intercepted a delivery truck carrying 265 pounds of high explosive en route to blow up the Bui Vien officers' billet in Cholon, just two blocks from the wrecked Metropole.[25] But the illusion of improved security was shattered on April 1, 1966 by the bombing of the Victoria Hotel in Cholon which housed some 200 American junior officers. As the *New York Times* noted, "the latest attack was hard to reconstruct because all the men who had witnessed the terrorists approach were killed." But what US investigators did discover about the bombing testified to a complex, 18-person operation that showcased F-100's superlative planning and operational audacity.

At about 5:15 AM, a group of terrorists approaching the Victoria began firing automatic weapons at the Americans and South Vietnamese guards at the entrance. Under the covering fire, one terrorist drove a gray panel truck to the entrance. The squad then ran down the street. A small explosion, possibly caused by a grenade, occurred across the street from the Victoria. Then about 200 pounds of explosives in the panel truck went up, blowing the truck to bits and shattering the front of the Victoria. On the corner south of the hotel, the terrorists ran into an American military-police lieutenant and his driver patrolling the area in a jeep. A furious gun battle ensued. When we found the dead MPs, their guns were empty.[26]

One member of the Viet Cong special action team was captured, but 6 American MPs and Vietnamese guards were killed (some accounts say 8), and 110 US officers were wounded. The next month (May 10), the urban guerrillas of F-100 tried to blow up the Brink Hotel again, but their truck was intercepted by police and the bomb it was carrying exploded prematurely. Amidst flaming debris, the wounded Viet Cong fought a ferocious gun battle with American MPs who arrived in machine-gun-mounted jeeps. Eight Americans were killed or wounded, along with 29 passersby.[27]

A month after the Victoria bombing, Defense Secretary Robert McNamara decided that the only solution to the continued threat of the Viet Cong's car bombs was to move as many Americans as possible out of Saigon. To facilitate this, he ordered the construction of a vast, self-contained "military suburb" 15 miles northeast of the city. The $130 million Long Binh complex, sprawling across 10 square miles of former French rubber plantations near the Bien Hoa Airbase, was designed to be both fortress and "Little America." "On blueprints," wrote the *New York Times* in fall 1966, "some of Long Binh's streets are already named – from Fargo Street to Eisenhower Loop. Troops will be housed in two-story wooden 'hootches' and have facilities from baseball diamonds to refrigerated warehouses and movie houses. The generals will have air-conditioned bungalows."[28]

Although car-bombings subsided in 1967 with the arrests of top F-100 cadre and the construction of Long Binh, the Battle of Saigon had hardly been declared an American victory before Tet 1968 arrived and sappers of the Viet Cong's C-10 battalion were suddenly inside the new US embassy. The stunning Tet Offensive – an enormous human sacrifice by the National Liberation Front in order to break American morale – has tended to overshadow the

1963–66 car-bombing campaign; indeed these audacious attacks barely rate footnotes in most histories of the long Indochinese conflict. Yet it was F-100 – the lost command of Brother Hoang and his hundreds of anonymous commandos – that established the decisive template for the future of urban guerrilla warfare.[29] Their operations were the direct inspirations, for instance, for the devastating Hezbollah truck-bombings of the US and French embassies and Marine barracks in Beirut in 1983. US strategists may have quickly forgotten the lessons of Saigon, but for future enemies, the Viet Cong attack on the American embassy in 1965, together with the Brink, Qui Nhon, Metropole, and Victoria bombings, were classical models to be emulated and refined.

9

"The Black Stuff"

By 1947, the conflicted history of ammonium nitrate could no longer be ignored by government and military leaders across the world. They either knew that extraordinary history – or should have known the history.

historian Bill Minutaglio[1]

The next stage in the evolution of the car bomb's lethality owes something to the Wisconsin Fish and Game Department and the innocent author of *Pothole Blasting for Wildlife*. The pamphlet – pored over by a small group of angry student radicals at the University of Wisconsin in 1969 – explained how farmers could cheaply excavate duck ponds with a powerful homemade explosive concocted from ammonium-nitrate fertilizer and fuel oil.

Ammonium nitrate, whose industrial synthesis from ammonia had freed world agriculture from dependence upon natural manures and guanos, has been responsible for the largest accidental explosions in history. In September 1921, for instance, a cleanup operation at the great BASF ammonium-synthesis complex in Oppau, Germany detonated a silo filled with 4500 tons of fertilizer: the shock waves of the explosion were felt 150 miles away and the plant was replaced by a vast crater 60 feet deep. Twenty-six years later, bags of ammonium nitrate loaded for France spontaneously combusted aboard a rusted ex-Liberty ship in the port of Texas City, Texas. The ensuing explosion of the 5 million pounds of fertilizer in its holds vaporized the S.S. *Grandcamp* and reduced the port and adjoining neighborhoods to burning rubble, killing 581 workers and residents and injuring at least 5000 others.[2]

Was the splinter group from the Madison Students for a Democratic Society (SDS) chapter, led by Karl Armstrong and Leo Burt, aware of this "extraordinary history"? They had already achieved local notoriety by fire-bombing the campus Reserve Officer Training Corps office in protest against the Vietnam War, but it is unclear whether they truly appreciated the sinister chemistry of fertilizer-based explosives. Nonetheless, they were quickly mesmerized by the vision of blasting some "duck ponds" of their own in the local military-industrial complex with ingredients easily available, no questions asked, from any farm co-op and filling station.[3]

Their first experiment with ammonium nitrate/fuel oil explosive (ANFO) was a New Year's Eve air raid in a stolen Cessna 150 against the Badger Ordnance Works. The mayonnaise jars of ANFO that they dropped from the sky did little damage to the munitions plant, but the comically daring attack made the "New Year's Gang" the underground heroes of the Madison anti-war movement. They were seen by the student Left less as proto-terrorists than as a guerrilla theater troupe whose harmless explosions mocked the Nixon administration's deadly bombing of Indochina. But the Gang's next exploit – the improvization of a massive ANFO car bomb to blow up the campus-based Army Mathematics Research Center – was anything but mere theater.[4]

The group loaded a stolen Ford Econoline van with 1750 pounds of ammonium nitrate (purchased from the Farmers Union Co-op for $48) mixed with 20 gallons of fuel oil according to the simple instructions from the Fish and Game Department pamphlet; the detonator was some Primacord that they had purloined from a mine. Early on the morning of August 23, 1970, when the Gang surmised the building would be empty, they left the van outside of Sterling Hall, the home of Army Math as well as the Physics Department. Although they were aware that the barrels of ANFO in the back of the van were the theoretical equivalent of 3400 sticks of dynamite, the "Vanguard of the Revolution," as they now styled themselves in an infantile note to the authorities, seemed to have had little comprehension of the actual destructive power they were about to unleash. They phoned a warning to campus police to evacuate the building, but the van exploded prematurely before cops could reach Sterling Hall.[5] One policeman (interviewed by Tom Bates for his book on the bombing) was Jack Schwichtenberg:

> He was nearing the intersection of University and Charter, separated from Sterling by the bulk of Old Chemistry, when the bomb went off with strobe-like flash and a deafening noise. Struggling to keep his vehicle on the road, he glimpsed a Toyota that had pulled over to get out of his way hurtling through the air, coming to rest in the bus lane. Schwichtenberg veered right onto Charter and found himself staring into a holocaust. The air was full of flying glass, and Sterling Hall appeared to be engulfed in flames. An orange column of fire rose hundreds of feet over the building, with a mushroom cloud of swirling objects at its top. Schwichtenberg had served in the Marines and had seen a lot of ordnance expended in Vietnam; nonetheless, he was stupefied. *It's like an atomic bomb!* he thought.[6]

Indeed, the huge explosion rocked the entire campus, blowing the outer wall off one wing of Sterling Hall and seriously damaging two dozen other buildings. A young physicist − an opponent of the Vietnam War who had absolutely no connection with Army Math − was working late in his lab and was killed, and several other graduate students were seriously injured. Dozens of labs were wrecked and decades of important research were lost. And thanks to the reckless stupidity of the New Year's Gang, the Madison New Left suddenly found itself with innocent blood on its hands.

From a bombmaker's perspective, however, the Army Math bombing was the shape of things to come. The first-generation car bombs − in Jaffa, Jerusalem, Saigon, Algiers, and Palermo − were deadly enough (with a maximum yield usually equal to several hundred pounds of TNT), but they required stolen industrial or military high explosives. ANFO, in contrast, was easily (if somewhat dangerously) blended from cheap, universally available ingredients, and it exponentially raised the maximum explosive yield of a van or truck bomb to several tons of TNT – comparable to the very biggest conventional weapons. Moreover, if mere schoolboys in Wisconsin could blow up half their university campus with an ANFO bomb, what might professional urban guerrillas achieve?

Whether cognizant of the Madison explosion or not, the Provisional IRA soon found itself under the spell of ANFO car bombs and their virtually unlimited destructive power. According to Belfast journalist Ed Moloney in his *Secret History of the IRA:* 'The car bomb was discovered entirely by accident, but its deployment by the Belfast IRA was not. The chain of events began in late December 1971 when the IRA's quartermaster general, Jack McCabe, was fatally injured in an explosion caused when an experimental fertilizer-based homemade mix known as the 'black stuff' exploded as he was blending it with a shovel in his garage on the northern outskirts of Dublin. GHQ warned that the mix was too dangerous to handle, but Belfast had already received a consignment, and someone had the idea of disposing of it by dumping it in a car with a fuse and a timer and leaving it somewhere in downtown Belfast."[7]

The resulting explosion made a profound impression upon the Belfast leadership. "We could feel the rattle where we stood. Then we knew we were onto something, and it took off from there."[8] The "black stuff" – which the IRA soon learned how to handle safely – freed the underground army from supply-side constraints: the car bomb enhanced destructive capacity yet reduced the likelihood of Volunteers being accidentally blown up or arrested. The ANFO car bomb, in other words, was an unexpected military revolution, but one (as the New Year's Gang had discovered) fraught with potential for political and moral disaster. "The sheer size of the devices," emphasizes Moloney, "greatly increased the risk of civilian deaths in careless or bungled operations."[9]

The IRA Army Council led by Sean MacStiofain were too seduced by the new weapon's awesome power to understand how easily it might backfire against them. Indeed, car bombs reinforced the illusion, shared by most of the top leadership in 1972, that the IRA was but a Tet Offensive away from victory over the British government. The car-bomb blitz began punctually on January 3 when three guerrillas left a hijacked beer truck outside one of the large Royal Avenue department stores, thronged with women and girls for the annual New Year's sales. Although the bomb was small enough to be concealed inside a single beer barrel and was probably not intended to kill, the explosion shattered the large display windows along the Avenue, and put 63 shoppers – all but 10 of them women – in hospital with glass lacerations. ("It was like being hit by glass bullets," one woman said.) A month later, IRA volunteers hijacked a fuel tanker carrying 4000 gallons of gasoline and parked it in front of the *Belfast Telegraph* building with a time bomb in the front seat. They called in a warning to the newspaper (the voice of ruling Unionism), and an Army bomb squad defused the device in time to save the city center from a cataclysm.[10]

Downtown was again attacked in March; this time with two car bombs. Garbled phone warnings led police to inadvertently evacuate people, including many children, in the direction of one of the explosions (Donegall Street): five civilians were killed along with two members of the security forces. Despite the public outcry as well as the immediate closure to traffic of the Royal Avenue shopping precinct, the Belfast Brigade's enthusiasm for car bombs remained undiminished and in May the leadership authorized a deceitful attack on Protestant factory workers in the Jennymount Industrial Estate. A phone call warned that a gelignite bomb had been placed in the factory, but as workers promptly evacuated outside into the parking lot, 60 of them were lacerated by glass and metal shards from an exploding car bomb.[11] With such "successes" to the credit of his leadership, MacStiofain now apparently believed that the IRA had the means to inflict a mortal blow on the status quo in Northern Ireland. Almost ranting, he envisioned a bombing offensive of "the utmost ferocity and ruthlessness" that would literally wreck the "colonial infrastructure" and overthrow the Unionist government in Stormont.[12]

On Friday, July 21 IRA Volunteers left 22 ANFO car bombs or

concealed gelignite[13] charges on the periphery of the now-gated
city center, with detonations timed to follow one another at
approximately five-minute intervals. The first car bomb (2:40
p.m.) exploded in front of the Ulster Bank in north Belfast and
blew both legs off a Catholic passerby; successive explosions
damaged two railroad stations, the Ulster Bus depot on Oxford
Street, various railway junctions, and a mixed Catholic–Protestant
residential area on Cavehill Road. "At the height of the bombing,
the center of Belfast resembled a city under artillery fire; clouds of
suffocating smoke enveloped buildings as one explosion followed
another, almost drowning out the hysterical screams of panicked
shoppers."[14] A series of telephoned IRA warnings only created
more chaos, as civilians fled from one explosion into the maw of
another. Seven civilians and two soldiers were killed and more than
130 people were seriously wounded.

Although not the economic knockout punch envisioned by
MacStiofain, "Bloody Friday" was the beginning of a "no business
as usual" bombing campaign that quickly inflicted significant
damage on the Northern Ireland economy, particularly its ability
to attract private and foreign investment. The terror of that day also
compelled authorities to tighten their anti-car-bomb "ring of steel"
around the Belfast city center, making it the prototype for other
fortified enclaves and future "green zones." In the tradition of their
ancestors, the Fenians, who had originated dynamite terrorism in
the 1870s, Irish Republicans had again added new pages to the
textbook of urban guerrilla warfare. Foreign aficionados, particularly in the Middle East, undoubtedly paid close attention to the
strategic employment of ANFO car bombs in a protracted bombing
campaign against an entire urban–regional economy.

What was less well understood outside of Ireland, however, was
the enormity of the wound that the IRA's car bombs inflicted on
the Republican movement itself. Bloody Friday destroyed much of
the IRA's heroic-underdog popular image, produced deep revul-
sion amongst ordinary Catholics, and gave the British government
an unexpected reprieve from the worldwide condemnation it had
earned for the Bloody Sunday massacre in Derry and the policy of

Figure 3   Bloody Friday, July 21, 1972. BBC Film Archive.

internment without trial. Moreover it gave the British Army the perfect pretext to launch the massive Operation Motorman: 13,000 troops led by Centurion tanks entered the "no-go" areas of Derry and Belfast, smashed the barricades, and reclaimed control of the streets from the Republican movement. (The same day that the tanks rolled into the ghettos, a bungled car-bomb attack on the village of Claudy in County Londonderry killed nine people.)

The debacle in Belfast led to a major turnover in IRA leadership, but failed to dispel their almost cargo-cult-like belief in the capacity of car bombs to turn the tide of battle. Forced on the defensive by Operation Motorman and the backlash to Bloody Friday, they decided to strike at the very heart of British power: the Belfast Brigade planned to send ten car bombs to London via the Dublin – Liverpool ferry using fresh volunteers with clean records, including two young sisters, Marion and Dolours Price. Snags arose and only four cars arrived in London; one of these was detonated in front of the Old Bailey, another in the center of Whitehall, close to Number 10 Downing Street. The toll was 180 Londoners injured and one dead of a heart attack. Although the eight IRA bombers were quickly caught, "the extent of the subsequent media coverage," Ed Moloney points out, "taught the IRA a lesson its members would never forget: one bomb in London was worth a dozen in Belfast."[15] Indeed the operation became the template for future Provisional bombing campaigns in London that would culminate in the huge explosions that shattered the City of London and unnerved the world insurance industry in 1992 and 1993.

10

Laughing at the Dead

There are grounds for suspecting that the bombers may have had
assistance from members of the security forces.

2003 Irish parliamentary report[1]

The 1972 London bombings may have also instigated elements of
the British military to send a brutal message to a government in
Dublin that was accused, however unfairly, of failing to crack down
on IRA activities in the Republic. Irish Republicans have long
suspected that the sophisticated car bombs – usually attributed to
Protestant terrorists from Northern Ireland – that devastated three
crowded shopping streets in Dublin, as well as a pub in Monaghan
Town, in May 1974 required the technical expertise of the Special
Air Services (SAS) or some other elite unit of the British Army.
Although these explosions claimed the highest one-day human toll
(33 dead, more than 240 hospitalized) in the history of the
"Troubles," the parallel police investigations in Belfast and Dublin,
despite early identification of leading suspects, ran into mysterious
obstacles and were quickly shelved without arrests or prosecutions.

Indeed the mass murders – the victims were mostly women
shoppers and their children – were almost forgotten until Yorkshire
Television in 1993 broadcast an hour-long special report – *Hidden
Hand: The Forgotten Massacre* – that offered sensational evidence of
Army collusion with the Loyalist bombers. Thanks to independent
British television, the formerly far-fetched idea that Her Majesty's

Forces (or some cohort thereof) could have helped Loyalists bomb Dublin suddenly became a serious hypothesis that the retired generals and relic politicians surviving from this period have yet to convincingly refute.

The background of the Dublin and Monaghan bombings was the epic collision in May 1974 between Prime Minister Harold Wilson's Labour government, championing the Sunningdale Agreement that provided for token power-sharing between Official Unionists and moderate Catholics in the Northern Ireland Parliament (Stormont), and the so-called Ulster Workers' Council, representing Loyalist paramilitaries and hardliners, who paralyzed the economy with a "general strike" enforced by Protestant mobs and gunmen in balaclavas. The British Army in Northern Ireland, whose largest contingent (the Ulster Defence Regiment or UDR) was notoriously infiltrated by Loyalist paramilitaries, repeatedly undercut the efforts of the Wilson government to end the sectarian strike, refusing to launch even a limited version of Operation Motorman to take back control of vital public utilities. A powerful faction, at least, of the Army and police were bitterly opposed to any political solution short of the total defeat of the IRA. A generation later, Merlyn Rees, the embattled Northern Ireland Secretary at the time, would complain to a television interviewer that "his 1974 policies were being undermined by a subversive faction in Army Intelligence . . . It was a unit – a section – out of control. There's no doubt it reflected the views of a number of soldiers – 'let's go in and fix this lot', and so on."[2]

"This lot" apparently included the Southern public. Yet, ironically, as far as most ordinary Dubliners were concerned, the near-insurrectionary events in Belfast (reminiscent of Algiers in 1960) could have been storms on another planet.[3] Their more immediate preoccupation on Friday, May 17, 1974, was the local bus strike that was creating chaos in the city center for employees and shoppers trying to negotiate the evening rush hour. Then within the terrifying span of just 90 seconds, the whole world seemed to blow up. Large car bombs exploded in Parnell Street, Talbot Street, and South Leinster Street (near the Dail, the Irish parliament), leaving the city center strewn with maimed bodies, screaming children, mangled burning cars, and smoldering debris from shattered shops. In his collection of eyewitness tales (certainly the largest and most poignant compilation of victim testimony about a car-bombing that I know of), Irish journalist Don Mullan introduces Bridget Fitzpatrick, one of the "luckier" survivors.

I was after collecting my children from school, gave them their dinner, clean up and took two of my sons, Derek and Tommy, along with my sister Kathleen to Hamill's clothes shop in Parnell Street to collect Derek's Holy Communion clothes. It was a happy day for my boys. They knew I would buy them a treat and we were excited . . .

I was in the middle of the road facing Westbrook Garage, holding my sons by each hand, and Derek's clothes under my arm, when this horrible bang went off in my head. At that very same moment I could see the front walls of the garage coming out and what I can only described as some kind of baby's pram lifting into the air. Then, in panic, there was nothing to do even though I knew I was badly hurt, with every thought I had to run as I realized it was a bomb. I grabbed my sons' hands as hard as I could and ran through thick blinding smoke and glass, cutting my legs, straight for the Rotunda Hospital. My poor son Tommy was shouting "Ma, Ma, stop. The bomb got me in the leg." He was only 5 years old.

. . .

When I got inside the door of the Rotunda Hospital I was taken into a room and put on a bed. My boys were being looked after by nurses. I saw a young man on the floor. The top of his head seemed to be gone. An elderly woman sitting on a chair with a pair of glasses but the glass was sticking in her eyes which were bleeding, and a nurse washing a young boy's arms covered in blood.[4]

If such carnage produced shock and incomprehension in Dublin, it was greeted with macabre glee by certain hardcore circles in the

North. Sammy Smith, the press officer for the Ulster Workers' Council, bragged to the British press: "I am very happy about the bombings in Dublin. There is a war with the Free State and now we are laughing at them."[5] It was quickly established that the three cars used to bomb Dublin had been purloined from Protestant neighborhoods in Belfast the morning of the attacks. The Garda, the Irish national police, obtained positive identifications of several of the bombers from eyewitnesses, pointing to leading members of the Ulster Volunteer Force (UVF) from the town of Portadown, southwest of Belfast in County Armagh. But the investigation soon ran afoul of poor cooperation from the Garda's northern counterpart, the Royal Ulster Constabulary (RUC), as well as diminished enthusiasm within the Dublin government for pressing ahead at all cost. Crucial forensic evidence was also mishandled, then lost.[6] The Garda, moreover, had difficulty resolving the contradiction between the apparent role of the Portadown UVF and their well-known lack of expertise and munitions to carry out such a complex serial bombing.

In the event, the Garda cracked down instead on the Republican movement in a nationwide series of raids, while the Dublin and Monaghan investigation lost momentum and then was quietly abandoned; as were, indeed, the victims and their families whose demands for justice were officially ignored for an entire generation. *Hidden Hand*, the 1993 documentary by Yorkshire Television's *First Tuesday* investigative team, implied that the Irish government might have been trying to avoid a conflagration of its relations with London. According to the sources interviewed by *First Tuesday* – including two former British undercover officers, five veteran Portadown paramilitaries, and "a senior source in the RUC Special Branch" – the actual planners of the bombing were not only "former or serving members of the British Army's biggest regiment, the UDR," but also assets of a top-secret British intelligence unit engaged in dirty-war-type operations inside the Irish Republic.[7]

Colin Wallace, an ex-British Intelligence operative, whom Irish parliamentary investigators later confirmed as "a highly knowledgeable witness,"[8] told millions of television viewers that the leaders of the bombers were "probably members of the special duties team, who were linked to SAS personnel." "That special duties team was based in the rolling countryside of County Armagh, at Castledillon, in the grounds of a stately home. The team was a group of SAS-trained undercover soldiers who formed the most secret unit of the British Army in Northern Ireland." Philip Tibenham, the program's narrator, then added: "The team's cover name was Four Field Survey Troop. Officially, they were answerable to Army Headquarters in Lisburn. But routinely, they operated in virtual isolation. Ultimately, their chain of command led to MI5." A former member of the team – his face blocked out – explained: "We were a specialist unit with training in surveillance and anti-surveillance, silent weapons, breaking and entering. We were also trained in weapons for sabotage with explosives and assassination. We also crossed the Irish border with explosives to booby-trap arms dumps and other missions."[9] (Later investigation by Irish television's *Prime Time* program established that "at the time of the Dublin and Monaghan bombings, a fully armed plain-clothes unit of trained SAS soldiers was operating in Ireland's capital city.")[10]

If the Irish Taoiseach (premier), the rabidly anti-Republican Liam Cosgrave, had any inkling of SAS involvement (as was likely the case), he and his cabinet would have confronted an unsavory choice between pressing forward with the investigation and risking public outrage against London at the very moment when both governments were desperately trying to save the Sunningdale Accord, or, conversely, backing off the case and betraying the victims. The cold logic of the government's collaboration with Westminister, as well as Cosgrave's personal stake in laying all blame at the feet of the Republican movement, dictated silence. No one in the ruling Fine Gael Party, presumably, wanted to vindicate the IRA's claims about British collusion with Loyalist terrorism. As a 2003 investigation by the Dail would conclude, "the Government of the day showed little interest in the bombings. When information was given to them suggesting that the British authorities had intelligence naming the bombers, this was not followed up."[11]

But, from the other side, what rational objective might have led the SAS or their bosses in MI5 to collude in the Dublin and Monaghan outrages – acts of sabotage against the Labour government in London as much as the Irish people? To answer this crucial question, *First Tuesday* reporters evoked the repressed memory of an earlier car-bombing: "In December 1972, two car bombs exploded in Dublin, killing two people as the Irish Parliament was debating new anti-terrorist laws. The Irish opposition was against the measures but now voted for them believing the IRA had planted the bombs. Yet within weeks, rumours that the British were responsible were rife. Even Jack Lynch, the Irish Prime Minister at the time of the bombs, suspected British involvement."[12] (Years later, Irish parliamentarians would complain about the refusal of the British government to cooperate in any way with a new investigation of the 1972 bombings.)[13]

Similarly, *First Tuesday* argued, the Dublin and Monaghan bombings by giving the Irish public "a taste of the carnage already suffered in Northern Ireland for five years" discouraged any desire in the South to become more involved in resolving the "Troubles." Thanks to both the Northern general strike and the bombings in the South, "the loyalists had destroyed much of the political will in Dublin and London. Sunningdale was dead."[14] And Northern Ireland was thereby doomed to a further 25 years of political assassinations, car-bombings, sectarian atrocities, miscarriages of justice, and economic decline.

11

Hell's Kitchen

This war was waged against the background of an ever-present fear of car bombs.

Rashid Khalidi[1]

Never in history has a single city been the battlefield for so many contesting ideologies, sectarian allegiances, local vendettas, foreign conspiracies and interventions as was Beirut in the early 1980s. Belfast's triangular conflicts – three armed camps (Republican, Loyalist, and British) and their splinter groups – seemed straightforward compared to the fractal or Russian-doll-like complexity of Lebanon's factional wars (Abu Nidal versus Abu Iyad, or Franjieh versus Gemayel) inside civil wars (Shiite versus Palestinian) within confessional wars (Maronite versus Moslem and Druze) inside regional conflicts (Israel versus Syria) and surrogate wars (Iran versus the United States) within, ultimately, the Cold War. In the fall of 1981, for example, there were 58 different armed groups in West Beirut alone.[2] With so many people trying to kill each other for so many different reasons, Beirut became to the technology of urban violence what a tropical rainforest is to the evolution of plants and insects.

Before 1981, car bombs were a dramatic but infrequent means of mass homicide in Beirut. The first bombing in July 1972 was organized by the Israeli Mossad to kill Ghassan Kanafani, famed novelist and spokesperson for the Popular Front for the Liberation of Palestine.[3] Then just before Christmas 1976, and shortly after the truce ending the Lebanese civil war, a car bomb was detonated near the home of Kamal Jumblatt – sparing the leader of the Palestinian–Lebanese Left alliance but killing three other people. At the New Year, Jumblatt's followers retaliated with a car bomb in front of the East Beirut headquarters of the Phalange Party's security service which killed more than 25 and wounded at least 70.[4] Two years later (and 7 years after the deaths of 11 members of the Israeli Olympic team in Munich) Mossad agents went after the chief organizer of Black September, Ali Hassan Salameh, in Beirut. The "Red Prince," as he was code-named by his Israeli hunters, was driving down the Rue Verdun in West Beirut in a Chevrolet station wagon when the Israelis detonated plastic explosives concealed in a parked Volkswagen. The car bomb – greeted with public celebration in Israel – killed Salameh and four associates, as well as four innocent passersby, including a German nun and a British student.[5]

These sporadic atrocities were just prelude to the sustained terrorization of Moslem West Beirut from late summer 1981 through early 1983: a succession of car-bombings that were evidently part of the joint Israeli–Phalangist campaign to evict the Palestinian Liberation Organization from Lebanon. For 18 months, a hellish chess game was played out with TNT-packed taxis and trucks in a vain attempt to intimidate the popular anti-Israeli forces in the Levant: in 1981 alone more than 200 civilians were killed in 18 car-bomb explosions in the Lebanese capital.[6] In the same period Damascus was also rocked by a series of deadly car-bomb explosions that the Assad regime blamed on the underground Moslem Brotherhood, but which plausibly might also have involved the Lebanese Christian militias, Iraq, Jordan, and/or Israel. The warring neighbors, Iran and Iraq, acting through their respective allies, the Al Dawa Party and the Peoples' Mujahedeen, also exchanged several volleys of car bombs in 1981–82 amidst a hurricane of regular munitions.[7]

The wave of bombings in Lebanon began on September 17, 1981 when a vehicle exploded outside the headquarters of the Palestinian–Lebanese Leftist alliance in the port city of Sidon, killing

29 (mainly passersby, including women and children, rather than guerrillas) and wounding 108; almost simultaneously, a cement factory in the northern town of Chekka, owned by the pro-Syrian ex-president of Lebanon, Suleiman Franjieh, was wrecked by another car bomb, leaving ten dead.[8] Responsibility for both explosions was claimed by the "Front for the Liberation of Lebanon from Aliens" – which the PLO immediately declared was simply "a name used to cover Israeli actions in Lebanon." The next day, an anonymous spokesman for the same group called news media to take credit for a car bomb that killed three people in the largely Shiite quarter of Chiya, on the southwestern edge of Beirut. He warned that the Front would keep bombing "until there no longer are any foreigners or plotters alive on the territory of greater Lebanon" – Palestinians and Syrians were specifically singled out. The shadowy group blew up a cinema in West Beirut (at least four dead), but police defused a large car bomb left the next day (September 21) in front of a hotel in the Moslem sector. Then, a week later, a Mercedes booby-trapped with a potent mixture of high explosives and incendiaries blew up in front of a crowded restaurant next to a Palestinian checkpoint, killing 16 and wounding 40, including many women and children.[9]

In response, the PLO introduced new anti-car-bomb security measures at its offices and began using police dogs from East Germany trained to detect the slightest trace of explosives.[10] But the bombers, the beneficiaries of exceedingly accurate on-the-ground intelligence, were undeterred. The deadliest attack came on October 1. As *New York Times* correspondent John Kifner reported from West Beirut:

A car packed with more than a hundred pounds of explosives blew up today outside Palestinian guerrilla offices in a crowded street, killing at least 50 people and wounding more than 250, according to officials. The explosion, the sixth and worst of its kind in two weeks, tore the façade from five buildings and squashed cars in the Fakhani neighborhood of Moslem West Beirut. As ambulances fought their way through traffic and guerrillas fired sub-machine guns into the air, Palestinian forces reported finding three other booby-trapped cars in the area.

The Fakhani neighborhood, on the southern edge of West Beirut, is controlled and policed by Palestinian guerrillas. Armed young men crowd the streets amid the bustle of a vegetable market and Beirut Arab University. It is the neighborhood that was bombed July 17 in an Israeli air raid that killed some 300 people, mostly civilians. Prime Minister Chafik Wazzan, on his way to a meeting at the presidential palace, said he blamed "agents of Israel" for today's explosions.

"Now that Israel has been prevented from persisting in its acts of destruction and killing in Lebanon through its air forces or other attacks," Mr. Wazzan said, "it is looking for other tactics, the cowardly ones to which it is currently resorting either directly or through agents."[11]

Car-bombings resumed in December with 18 incidents, including a dual attack just before Christmas that killed 13 people near the offices of Palestinian guerrilla organizations. "Lebanese police statistics," writes Yezid Sayigh, "showed that Israeli attacks, internecine clashes, and car bombs had caused 2100 deaths by the end of the year."[12] Then on February 23, 1982, two car bombs, exploding a few minutes apart, devastated the ramshackle outdoor market along the seaside highway that had replaced Beirut's famous *souk*, destroyed at the beginning of the civil war six years earlier. Crowded with thousands of shoppers and traders, the Corniche market was "perched precariously along a cliff, once one of the city's choicest views," and offered an inviting target to anyone interested in sowing maximum terror amongst the civilian Moslem population. "The blasts," reported the *New York Times*, "damaged about 200 cars, destroyed a gas station, set fire to other nearby buildings and ripped through the flimsy tin shops. Hospital wards were full of victims as local militia men waved automatic rifles and fired into the air to clear the way for ambulances." Once again the shadowy Front claimed responsibility for the nearly 100 casualties as it did for the car bomb that killed eight people in the Shia slum of Ouzai a few days later during a visit to Beirut by Reagan envoy Philip Habib.[13]

During the Israeli siege of Beirut that June, car bombs added to the terror caused by the Israeli Air Force's cluster bombs and Israeli artillery's use of white phosphorous shells against Moslem neighborhoods. The first of a new wave of car-bombings killed 60 refugees on June 24; another three days later killed 23 civilians. Three weeks later, as General Sharon pressed toward his goal of "the destruction of the refugee camps in Lebanon and the mass deportation of the 200,000 Palestinians," 32 people in West Beirut were killed or wounded by another vehicle bomb. Unexpectedly stiff Palestinian resistance (Arafat had vowed to make West Beirut the "Arab Stalingrad"), however, led to redoubled efforts to kill the PLO leadership. In what was apparently a synchronized assassination attempt in August, Israeli bombers destroyed an apartment building briefly used by the PLO, killing more than 200 refugees. When Arafat arrived on the scene to console survivors, he narrowly escaped being blown up by a hidden car bomb.[14]

Was Tel Aviv directly or indirectly responsible for this carnage? There was little surprise when the Palestinian–Lebanese Left coalition offered provocative evidence that Israel was the chief sponsor of the car-bombings in West Beirut. According to scholar Rashid Khalidi (who cites contemporary reports by *Newsweek* and *Guardian* journalists), "a sequence of public confessions by captured drivers made clear these [car-bombings] were being utilized by the Israelis and their Phalangist allies to increase the pressure on the PLO to leave."[15] Tabitha Petran also blames Israel for the explosions that caused more than 500 civilian casualties, claiming that the car bombs were rigged in Saad Haddad's Israeli-protected enclave in southern Lebanon then driven to East Beirut before being moved to the western sector of the city.[16] The PLO itself fingered Johnny Abdo, the head of Lebanese Army Intelligence, as Israel's co-conspirator in the attacks.[17]

The Palestinian historian Yezid Sayigh has no doubt that "hostile intelligence agencies were also actively involved." "A car bomb that was defused at the 'Ayn al-Hilwa refugee camp on 13 March contained 200 kilograms of explosives with Hebrew markings."[18] Other credible evidence of Israeli complicity emerged in the wake of an attack on a Shiite neighborhood in June 1982. British journalist Robert Fisk was not far from the scene when an "enormous [car] bomb blew a 45-foot-crater in the road and brought down an entire block of apartments. The building collapsed like a concertina, crushing more than 50 of its occupants to death, most of them Shia refugees from southern Lebanon." Several of the car bombers were captured and confessed that the bombs had been rigged by the Shin Bet, the Israeli equivalent of the FBI or the British Special Branch. "One of the men," relates Fisk, "said his brother had been arrested by the Israelis who had threatened to kill him if he did not help plant the bomb. The explosives – which we saw the following day – all had printed Hebrew words on them."[19]

But who was responsible for the parallel car-bombing campaign inside Syria? Answering this question is rather like solving a murder in an Agatha Christie novel where all the passengers on the train or guests at dinner have sufficient motives for homicide. Most of the major players in the Middle East – the Phalangists, the Israelis, the Iraqis, the Jordanians, the majority faction of the PLO as well as France and the United States – had grievances against the Baathist regime of President Hafez Asad in Damascus. With discreet permission from Kissinger and Israel, Syrian armor columns had entered Lebanon in June 1976 to rescue the Phalangists from almost certain defeat at the hands of the PLO and the Lebanese Left led by Kamal Jumblatt. Asad's "treason" was subsequently denounced throughout the Arab world, yet the savior of the Christians was soon in violent conflict with the Phalangists over their ties to Israel. Furthermore, as British journalist Patrick Seale points out, "He had exasperated Washington by his attacks on the Egypt–Israel peace treaty. He had broken with Iraq and after the emergence of Ayatollah Khomayni had sided with revolutionary Iran. He was on the worst possible terms with King Husayn of Jordan. He had tangled dangerously with Israel in Lebanon."[20]

Some combination of these antagonists became deeply involved in provisioning the terrorist campaign inside Syria which was being

waged by Asad's truly most implacable enemy: the Moslem Brotherhood (*ikhwan*). By 1979 this Sunni underground group was
engaged in the wholesale assassination of the Baathist cadre –
especially those, like the President himself, who hailed from the
Alawite (a Shiite sect) minority. Seale argues that the *ikhwan*'s
astonishing efficiency in terrorism (it killed 300 Baathists in Aleppo
alone) owed much to covert subsidies. " [They] had a fortune in
foreign money, sophisticated communications equipment and large
arms dumps – no fewer than 15,000 machine guns were captured.
And as soldiers they were not novices. About half of those captured
had been trained in Arab countries, mainly in Jordan." Asad himself
accused Israel, the CIA, Jordan, and Iraq: a claim made more
plausible by Saddam Hussein's brazen admission that he had
supplied arms to the guerrillas, as well as by the discovery in *ikhwan*
hideouts of sophisticated equipment with Israeli and US markings.[21]

In any event, the car-bombing of Damascus began in earnest in
August 1981 with an explosion outside the Prime Minister's office.
This was soon followed on September 3 by an attack on the
headquarters of the Syrian Air Force which left at least 20 dead.
In October, a car bomb killed several Soviet advisors outside their
compound, and Damascus became "stiff with troops, the city was
turned into an armed camp. Checkpoints were everywhere, body
searches became routine."[22] On November 29 – while Asad was
meeting with other Arab leaders in Fez – security agents confronted
someone attempting to abandon a car in the busy Ezbekieh district
not far from the Central Bank. When the driver pulled out a gun,
the agents shot him dead, but an accomplice hidden somewhere in
the neighborhood, detonated the several hundred pounds of TNT
inside the car by remote control. The huge explosion brought
down four nearby apartment blocs and devastated a school: many of
the more than 200 dead and 500 wounded were children. To that
date, it was the deadliest car-bombing in history. The government
immediately blamed the Moslem Brotherhood, but the anti-alien
Front – the erstwhile bombers of Beirut – phoned the Agence
France-Presse to claim credit.[23]

Asad, however, decided to punish the Iraqis first. In a preview of what lay ahead for his other enemies, the impressive seven-story Iraqi embassy – according to *Le Monde*, "the most well guarded building in Beirut" – was obliterated by a suicide car bomber who managed to crash through several layers of security barriers. The ambassador was killed, along with 65 members of his delegation. *Le Monde* found it "inexplicable" that the supposedly unassailable structure surrounded by concrete sentry posts, a high security wall, and a large contingent of armed guards, could have fallen "like a house of cards." The destruction was so complete that it took rescue workers 27 days to excavate all the bodies from the ruins. Some speculated that explosives must also have been concealed inside the building, but the more obvious explanation was the location of the embassy in a neighborhood controlled by Syrian troops. Iran – then fighting for its life against Saddam Hussein's armies – was a likely co-conspirator, and Baghdad radio blamed both countries.[24] (The following August, a van blew up outside the Iraqi embassy in Paris, setting fire to the building and injuring six – both Syrian and Iranian intelligence services were immediate suspects.)[25]

The *ikhwan*'s turn came two months later, following the ambush of an army patrol, when Asad unleashed his brother Rifaat's ruthless Saraya al Difa (Special Defense Brigades) on the Brotherhood citadel of Hama, a picturesque old town on the Orontes River 120 miles from Beirut. The battle lasted for more than a month, and when journalist Robert Fisk visited Hama a year later, it had become a latter-day Carthage: "the old city – the walls, the narrow streets, the Beit Azem museum – had simply disappeared, the ancient ruins flattened and turned into a massive car park." Fisk estimates that Rifaat's commandos killed as many as 10,000 supporters of the *ikhwan* (other accounts suggest 20,000).[26] In a speech in Damascus shortly after the Hama battle, President Asad accused "the butcher of Baghdad," Saddam Hussein, of inciting the Brotherhood, while Syrian television displayed captured cases of arms stenciled "Property of the Government of Iraq" as well as others with American markings.[27]

As he was destroying the *ikhwan*, Asad was also secretly at war against the French. France, the historic architect of Maronite supremacy, had returned in force to Lebanon in 1978 when a battalion of troops wearing UN blue helmets marched into Tyre, and relations with Syria became openly poisonous in 1981 when Paris rejected demands to turn over exiles accused of masterminding the car-bomb attacks in Damascus. That September, accordingly, the French ambassador in Beirut was assassinated by Shiite gunmen whom the Lebanese press, then French television, linked to the Syrian secret service. "Syrian responsibility in the murder of the French ambassador," reported the *Washington Post*, "was considered a foregone conclusion by many informed Lebanese." Then in March 1982 a car bomb shattered the neighborhood around the French Cultural Center in West Beirut. A month later, during the morning rush hour, another car bomb exploded in front of the Paris office of the anti-Syrian, Arab-language newspaper *Al-Watan Al-Arabi,* killing a pregnant pedestrian and injuring 60 others.[28]

French investigators quickly came to the horrifying conclusion that the Paris bomb had been intended to kill as many innocents as possible. As Henry Tanner reported in the *New York Times*:

> The police said that 11 of the 46 wounded were in critical condition, including a teenage boy whose leg was shattered by the blast. Police sources said that the car had been left in a spot where the explosion necessarily would wound or kill a maximum number of passersby rather than do damage to the newspaper office across the street. The car was carrying Vienna licence plates, but had been rented in Ljubljana, in northern Yugoslavia, the police said. It was totally destroyed by the explosion. More than a dozen other parked cars were also destroyed or heavily damaged. The fronts of shops were shattered and even windows on the higher floors of nearby buildings were broken.[29]

Although there was some press speculation that the bombing might be linked to the opening of the trial of two terrorist associates of Carlos "The Jackal," the Elysée quickly expressed its official opinion by expelling two Syrian diplomats identified as members of the secret service and recalling its ambassador from Damascus. The French could scarcely have imagined what would come next on May 25.

The French embassy in Beirut, which like the Iraqi compound, was considered almost impregnable and was guarded by a recently reinforced contingent of elite *paras*, was blown up by a bomb concealed in the car belonging to the ambassador's secretary. During the preceding weekend, someone had managed to hide 50 kilos of explosives in her trunk, which was then detonated by remote control when she drove unsuspectingly into the diplomatic compound on Monday morning. Aside from the secretary and a *para*, the rest of the dozen dead were Lebanese lined up to apply for French visas. Although a previously unknown group, the "Liberal Nasserite Organization," claimed credit for this highly sophisticated operation, most of the French press logically assumed it was the further handiwork of Syrian intelligence.[30] *Le Monde,* moreover, revealed that the French secret service, the SDECE, had been lobbying for the authority to follow "Israel's muscular example" and strike "secretly and with punctual violence" against France's enemies – Syria and its local allies.[31] Had France already done so? Was the SDECE one of the patrons of the shadowy anti-alien Front? Clearly Asad thought so.[32]

In September, another of Asad's *bêtes noires*, newly elected Lebanese President Bashir Gemayal, was blown up (by a suitcase bomb) along with 25 of his followers at the heavily fortified East Beirut headquarters of the Phalange Party – an event that set in motion the infamous massacres of Palestinians in the Sabra and Chatila camps. "The bombing," according to former Mossad agent Victor Ostrovsky, "was traced to Ptabib Chartouny, 26, a member of the Syrian People's Party, rivals of the Phalangists. The operation had been run by Syrian intelligence in Lebanon under Lieutenant Colonel Mohammed G'anen." (But Ostrovsky – another Agatha Christie fan – also implies the alternate possibility that the Mossad might have colluded with Phalangist security chief Elie Hobeika, an Israeli protégé and enemy of Bashir to either kill the president–elect or leave him unprotected in face of a known Syrian plot.)[33]

The Syrian president, who obviously liked to settle scores in comprehensive Michael Corleone-fashion, was probably also responsible for the huge car bomb in January 1983 which blew up a three-story building in the Syrian-controlled Bekaa Valley housing Al-Fatah's military intelligence organization (simply known as "17"). The day before, a Syrian-controlled Palestinian splinter group had publicly threatened Yasir Arafat with assassination. "Al-Saiqa's statement," reported Thomas Friedman in the *New York Times*, "described Mr. Arafat as a traitor for pursuing diplomatic options with King Hussein of Jordan and warned the P.L.O. chief of the fate that King Hussein's grandfather, King Abdullah, and President Anwar el-Sadat of Egypt met when they tried to make peace with Israel. Both were assassinated."[34]

To make sure that Arafat understood Damascus's anger, a second car bomb a week later destroyed the Palestine Research Center, the last remaining PLO office in Beirut, as well as the adjacent Libyan embassy. In addition to at least 20 dead and 136 wounded, the blast destroyed what remained of the PLO's national archive of Palestinian culture (earlier defaced and looted by the Israeli Army). Although the PLO officially blamed Israel and its "Front," sophisticated observers inclined toward the belief that the explosion was probably the capstone to the cold vengeance of Hafez Asad.[35] In the course of a long year, his secret services (which a generation later, in February 2005, would be universally suspect in the truck-bomb assassination of Lebanese Premier Rafik Hariri) had proven themselves even more adept than the Mossad in using anonymous car-bombings as a murderous arm of state power. But both secret services would soon be overshadowed by Iran's Lebanese protégés and Syria's reluctant allies, the slum-grown suicide bombers of Hezbollah.

12

The Beirut Hilton

We are soldiers of God and we crave death. We are ready to turn
Lebanon into another Vietnam.

Hezbollah[1]

Amongst the myriad martyrs and sectarian heroes of Lebanon's
bloody ground, Sheik Ahmed Qassir, a Shiite militant from the
southern village of Dair Qanoun al-Nahr, is one of the most
renowned. Hezbollah venerates him as the "first suicide car bomber," an unstoppable warrior who managed to kill or wound 141
Israelis in an attack on their eight-story headquarters in Tyre on
November 11, 1982 (a year later another Hezbollah car bomber
blew up the building again, killing 60, including some top Shin Bet
officials). The attack remains "the deadliest single disaster in Israel's
history."[2] Although the anonymous driver of the bomb-laden
vehicle that destroyed the Iraqi embassy the previous December
actually had priority, it is Sheik Qassir who has become enshrined in
Middle Eastern popular culture as the Edison or Lindbergh of the
suicide car bomb: a celebrity that owes much to Hezbollah's shrewd
innovation of video-recording the operation.[3] The anniversary of
his attack is now Hezbollah's major holiday – "Martyrs' Day" –
celebrated throughout southern Lebanon and in the slums of
Beirut.[4]

Indeed the Tyre attack, and the myth that has arisen around it,
probably constitute the single most important watershed in the car

bomb's slouching-toward-Bethlehem to become a universal weapon of mass destruction. To the Madison/Belfast recipe of vehicle plus ANFO was now added a third and decisive ingredient from Beirut cuisine: the grimly determined *kamikaze* ready to crash through security barriers and past startled guards in order to bring his deadly payload into the very lobby of an embassy or barracks.

The Shiite suicide bomber, however, was largely a Frankenstein monster of Ariel Sharon's deliberate creation. The Israeli invasion of Lebanon in June 1982, followed by the destruction of the Syrian Air Force, the indiscriminate cluster bombing of Moslem districts of Beirut, and then the entry of Israeli paratroopers into the outskirts of the city in August, produced a fundamental realignment of forces.[5] Defense Minister Sharon's iron heel in southern Lebanon and Beirut – scarcely a household was spared injury, property damage, or the arrest of a male member – quickly converted the Shiites (an estimated 40 percent of Lebanon's population) from Israel's informal allies into their most resolute and skillful opponents.[6] (Twenty years later, Israeli Prime Minister Sharon, under investigation for war crimes by a tribunal in Belgium, would be accused by Lebanese officials of ordering the car-bomb assassination in Beirut of the key witness preparing to testify against him.)[7]

The new Shiite militancy was incarnated in Hezbollah, formed in mid-1982 out of an amalgamation of Islamic Amal (a splinter group of the larger Amal movement) with other pro-Khomeini *groupuscules*. Trained and advised by the Iranian Pasdaran, who based themselves with Damascus's permission in the Syrian-controlled Bekaa Valley, Hezbollah was both an indigenous resistance movement with deep roots in the Shiite villages and slums, and, at the same time, the long arm of Iran's theocratic revolution. Although some experts espouse alternative theories, Islamic Amal/Hezbollah is usually seen as the author, with Iranian and Syrian technical assistance, of the devastating attacks on American and French forces in Beirut during 1983. With the Iraqi embassy and Tyre attacks as templates, and with some obvious understanding of Viet Cong tactics during the Battle of Saigon, Hezbollah used suicide vehicle-bombings to transform the balance of power in the Middle East.[8]

The United States and France became targets of Hezbollah and its Syrian and Iranian patrons after the Multinational Force (MNF) in Beirut, which was supposedly landed to allow safe evacuation of the PLO, evolved first into the informal, then the public ally of the Christian Maronite government in its civil war against the Moslem–Druze majority. "By the spring of 1983," explains Robert Fisk, "the MNF was supporting a Phalangist administration, openly acknowledging links with Israeli forces and, through the Americans, encouraging an unofficial peace treaty between Israel and Lebanon."[9] Despite a premonitory series of grenade, rocket, and sniper attacks on the American embassy in Beirut between 1979 and 1982, the Reagan administration seemingly took little heed of Hezbollah's emergence or Shiite grievances, much less the threat posed by *kamikazes* in trucks.[10]

Payback for Washington's blatant support of the Maronites came on April 18, 1983, when a pickup truck carrying 2000 pounds of ANFO explosive suddenly swerved across traffic into the driveway of the seafront US embassy in Beirut. The driver gunned the truck past a startled guard and crashed through the lobby door. "Even by Beirut standards," writes former CIA agent Robert Baer, "it was an enormous blast, shattering windows. The USS *Guadalcanal*, anchored five miles off the coast, shuddered from the tremors. At ground zero, the center of the seven-story embassy lifted up hundreds of feet into the air, remained suspended for what seemed an eternity, and then collapsed in a cloud of dust, people, splintered furniture, and paper."[11]

Robert Fisk, whose apartment was just a few blocks from the embassy, was an eyewitness to the extraordinary destruction.

A sudden, gentle breeze had moved in from the sea and drawn the curtain of smoke aside. The centre of the Embassy was missing. The bottom of the two wings of the Embassy had disappeared. One half of the building had disintegrated and the upper floors of the centre now hung down in slabs as if someone had cut through it with a knife and removed the outer portion. Behind each dangling slab of floor were trapped desks, telephones, carpets and chairs. And suspended by the feet from one of the slabs, upside-down, still in his business suit, his arms dangling cruelly round his balding head, hung a dead American diplomat.

We tripped over corpses. The roadway was slippery with water, glass and blood and other, more terrible objects which a team of Lebanese Red Cross men and women were shoveling onto stretchers. In the visa section, where dozens of Lebanese men and women had been queuing for permission to visit the United States, every living soul had been burned alive. They were brought out not as bodies but as torsos, legs, lumps of intestines piled on stretchers, individual heads heaped inside a blanket. A Red Cross girl was scooping up remains in a bucket. An American Embassy security guard, still alive but temporarily deranged by the explosion which had broken his ear-drums began walking up and down in front of the smoking wreckage yelling "It's gonna blow, it's gonna blow" over and over again. We could see several bodies – and parts of bodies – floating in the Mediterranean.[12]

Whether as a result of superb intelligence or sheer luck, the bombing coincided with a visit to the embassy of Robert Ames, the CIA's national intelligence officer for the Near East and Washington's key liaison to the PLO leadership (who often supplied him with invaluable intelligence). It killed him ("his hand was found floating a mile offshore, the wedding ring still on his finger") and all six members of the Beirut CIA station. "Never before had the CIA lost so many officers in a single attack. It was a tragedy from which the agency would never recover."[13] It also left the Americans blind in Beirut, forcing them to scrounge for intelligence scraps from the French embassy or the British listening station offshore on Cyprus.[14]

Pentagon and National Security Agency officials agreed about Iranian complicity in the bombing (supposedly organized by their ambassador to Damascus, Mohammed Mohtashami-Pur), but there was no consensus about the role of the Syrians. According to the

Washington Post's Bob Woodward, Director William Casey "had sent some CIA officers to Beirut to conduct an investigation, and they had traced it right to Syrian intelligence," but one of the US agents tortured a suspect to death and the investigation was forced to close down.[15] The Pentagon's top-secret Intelligence Support Activity ("an officially non-existent unit") had also visited Beirut and returned with warnings that more heavy weather was on its way. But General John Vessey, the Chairman of the Joint Chiefs of Staff, was skeptical about these reports and dismissed the embassy bombing as an "inexplicable aberration."[16] As a result, the Americans never foresaw the coming of the mother of all vehicle-bomb attacks. (There is also the unsavory possibility that the Israelis deliberately withheld crucial intelligence about forthcoming attacks from their US counterparts – a charge made by former Mossad agent Victor Ostrovsky in a memoir that Tel Aviv tried to suppress.)[17]

From a Syrian or Shiite point of view, meanwhile, Washington was engaged in a policy of brazen provocation. In September, over the protests of Colonel Timothy Geraghty, the commander of the US Marines onshore in Beirut, President Reagan's senior representative, Robert McFarlane, ordered US destroyers to bombard the Druze militia who were storming Lebanese Forces' positions in the hills above Beirut. This action brought the United States into the conflict on the side of the reactionary government of Amin Gemayel. "[T]he moment the Sixth Fleet opened fire to help Gemayel's forces," Robert Fisk explained, "the Marines in Beirut would become participants in the civil war. The very second that the first U.S. Navy shell landed among the Druze at Souq al-Gharb, the Americans would have aligned themselves with the Phalange in open war against the Muslims of Lebanon. Every self-imposed rule of the 'peace-keeping' force would have been broken."[18]

There was also a more direct incitement to Shia anger: a month after the US bombardment (October 16), the Lebanese Army attacked inhabitants of a sprawling Shiite shantytown that adjoined the US Marine encampment at the Beirut International Airport; the Marines had long complained about rock-throwing by the squatters, as well as the hazard their shacks supposedly posed to aircraft during landings. The residents, mostly poor refugees who had fled Israeli bombing in the south, rioted when the soldiers tried to bulldoze their homes and a half-finished mosque. A woman was crushed to death by a troop carrier and several others, including a young teenager, were shot dead.[19] Although this little massacre as well as the resulting destruction of the mosque hardly figures in most histories of the American experience in Lebanon, it probably enraged local Shias – including a prominent resident of the airport slums named Imad Faiz Mugniyah – more than the shelling of the Druze in September.

Mugniyah, who had fought with Al-Fatah and served as a bodyguard to Arafat, was Hezbollah's chief of operations and arguably the world's master car bomber. In response to McFarlane's escalation of US support for the Christians and Israelis, he now planned a Shiite version of Pearl Harbor.[20] The timing, moreover, was virtually the same as in 1941: just after 6 a.m. on a sleepy Sunday morning (October 23), a speeding Mercedes dump truck, its driver grinning maniacally at the wheel, hurtled past sandbagged Marine sentries and smashed through a guardhouse into the ground floor of the so-called "Beirut Hilton," the US military barracks which occupied a former PLO headquarters next to the international airport. The truck's payload was an incredible 12,000 pounds of high explosives (probably Hexogen)[21] along with tanks of butane or propane designed to magnify the explosive force.

"The FBI Forensic Laboratory," according to the official Pentagon report, "described the bomb as the largest conventional blast ever seen by the explosive experts community . . . [Indeed] the Commission believes that major damage to the BLT [Battalion Landing Team] Headquarters building and significant casualties would probably have resulted even if the terrorist truck had not penetrated USMNF [US Multinational Force] defensive perimeter but had detonated in the roadway some 330 feet from the building."[22]

In any event, the truck exploded inside the entrance with enough force to instantly kill 70 percent of the occupants and rewrite every textbook on the physics of demolition. Despite initial incredulity, the DOD Commission's engineers came to the startling conclusion that the huge barracks, like the US embassy before it, had been literally elevated off the ground by the blast.

> When the truck exploded it created an oblong crater measuring 39' by 29'6" and 8'8" in depth. The southern edge of the crater was thirteen feet into the lobby. To create such a crater, the explosion penetrated and destroyed the concrete floor which measured 7 inches in thickness and which was reinforced throughout with $1^3/_4$" diameter iron rods. Because of the structure of the building – it had a large covered courtyard extending from the lobby to the roof – the effect of the explosion was greatly intensified. This was caused by the confinement of the explosive force within the building and resultant convergence of force vectors. This "tampering effect" multiplied the blast effect to the point that the bottom of the building was apparently blown out and the upper portions appeared to have collapsed on top of it. *The force of the explosion initially lifted the entire building upward*, shearing the base off its upright concrete columns, each of which was 15 feet in circumference and reinforced throughout with $1^3/_4$" diameter iron rods. The building then imploded upon itself and collapsed toward its weakest point – its sheared undergirding.[23]

A couple of men sleeping on the roof simply "surfed the blast" and rode the collapsing structure down to the ground with little injury.[24] But so many Marines were killed or wounded that there were initially only a few dozen men available to help pull survivors from the ruins. One member of a later work party thought he had been sent to a landfill. The rescue effort was considerably hampered by exploding ordinance as well as Shiite snipers in the nearby slum that Marines had nicknamed "Hooterville." A military chaplain, meanwhile, performed the last rites on mere shards of bodies and torsos dangling from the remains of an upper floor.[25] The ultimate death toll of young Marines and Navy corpsmen was 241, the highest single-day loss since Iwo Jima in 1945.

Figure 4 US Marine barracks, Beirut 1983. The cleanup begins after a truck bomb killed 241 US Marines.

Marine landing-force commander Geraghy was reprimanded for his failure to anticipate or stop the bombing, but many journalists, including the *New York Time*'s Thomas Friedman, were sympathetic when the colonel lamented the impossibility of envisioning such an enormous attack:

> It was new, unprecedented. We had received over 100 car-bomb threats – pickup trucks, ambulances, U.N. vehicles, myriad types. Those . . . things we had taken appropriate countermeasures toward. But never the sheer magnitude of the 5-ton dump truck going 50–60 miles an hour with an explosive force from 12,000 to 16,000 pounds. [That] was simply beyond the capability to offer any defense. When was the last time you heard of a bomb that size? . . . There may have been a fanatic driving that truck, but I promise you there was a cold, hard, political, calculating mind behind the planning and execution of it.[26]

The "mind," of course, was Mugniyah's, and he had planned a double-header that Sunday morning. Two minutes after the destruction of the "Hilton," another of his *kamikazes* crashed an explosive-laden van into the high-rise French barracks in West Beirut. Robert Fisk was again one of the first journalists on the scene:

> Lieutenant-Colonel Philippe de Longeaux gazes fearfully into the burning crater, staring at the catastrophe that has struck his men. He talks slowly in a dreamy kind of way, in shock: "We have found three people who are alive. There are about a hundred soldiers still under there. The bomb lifted up the building. Right up, do you understand? And it put it down again over there."
>
> He points vaguely to the wreckage. *The bomb lifted the nine-storey building into the air and moved it 20 feet. The whole building became airborne. The crater is where the building was.* How could this be done? "It was a car bomb," he says. "A suicide driver, just like the American Embassy."[27]

If the airport bomb repaid the Americans for saving Gemayal and inflaming the Shiite slums, this second explosion was probably a response to the French decision to supply Saddam Hussein with Super-Etendard jets and Exocet missiles to attack Iran. The hazy distinction between local Shiite grievances and the interests of Tehran and Damascus was further blurred when 2 members of Hezbollah joined with 18 members of the (pro-Iranian) Iraqi Islamic Dawa Party to truck-bomb the US embassy in Kuwait in mid-December. The embassy had taken the precaution of excluding all vehicles, except garbage trucks, from the compound, so the two suicide bombers punctually arrived in a garbage truck. Kuwaiti guards reacted too late to prevent the truck from gaining access to the courtyard where it exploded in front of the consular building and chancellery, killing 8 and wounding 63. The French embassy, the control tower at the airport, the main oil refinery, and an expatriate residential compound were also targeted by remotely detonated car bombs in what was clearly intended to be a stern warning to the enemies of Syria and Iran.[28]

Following another truck-bombing against the French in Beirut, as well as further deadly attacks on Marine outposts and a brief air war between US carrier pilots and Syrian anti-aircraft batteries, the Multinational Force began to withdraw from Lebanon in February 1984. It was the Reagan administration's most stunning geopolitical defeat, as well as the worst setback for the Western powers in the Arab world since the victory of the Algerian revolution. In the impolite phrase of Bob Woodward, "Essentially we turned tail and ran and left Lebanon." American power in Lebanon, added Thomas Friedman, was neutralized by "just 12,000 pounds of dynamite and a stolen truck."[29] Deserted by his Western backers, President Amin Gemayel, the Phalangist butcher of the Palestinian refugee camps, was forced to abrogate his treaty with Israel and fly to Damascus to beg Asad's forgiveness.

From the safety of their aircraft carriers and battleships, however, the Americans and French still harried the Syrians, the Druze, and Hezbollah. Washington also continued to veto every UN resolution condemning the brutal Israeli occupation of Shiite-majority southern Lebanon. The Reagan administration, moreover, began to provide satellite intelligence and military aid to Iraq, the original aggressor, in its endlessly bloody war with revolutionary Iran. This Washington–Baghdad rapprochement became brazen with Donald Rumsfeld's pilgrimage to Saddam Hussein in December 1983. Imad Mugniyah, accordingly, looked for his next target. The Defense Intelligence Agency soon warned of imminent threats to the remaining American personnel in Beirut. "Intelligence also picked up the fact that Iran was shipping explosives into Lebanon through its embassy in Damascus."[30]

Table 2   Car-Bombed Embassies*

Date	Place	Dead	Culprit
1965	USA (Saigon)	6	(Viet Cong)
1981	IRAQ (Beirut)	66	(Syria)
1982	FRANCE (Beirut)	14	(Syria)
	IRAQ (Beirut)	—	(Syria/Iran?)
1983	USA (Beirut)	63	(Hezbollah)
	USA (Kuwait)	8	(Hezbollah and Dawa)
	LIBYA (Beirut)	20	(?)
1984	USA (Beirut)	23	(Hezbollah)
	USA (Bogotá)	1	(?)
	ISRAEL (Nicosia)	—	(Al-Fatah)
1986	USA (Lima)	—	(Tupac Amaru)
	USA (Lisbon)	—	(25 April group)
1987	USA (Rome)	—	("Anti-imperialist Brigades")
1988	ISRAEL (Nicosia)	3	(Al-Fatah?)
1992	USA (Lima)	2	(Sendero Luminoso)
	ISRAEL (Buenos Aires)	29	(Hezbollah)
1994	ISRAEL (Ankara)	1	(Hezbollah)
	ISRAEL (London)	—	(Hezbollah)
1995	EGYPT (Islamabad)	16	(?)
1998	USA (Nairobi)	213	(Al Qaeda)
	USA (Dar-es-Salaam)	11	(Al Qaeda)
2002	USA (Lima)	9	(Sendero Luminoso)
2003	JORDAN (Baghdad)	11	(al-Zarqawi)
	TURKEY (Baghdad)	1	(al-Zarqawi)
2004	AUSTRALIA (Jakarta)	9	(Jemaah Islamiyah)
2006	USA (Damascus)	4	(?)

* including ambassadors' residences

US officials, however, were lulled by the false belief that the new, heavily fortified embassy annex in a suburb of Christian East Beirut, guarded by Maronite mercenaries, was invulnerable to car bomb attacks. On September 20, 1984, however, the driver of a large American station wagon astonished guards with his racetrack-like skill in manuevering around the concrete "dragon teeth" barriers that protected the embassy. Once again there was a devastating explosion ("the blast was heard in seafront districts of West Beirut, more than 10 miles away"), killing 16 people and injuring 69 others, including the visiting British ambassador, David Miers.[31] Within 24 hours of the attack, the CIA had furnished the White House with startling reconnaissance photographs of the Sheik Abdullah Barracks near Baalbek in the Bekaa Valley, where the Iranian revolutionary guards (Pasdaran) supposedly trained Hezbollah members and where various kidnapped Western hostages were believed to be held. The photographs showed an exact mockup of the concrete protective barriers in front of the US embassy annex. "A closer look revealed tire tracks running through the obstacles: the suicide driver had practiced navigating his way through the maze."[32] Hezbollah and the Iranians were running a professional car-bombing school.[33]

13

Car-Bomb University

"Jesus, fuck, I like that – keeper of the faith" Casey said. "Oh fuck, I like that – keeper of the faith."

CIA director William Casey[1]

Soon the CIA and its friends would soon be underwriting even bigger urban terrorism academies of their own. Gunboat diplomacy had been defeated by car bombs in Lebanon, leaving the Reagan administration and, above all, CIA director William Casey, thirsting for revenge against Hezbollah. The obvious temptation was to revert to Saigon-*circa*-1952 tradition and give Hezbollah a dose of its own medicine. Indeed National Security Decision Directive (NSDD) 138, originally drafted by Colonel Oliver North in 1983, provided presidential sanction for special operations to "neutralize" foreign terrorists.[2] (According to Bob Woodward, North had argued in his inimitable fashion that "it was time to kill the 'cocksucker' terrorists.")[3] But the hot-tempered Casey had a frustrating time overcoming the objections of the more cool-minded Defense Secretary Caspar Weinberger who rightfully feared that tit-for-tat attacks would simply slaughter civilians and generate more hatred toward the United States.[4]

Casey, however, was persistent. "Finally in 1985," explains Woodward, "he worked out with the Saudis a plan to use a car bomb to kill [Hezbollah leader] Sheikh [Mohammed Hussein] Fadlallah who they determined was one of the people behind, not only the Marine barracks, but was involved in the taking of American hostages in Beirut . . . It was Casey on his own, saying, 'I'm going to solve the big problem by essentially getting tougher or as tough as the terrorists in using their weapon – the car bomb.'"[5]

The CIA's local assets, however, proved woefully incompetent to carry out the bombing, so Casey subcontracted the operation to Lebanese operators; these agents were led by a former British SAS officer recommended by Saudi Ambassador Prince Bandar, who also deposited $3 million in a CIA Swiss bank account to finance the bombing.[6] As Woodward reconstructs the operation:

> The Englishman established operational compartments to carry out separate parts of the assassination plan; none had any communication with any other except through him. Several men were hired to procure a large quantity of explosives; another man was hired to find a car; money was paid to informants to make sure they knew where Fadlallah would be at a certain time; another group was hired to design an after-action deception so that the Saudis and the CIA would not be connected; the Lebanese intelligence service hired the men to carry out the operation.[7]

On a sunny March afternoon in 1985, Casey's hirelings parked a Datsun pickup truck with 750 pounds of high explosives concealed under crates of vegetables across from Sheikh Fadlallah's home, near a mosque in the crowded Bir al-Abed neighborhood in south Beirut. According to journalist Nora Boustany, who interviewed eyewitnesses: "About 250 girls and women in flowing black chadors, pouring out of Friday prayers at the Imam Riad Mosque, took the brunt of the blast. At least 40 of them were killed and many more were maimed." The enormous explosion blew the façades off four nearby apartment buildings and damaged 20 others up to 600 feet away. "It burnt babies in their beds. It killed a bride buying her trousseau in a lingerie shop. It blew away three children as they walked home from the mosque and it left a 9-year-old girl permanently disabled with a chunk of shrapnel in her brain that cannot be removed." In all, it killed 80 residents and seriously wounded 256, but the principal target, Mohammed Hussein Fadlallah, walked away unscathed.[8]

Despite the CIA's various deceptions and eventual lies to Congress, Hezbollah had no doubt about the provenance of the bomb, and they immediately hung a large banner over the rubble: MADE IN THE USA. Shiite vengeance followed punctually. Three months later, militants threw the body of an American sailor out of the door of hijacked TWA Flight 847 at Beirut Airport, shouting "We have not forgotten the massacre of Bir al-Abed!"[9] That fall Hezbollah boasted of apprehending and executing 11 members of the Lebanese Army's secret "Foreign Work and Analysis Unit" after they confessed to carrying out the Fadlallah attack and many of the earlier car-bombings claimed by the mysterious Front for the Liberation of Lebanon from Aliens. According to the condemned men, Lebanese Army Intelligence, under control of the Phalange Party, had closely coordinated its campaign of terror with both the Mossad and the CIA.[10]

The Fadlallah fiasco and its aftermath might have dispirited a lesser man, but William Casey remained enthusiastic about using urban terrorism to advance Reagan administration goals, and so his attention now turned to the Soviets and their allies in Afghanistan. According to journalist Stephen Coll, the CIA sirector had a singular vision of unleashing religious fanaticism against the Soviet Union. A fervent Franco supporter during his college days in the 1930s, Casey "saw political Islam and the Catholic Church as natural allies" in a covert crusade to defeat the Kremlin and its various franchises.[11] Texas Democratic congressman Charlie Wilson, whose own passions were collecting blondes and killing Russians, ran interference for Casey, and incessantly badgered Congress to increase appropriations for clandestine operations in Afghanistan. A year after the Bir al-Abed massacre, Casey convinced President Reagan to sign NSDD 166, a secret directive that, according to Coll, inaugurated a "new era of direct infusions of advanced U.S. military technology into Afghanistan, intensified training of Islamist guerrillas in explosives and sabotage techniques, and targeted attacks on Soviet military officers."[12] The aim was not only to inflict maximum damage on Soviet forces – revenge for Vietnam – but also to derail UN efforts to negotiate an end to the intervention.[13]

Again, Casey created a compartmentalized chain of command to disguise his own role as chief terrorist. At the top of the hierarchy were Casey and Prince Turki, the head of Saudi intelligence; just below them, were President Muhammed Zia, the dictator of Pakistan (who undoubtedly believed himself to be the ultimate master of the situation), and his Islamist intelligence chief, Brigadier Mohammed Yousaf. US Special Forces experts secretly taught state-of-the-art sabotage techniques, including the fabrication of ANFO car bombs, to officers of Pakistani Inter-Services Intelligence (ISI) under the command of Yousaf. The ISI officers (with a few CIA types hovering in the background), in turn, tutored thousands of Afghan and foreign *mujahedin*, including the future cadre of Al Qaeda, in scores of training camps financed by the Saudis and Gulf emirates. The ISI, however, vetted the selection of trainees and generally restricted the flow of arms and explosives to the four most extreme Islamist groups, fatally weakening more moderate and modern factions. "By the late 1980s," writes Coll, "the ISI had effectively eliminated all the secular, leftist, and royalist political parties that had first formed when Afghan refugees fled Communist rule."[14]

Car bombs were part of the core curriculum at training camps such as the "University of Dawa and Jihad" outside of Peshawar.[15] "Under ISI direction," writes Coll, "the *mujahedin* received training and malleable explosives to mount car bomb and even camel bomb attacks in Soviet-occupied cities, usually designed to kill Soviet soldiers and commanders. Casey endorsed these techniques despite the qualms of some CIA career officers."[16] CIA and Special Forces instructors were supposedly told by Casey's man-on-the-spot, Gust Avrakotos: "Teach the mujahideen how to kill: pipe bombs, car bombs. But don't ever tell me how you're doing it in writing. Just do it." Likewise Coll claims that "the CIA officers that [General] Yousaf worked with closely impressed upon him one rule: never use the terms *sabotage* or *assassination* when speaking with visiting congressmen."[17]

The *mujahedin* car-bombed and sabotaged Kabul for almost four years. Reportage of the explosions was censored by the Russians, but enough news crept out of Kabul to suggest carnage on a Beirut scale. In early April 1986, a car bomb near the Kabul Hotel claimed 22 casualties, while the following February, a car bomb outside the Indian embassy killed several children at an adjacent girls' school and wounded a dozen diplomats. In October 1987 a powerful car bomb outside a mosque frequented by government officials killed 27 people and wounded 35 during evening prayer.[18] Other bombs targeted the haunts of the leftwing intelligentsia. "Yousaf and the Afghan car-bombing squads he trained," observes Coll, "regarded Kabul University professors as fair game, as well as movie theaters and cultural events."[19]

As the Soviets prepared to withdraw in 1988, the bombings intensified. A truck bomb on a downtown street on April 27 (one of three dozen explosive devices detonated or defused in a single month) killed spectators at a parade commemorating the tenth anniversary of the Communist revolution: "The blast, heard across the city, destroyed two buses and two taxis and shattered windows in buildings 300 yards away." A Pakistani license plate was exhumed from the wreckage.[20] A month later, another large truck bomb exploded near reviewing stands erected for the Red Army's farewell ceremony, killing 8 and injuring 20.[21] However, the biggest bomb, estimated to consist of one-half ton of high explosive in an American pickup, was saved for a bold attack on the compound housing post-Soviet President Mohammad Najibullah and his ruling People's Democratic Party's Central Committee. At least 22 people died and Najibullah sent a personal message to President George H. Bush imploring him to call off the terror campaign for which Washington and Islamabad (in the words of his foreign minister) were "financially, materially and morally responsible."[22]

Casey, says Coll, "was delighted with the results."[23] As were the *mujahedin* and *jihadis*. It was the greatest transfer of terrorist technology in history: there was no need for angry Islamists to take car-bomb extension courses from Hezbollah when they could matriculate in a CIA-supported urban-sabotage course in Pakistan's frontier provinces. An estimated 35,000 foreign Moslems were trained by the ISI between 1982 and 1992.[24] Some "blowback" – perhaps *big* blowback – was inevitable. "Ten years later," Coll says, "the vast training infrastructure that Yousaf and his colleagues built with the enormous budgets endorsed by NSDD-166 – the specialized camps, the sabotage training manuals, the electronic bomb detonators, and so on – would be referred to routinely in America as 'terrorist infrastructure.'"[25] Moreover, the alumni of the ISI camps such as Ramzi Yousef, who plotted the first 1993 World Trade Center attack, or his uncle, Khalid Sheikh Mohammed, who was allegedly the architect of the second attack, would soon be applying their expertise on almost every continent.

(Jason Burke, the veteran Middle East correspondent for the *Observer*, rightly criticizes the current practice of labeling these camps, which continued to train thousands of militants in sabotage techniques through the middle 1990s, as "bin Laden camps" or "Al Qaeda camps." "There is no evidence," he emphasizes, "for any significant involvement of bin Laden in the dozens of establishments set up by Afghan and Pakistani religious hardliners at the time . . . The simple truth is that bin Laden was a marginal player at the time."[26] The real patronage continued to be provided by the Saudis and the ISI, with the latter using the camps to train guerrillas to fight in Kashmir.)

It must be noted, of course, that the KGB did not sit quietly by while the CIA, Saudis, and ISI car-bombed the Red Army and its friends in Kabul, or while Casey – who seemed to toy with the idea of starting World War Three all by himself – instigated the *mujahedin* to raid the USSR.[27] Several devastating car-bomb explosions in Pakistan were almost certainly Moscow's handiwork, as were perhaps some of the contemporary terrorist attacks against American installations in Europe. Coincident with Casey's secret war in Afghanistan (1985–88), a loose coalition of European far-Left groups – including Action Directe in France, the Red Army

Faction in Germany, and the November 17 group in Greece – unleashed their own mini-war against NATO. Such attacks as the August 1985 car-bombing of a US Air Force base outside of Frankfurt (2 dead, 20 injured), the February 1985 car-bombing of the US embassy in Lisbon (no deaths), the April 1988 explosion that killed 5 people outside the USO in Naples, and the June 1988 murder of the US military attaché in Athens by remote-controlled car bomb might actually have been messages from the KGB. In the rigorously reciprocal code of the Cold War, one car bomb deserved another.

14

The Suicide Tigers

They were believed to be superhumanly cruel and cunning and, like demons, ubiquitous

Sinhalese perceptions of Tamil Tigers[1]

So much nonsense has been written about the unfathomable mysteries of Japanese military culture during World War Two that it is often forgotten that the *kamikazes*, unlike the *banzai* charges and collective suicides, were the instruments of a brilliant strategy that, starting from a hopeless mismatch between available planes (lots) and veteran pilots (few), coldly calculated the most efficient way to inflict maximum damage on the approaching US Pacific Fleet. According to the US Air Force Historical Studies Office, "approximately 2800 Kamikaze attackers sunk 34 Navy ships, damaged 368 others, killed 4900 sailors and wounded over 4800."[2] Moreover, as Edwin Hoyt emphasizes in his history of US naval strategy in the Pacific, Americans "could not devise a really satisfactory defense against men who were willing to sacrifice their lives to hit a ship" (which they succeeded in doing an impressive 14 percent of the time). *Kamikazes* may not ultimately have turned the tide of war, but as the US Strategic Bombing Survey recognized, they were "macabre, effective, and supremely practical under the circumstances."[3]

Likewise, Hezbollah's suicide truck bombs in the 1980s proved to be one of the most surprisingly simple and deadly military innovations since the first *kamikaze* attack at Leyte Gulf in 1944. From the hindsight of the twenty-first century, it is arguable that the defeat of the US intervention in Lebanon in 1983–84 has had larger and more potent geopolitical repercussions than the loss of Saigon in 1975. The Vietnam War, of course, was a more epic struggle whose imprint upon domestic American politics remains profound, but it belonged to the era of the Cold War and bipolar superpower rivalry. Hezbollah's war in Beirut and south Lebanon, on the other hand, prefigured (and even inspired) the "asymmetric" conflicts that characterize the new millennium. (It is sometimes forgotten that the famous "Weinberger–Powell Doctrine" – the use of American force as a last resort and only in overwhelming preponderance – was a direct response to Hezbollah's truck bombs, not the fall of Saigon and lessons of Vietnam.)[4] Although rural guerrillas survive in rugged redoubts like the Himalayas, the Khyber Pass, and the Andes, the center of gravity of global insurgency has moved back to the cities and their slum peripheries. In this post-Cold War urban context, the Hezbollah bombing of the Marine barracks constitutes the gold standard of terrorism; the attacks of September 11, 2001 were only the inevitable scaling-up of the tactic: the weapons were, in effect, car bombs with wings.

Not all guerrilla movements or non-state combatants, however, are willing to put a *kamikaze* in the driver's seat: many movements, including the Afghan *mujahedin* in the 1980s, have deep-rooted moral or cultural aversions to suicide action. The popular image, of course, is that the typical suicide bomber is a simple-minded religious fanatic punching his admission ticket to a voluptuous afterlife. Although this stereotype may be true of some of the recent foreign car bombers in Iraq (a point I discuss later), the political scientist Robert Pape has shown in a celebrated study that most suicide terrorists are actually local patriots responding to collective injustice, above all the humiliation of foreign occupation, especially when the occupier is seen as seeking to impose an alien religion or value system.

Few suicide attackers are social misfits, criminally insane, or professional losers. Most fit a nearly opposite profile: typically they are psychologically normal, have better than average economic prospects for their communities, and are deeply integrated into social networks and emotionally attached to their national communities. They see themselves as sacrificing their lives for the nation's good . . . The bottom line, then, is that suicide terrorism is mainly a response to foreign occupation.[5]

Indeed, the first two groups to embrace Hezbollah's suicide car-bomb strategy were secular nationalist movements, albeit movements characterized by strong aspects of cultism. In the 1930s, the Partie Populaire Syrienne – romantically allied with Mussolini's vision of a fascist Mediterranean – fought the French in the name of the Greater Syria that the Sykes–Picot Treaty had dismantled. This antique fascist-nationalist party was resurrected in the 1980s as the Syrian Social Nationalist Party (SSNP) and became the pro-Syrian, but non-Baathist wing of resistance to the Israeli occupation of southern Lebanon. Fighting side by side with Hezbollah, its membership was a mixture of Shiites, Christians, Sunnis, and (probably) Syrian intelligence agents. The SSNP's contribution to the history of the car bomb was the first female suicide driver: Sana' Usuf Muhaydli. In April 1985 Muhaydli told her parents that she was going out for a few minutes to buy some lipstick – instead she drove her white Peugeot, loaded with TNT, into an Israeli jeep, killing herself and two soldiers. The SSNP, like the Sicilian Mafia, had a car fetish, and another white Peugeot, driven by a woman killed 17 members of a pro-Israeli militia at a checkpoint. At the height of the SSNP car-bomb siege of the Israeli buffer zone in south Lebanon during the summer of 1985, the group was averaging one suicide car-bombing each week – quite a lot of white Peugeots.[6]

Hezbollah's most ardent accolytes, however, were the Liberation Tigers of Tamil Eelam (LTTE) in Sri Lanka, the secessionist movement led by Vellupillai Pirabhakaran which "made a strategic decision to adopt the method of suicide attack after observing its lethal effectiveness in the 1983 suicide bombings of the US and French barracks in Beirut."[7] Pirabhakaran – regarded by his devoted followers as a superhuman, almost godlike figure – established an elite *kamikaze* corps of co-ed "Black Tigers," highly trained and ready to die at his command. Since their inauguration of the tactic in 1984 with a truck-bombing of a police station, the Black Tigers, according to the Rand Corporation's Christine Fair, have been responsible for twice as many suicide attacks of all kinds as Hezbollah and Hamas combined.[8] A mass nationalist movement with a "liberated territory" on the Jaffna Peninsula, a sizeable army and even a tiny navy, the LTTE has integrated car-bombings into the full spectrum of its military operations, from stand-alone acts of terrorism to battalion-size offensives involving hundreds of fighters. A typical LTTE assault on a rural Sri Lankan army camp, for instance, will commence with a suicide truck driver crashing through the main gate. (In the Tamil secessionist capital of Jaffna there is a heroic statute of "Captain Miller," the Black Tiger who killed 70 soldiers in 1987 when he truck-bombed an army base in Vadamarachi.)[9]

The Sri Lankan capital of Colombo, according to Fair, has always been the Black Tigers' "most prized theater of operation." "A single blast in Colombo," a Defense Ministry official told her, "has more value psychologically than full-scale conflict in the north and northeast."[10] The first car bomb in the metropolis (April 21, 1987) was an act of almost unsurpassed horror. The explosion devastated the main bus terminal during evening rush hour, burning scores of passengers to death inside crowded buses. "The scene," wrote Barbara Crossette of the *New York Times*, "was one of unbelievable carnage, with human heads and limbs and the victims' possessions strewn over a wide area . . . In one bus, a driver leaned on the horn and screamed incoherently through the blown-away front of his vehicle." As word spread through the city of the terrible carnage (as many as 150 killed and 200 seriously injured), Sinhalese lynch mobs began to hunt for Tamils, forcing police to open fire and the government to declare a curfew throughout the city.[11] Like the Stern Gang before them, the LLTE waged war on peace, creating deliberate atrocities that made ethnic coexistence and peaceful reform struggle impossible.[12]

But unlike the pariahs of LEHI, the Tigers had friends in high places, notably Indira Gandhi. The Colombo car bombers, like thousands of other LLTE cadre, had received secret paramilitary training from 1983 to 1987, first in the Himalayan foothills, then in the southern Indian state of Tamil Nadu, courtesy of the Indian Prime Minister and her version of the CIA, the Research and Analysis Wing (RAW). At one point, there were reportedly 39 camps in Tamil Nadu where guerrillas from the Tigers and other Tamil extremist groups were tutored in espionage, explosives, and urban sabotage by the RAW. Although primarily trained to commit sabotage against military targets in Sri Lanka, there is some evidence that LLTE militants were also "offered money by RAW to massacre Sinhalese civilians" and that "Pirabhakaran was in radio contact with RAW agents both during and after . . . the Anuradhapura bus station massacre of 143 people."[13]

Such sponsorship literally blew up in Delhi's face when 100,000 Indian "peacekeepers" intervened in the Jaffna Peninsula in 1987 and quickly found themselves the targets of Tamil fury: car bombs and remote-controlled landmines, manufactured under the supervision of the LTTE's master bombmaker, "Yogaratma," were soon wiping out entire patrols, while captured Indian soldiers were summarily "necklaced" – burnt to death by flaming tires put around their necks by their former allies. The supreme revenge came in 1993 when Indira's son and successor, Rajiv Gandhi, was killed by a female Tiger suicide bomber.[14] (Two years later another Black Tiger assassinated Sri Lanka's President, Ranasinghe Premadasa.)

The LTTE has been accused of being a death cult for good reason: each member wears a cyanide capsule around her/his neck in case of capture (a route reportedly chosen by more than 1000 Tigers). Anita Pratap, the former Delhi bureau chief for CNN, is one of the few journalists to have won the trust of LTTE leader Pirabhakaran, and in her book *Island of Blood* she describes an atmosphere of monastic discipline that makes the Taliban seem like libertines.

Once recruited, cadres have to renounce their friends, their family, their home. The Tiger legion is their new family. They are not allowed to smoke, drink or have sex. Their prized

possession is their weapon, usually an AK-47 . . . They clean
their guns lovingly and painstakingly, much like an ardent lover
would stroke his beloved. Apart from their rifle and cyanide vial,
their worldly possessions comprise a change of clothes and a pair
of *chappals* [sandals] . . .[15]

After years of lobbying Pirabhakaran for permission, she became the
first journalist allowed to meet with a group of the legendary Black
Tigers as they prepared for a suicide mission:

They could have been lobotomized for all I knew . . . The only
time they showed some emotion was when they talked about
Pirabharkaran, their Annai. A Black Tiger named Sunil said with
something close to awe, "For us, he is mother, father and God all
rolled into one." But I detected one fear in all of them: the fear
that they might let Pirabhakaran down. They would die happily;
their only hope was their death would inflict the kind of damage
on the enemy that would make Pirabhakaran happy.[16]

Before leaving to truck-bomb a bus depot or army base, the Black
Tigers – like big-money contributors visiting the White House –
have the opportunity of a ceremonial photo session with their
leader. It becomes their small posthumous share of his nearly divine
celebrity.

15

Soft Targets

The blast caused panic among shoppers. Witnesses said they saw one woman running out of the supermarket with her hair in flames.

Barcelona bombing, 1987[1]

No account of the evolution of the car bomb during the 1980s would be complete without a brief consideration of the important Iberian franchise. Although revolutionary suicide has never been part of their agenda, the radical Basque nationalists of Euskadi Ta Askatasuna (ETA) have rivaled Hezbollah and the Tamil Tigers, as well as the Provisional IRA, in the sheer endurance of their bombing campaign. ETA, of course, is universally notorious, but its implacable hatred of the Spanish state was forged by a horrific history of official repression that includes several generations of mass arrests, beatings, torture, executions, and assassinations. In the last years of the Franco dictatorship, Madrid recruited former OAS "Deltas" (who, as we saw, received sanctuary in Spain in 1962) to stalk and murder ETA cadre. In a three-year period between 1978 and 1980, these death squads murdered 36 Basque nationalists, while another 41 activists were killed by the police in the course of demonstrations and street riots.[2]

A second, even dirtier "dirty war" was secretly mounted by the "socialist" Prime Minister Felipe Gonzales during the 1980s, when the so-called Grupos Antiterroristas de Liberación (GAL) were unleashed against ETA's supporters in France and Spain. Again led by OAS veterans, the killers of GAL, according to historian Robert Clark, included "Italian neo-fascists, Portuguese mercenaries, former members of the French Army in Algeria, Spanish undercover agents, [and] professional killers from Marseilles."[3] As both Clark and Paddy Woodworth have eloquently argued, the ferocity of Basque nationalism has evolved in almost lock-step response to this chronic state terrorism (under social-democratic as well as fascist auspices) which the rest of the world has seldom acknowledged or bothered to condemn.[4]

ETA's first sustained bombing campaign in 1979, moreover, was the product of a deep crisis in Basque nationalist ranks following the failure to achieve autonomy or independence in the post-Franco transition. ETA was bitterly split between a "political-military" wing [ETA(p-m)] that advocated forcing concessions from the Spanish state through bomb attacks on barracks and public spaces, and a "military" wing [ETA(m)] which persisted in a classical strategy of individual assassinations and *attentados*. ETA(p-m), which had stolen 1000 kilograms of GOMA-2[5] in Pamplona in early March 1979, set off the first car bomb in Spain outside a Guardia Civil barracks in Navarre, then planted a package bomb in a bathroom of a Barcelona branch of Spain's largest department store, El Corte Inglés. The following year, according to a Spanish chronicler of terrorism, "ETA(p-m) traded its package bombs for the first car bomb against El Corte Inglés, this time in Madrid."[6] For the next quarter century, *etarristas* would plow the same terrain over and over again: alternating between car-bomb attacks (without warning) on Guardia Civil barracks, buses, and parades, and bombings (with warnings) against Spanish department stores and malls.

ETA(p-m), however, was merely the pioneer, not the main protagonist. It suspended its bombing campaign after a dozen sensational detonations in the tourist resorts of Marbella and Benidorm, as well as a bloody trio of simultaneous explosions in Madrid (6 dead), brought universal public condemnation. Like the Official IRA in Ireland, ETA(p-m)'s real trajectory, under the leadership of the brilliant "Pertur" (Eduardo Moreno Bergareche), was toward legal working-class politics and it soon abandoned the armed struggle entirely. But ETA(m) quickly took its place, murdering the apostate Pertur but embracing the dual-track bombing campaign against Spanish cops and shoppers with a particularly ruthless zeal.[7] Like the Provisional IRA before them, the militarists of ETA (who didn't need to use fertilizer because they were so brilliant at stealing huge quantities of high explosives from Spanish and French mining companies) were seduced by the sheer ease and seeming invincibility of the car bomb. And just like their Irish comrades, they became blinded to its savage moral and political consequences.

ETA's car-bomb campaign against the Guardia Civil – the national paramilitary police so synonymous with fascist brutality – can be briefly summarized: In 1985 ETA car bombs killed a pedestrian in front of a police barracks in Barcelona and an American businessman jogging near a police van on a busy street in Madrid (16 members of the Guardia were wounded). The next year, a more powerful bomb that blew up beside a bus filled with traffic police trainees, killed 12 and wounded 50, including a passerby. This tactic was repeated in January 1987 against an army bus in Zaragoza: killing the driver and an officer, and wounding 39 soldiers and pedestrians. In May a massive car bomb shattered the front of the Guardia headquarters in Madrid, killing 1 and injuring many bystanders, including 2 children. In December it was Zaragoza's turn again: 12 died, including toddlers and mothers, when a 150-kilo car bomb devastated a police barracks housing 50 families. After a lull in the late 1980 – while ETA and the Spanish government secretly negotiated with little success in Algiers – attacks on the Guardia resumed in August 1990 when a car bomb injured 64 police and bystanders in Burgos. Over the next two years, ETA's car bombs would wreck Guardia barracks in Barcelona (12 dead, including 4 children), Alicante (4 dead), and Murcia (2 dead).[8]

By bombing barracks and police vehicles, of course, ETA was merely replicating the classical tactics of the Stern Gang and the Provisional IRA – the Basque group's diabolical originality was in singling out soft targets (the El Corte Inglés department-store chain and its Hipercor franchises) for sustained attack. The dual objectives were apparently to terrorize the Spanish public literally where it shopped and, at the same time, to coerce El Corte Inglés into paying the *impuesto revolucionario* (revolutionary tax) that financed ETA's guerrilla war. Unlike the deadly attacks on the Guardia, the package and car bombs that ETA delivered to the doorstep of El Corte Inglés were always preceded by telephoned warnings to the police and store management.

Thus on June 19, 1987, an ETA cell made three separate calls, beginning almost two hours before the timed detonation, to warn that a bomb had been placed in a huge Hipercor store in a blue-collar neighborhood of Barcelona. Store guards and police began to search the store, but they failed to notify or evacuate the 600 to 700 shoppers, most of them women and children, who crowded the aisles that Friday afternoon. (The police and store management would later trade recriminations over this failure to promptly evacuate the facility.) At 4:15 in the afternoon, 150 kilos of GOMA-2 (twice the usual ETA charge and, according to the police, perhaps mixed with a "napalm-like" compound) hidden inside a stolen Ford Sierra blew up on the first level of the underground parking structure, directly under the food section of the store. Carnage was followed by panic, then inconsolable grief: the 21 dead included 9 women and children, some of them burnt beyond recognition. Another 45 shoppers – ordinary working-class people – were seriously burned or maimed.[9]

Later, a "daughter of a Basque national hero" would tell Paddy Woodworth, the Irish journalist who helped expose the "dirty war" conducted by Felipe Gonzáles against ETA and its supporters, that the Hipercor atrocity was a terrible mistake, if not the fault of the police who refused to heed the telephoned warnings. "I know the people who bombed Hipercor, and if anyone is sorry for what happened it's them. Of course they are two of the most delightful people, and with the purest feelings anyone could have. And of course they are incapable of doing anyone any harm." But Wood-worth, despite his sympathies with Basque grievances, was more than skeptical. "It is not at all certain," he wrote, "that the Hipercor bombing was an 'accident' from ETA's point of view. It belongs to the period in ETA's campaign when (relatively) discriminate shootings were largely replaced by indiscriminate bombings, as part of a policy of 'accumulation of forces.'"[10]

Despite a vast gathering in Barcelona (an estimated crowd of 750,000) to condemn the bombing, ETA persisted in its soft-target campaign: two more El Corte Inglés stores were car-bombed in 1989. (Stores, however, were now immediately evacuated after receipt of warnings.) After another decade-long cycle of bombing, clandestine negotiation, and even a truce, ETA's war against shoppers reached its climax in 2002 when car bombs rocked half a dozen El Corte Inglés and FNAC (the French chain) stores in Madrid, Bilbao, and Zaragoza.[11] Although ETA itself, morally depleted and overshadowed by even fiercer Islamic terror, "permanently suspended" its revolutionary war in 2006, its 26-year-long campaign against El Corte Inglés undoubtedly has many secret admirers, some of whom won't bother to call the police when they leave the GOMA-2 in the parking lot of the local mall or big-box store.

16

Los Coches Bomba

> At first we used to get scared whenever a bomb went off, but now we are like the residents of Beirut – we just keep going.
>
> Medellín tax driver[1]

Car bombs, despite the early essay by the ABC movement in Havana in 1933, were not part of the Cuban-inspired "Second War of Independence" waged in the *selvas* and *sierras* by the Latin American New Left in the 1960s and early 1970s. It was only after the Guevarist *focos* were isolated and defeated, and guerrilla warfare was "reconceived in an urban milieu" under the influence of Iberian anarchist traditions, that bombings of presidential palaces, military barracks, and foreign corporations became relatively commonplace. But even then, the followers of Abraham Guillén and Carlos Marighella (the chief Latin American theorists of urban guerrilla warfare) never embraced the car bomb with the enthusiasm of the Viet Cong or the IRA.[2]

Thus, in the early 1980s, despite high levels of political violence throughout the hemisphere, there were only scattered instances of the weapon's deployment: an explosion near the office of the Guatemalan President in September 1980 (8 dead), a car bomb in San Salvador in March 1981 of unknown provenance (2 dead), a blast outside the presidential palace in Bogotá in March 1982 which was claimed by the M19 guerrillas (1 dead), a mysterious explosion near the presidential residence in Port-au-Prince on New Year's

Day 1983 (4 dead), a non-fatal attack on the US embassy in Bogotá in 1984, and an equally harmless explosion outside the Chilean War College in 1985 to celebrate dictator Augusto Pinochet's seventieth birthday.[3]

The true impresario of the car bomb in the Western Hemisphere was Pablo Escobar, the ex-car thief and lord of the coca leaf who became the wealthiest criminal in world history during the 1980s. Escobar, who fancied himself a narco-populist, redistributed some of the profits from North American cocaine addiction to build soccer fields and housing in the slums of his native Medellín. He also courted Colombia's traditional oligarchy by unleashing his assassins to kill suspected members and sympathizers of the revolutionary Left. But at the height of his glory, following his election in 1982 as an alternate representative of the Liberal Party to the Colombian Congress (a position that provided judicial immunity) Escobar became the chief target of Washington's new "War on Drugs" led by Vice-President George H. Bush. Under tremendous pressure from the United States, Colombian President Belisario Betancur declared a state of siege, sent the army to raid Escobar's jungle cocaine laboratories, and began to extradite Medellín henchmen to the United States. He also opened the door to direct US involvement in field operations against the cartel inside Colombia, a collaboration that would eventually become a full-scale dirty war with American Delta Force commandos, Navy Seals, Drug Enforcement Administration (DEA) agents, and the Colombian National Police death squads (the so-called Los Pepes) stalking both the cartel's rank and file and its *jefes*.[4]

Escobar's response to the Yanqui-instigated campaign was a decade-long hurricane of terror, beginning with the assassination of Justice Minister Rodrigo Lara Bonilla in 1984 and followed by ferocious onslaughts against the oligarchy that he blamed for betraying him and selling the country to the DEA. His declared goal was to make his enemies, from ordinary cops to presidents, fear the wrath of Medellín more than that of Washington. He organized his fellow *narcotraficantes*, including the notorious José Rodríguez-Gacha and the Ochoa brothers, into the so-called "Extraditables," who were soon issuing ghoulish and theatrical threats: "We are friends of Pablo Escobar and we are ready to do anything for him. We are capable of executing you at any place on this planet . . . in the meantime, you will see the fall, one by one, of all the members of your family . . . For calling Mr. Escobar to trial you will remain without forebears or descendants in your genealogical tree."[5]

The car bomb, outfitted from Escobar's huge private stock of high explosives, perfectly suited the Extraditables' dual campaigns against the DEA and the Colombian Establishment. The first car bombs, like the November 1984 explosion outside the US embassy in Bogotá, sent the message that the Cartel was ready to fight the DEA blow for blow, and indeed, in March 1985 the *Washington Post* reported that nervous Agency officials considered themselves everywhere under siege.

> The agency's Miami office, for example, has no identifying sign outside. A van blocks the front door to ward off car-bomb attacks. Inside the van, armed guards wait behind darkened windows. Parking spaces around the building's perimeter have been blocked to discourage bombing attacks. Newly installed closed-circuit television cameras pan the area. At the street entrance to the parking lot, an armed state wildlife officer – temporarily reassigned from hunting drug traffickers in the Everglades – guards the building.[6]

After his initial attacks on the DEA, Escobar (according to writer Mark Bowden) used his lawyers in 1986 to approach the Reagan administration "with an offer to trade information against Communist guerrillas, the FARC, ELN, and M-19, in return for amnesty from his drug crimes." President Reagan's response, however, was NSDD 221, ordering US Army Special Forces and Delta commandos to reinforce DEA operations inside Colombia. At the same time, the rival Cali cartel, which in the late 1980s enjoyed relative immunity from American attention, seized the opportunity to car-bomb Escobar's Medellín apartment complex, almost killing his family in a huge explosion in January 1989. (Bowden implies that the CIA were the instigators, skillfully "playing on murderous rivalries between the Cali and Medellín cartels.")[7]

Escobar and the Extraditables, in turn, fought back furiously: they bombed the drugstores owned by the Rodríguez Orejuela brothers (chiefs of the Cali cartel) and assassinated prominent "traitors" in the ruling factions of the Conservative and Liberal parties. At the end of May 1989, General Miguel Maza Márquez, the head of the Colombian secret police (DAS), miraculously escaped an Escobar car bomb that killed his bodyguards and injured more than 50 bystanders.[8] That July, following an abortive attempt by British mercenaries to kill Pablo, the Extraditables used a powerful bomb in a parked car in Medellín to kill the governor of the state of Antioquia, Antonio Roldán Betancur, a human-rights advocate who had recently condemned the murder of leftwing activists of the Unión Patriótica by the cartel's death squads.[9] The next month, while Escobar hid out in luxury in Panama, the Extraditables assassinated Luis Carlos Galán, the popular Liberal candidate for president who had earlier expelled Escobar from the party; in the fall, they blew up an airplane they mistakenly believed was carrying Galán's successor, killing 110 people, including several Yanquis. They also car-bombed the second-leading newspaper in Bogotá, *El Espectador*, and, a few weeks later, its sister daily in the large provincial city of Bucaramanga, killing a number of employees.[10]

In early December, the Medellín forces led by José Rodríguez Gacha mounted a Hezbollah-scale attack (*sans* suicide driver) on the Departamento Administrativo de Seguridad (DAS), the secret police directly responsible for a series of recent extraditions: a truck containing one-half-ton of dynamite was exploded by remote control outside the DAS headquarters in Bogotá during morning rush hour. "The explosion," reported the *New York Times*, "was so powerful that it broke windows in a building across the street from the United States Embassy, *seven miles away*." The largest car bomb ever detonated outside the Middle East left a 20-foot-deep crater in the street and devastated 23 city blocks. DAS commander, General Miguel Maza Márquez managed to survive the blast – which he described as a "mini-atomic bomb" – in his steel-plated ninth-floor office, but his secretary was killed, along with 58 other people. An incredible 1000 workers, residents, and pedestrians were injured (250 seriously), and at least 1500 homes and office buildings suffered significant damage. The toll might have been even more catastrophic had police not defused a second car bomb placed in front of judicial offices. In a statement to the media, the Extraditables warned that such bombings would continue until Colombian President Virgilio Barco Vargas allowed a popular plebiscite on extraditions to North America.[11]

Gacha, known as "El Mexicano," was soon killed by an elite police taskforce working with US Navy Seals, and a huge cache of dynamite was seized on one of Escobar's plantations, but hundreds of Escobar gunmen were still at large, and the Extraditables torqued up their vengeful rhetoric to an apocalyptic fever pitch: "We will not respect the families of those who have not respected our families. We will burn and destroy the industries, properties and mansions of the oligarchy."[12] The new wave of bombings and assassinations was not quite the end of the world for the cartel's enemies, but it must certainly have seemed like it at times. After Escobar announced in spring 1990 that he would pay a $4200 bounty for each dead cop, the city police in Medellín quickly became an endangered species, suffering 42 fatalities in one month at the hands of the city's underworld. (The grim total by 1991 would be 457.) Meanwhile, car bombs in April twice devastated convoys of elite federal police, killing 26 people and wounding almost 100.[13]

In mid-May, the Extraditables struck viciously at the well-heeled crowds shopping for Mother's Day gifts at the fashionable Niza and Cafam malls in Bogotá, killing 25 and wounding 150 with two simultaneous car bombs. Later that day, a third vehicle bomb exploded outside a fancy restaurant in the enemy citadel of Cali, killing six people.[14] At the end of May, a car bomb left a dozen dead in front of Medellín's best hotel, and a month later 330 pounds of explosives in a parked car devastated a police station and killed a news reporter, four children, a federal senator, and a half-dozen police.[15]

Faced with escalating carnage in their own streets and shopping centers, the Colombian middle-class cried "*basta!*" "Pablo's tactics," writes Mark Bowden, "were paying off. His bombing campaign had terrified the public, and polls showed growing support for striking a deal to end the violence."[16] Liberal President Cesar Gavira accordingly struck a plea bargain with Escobar and the other Extraditables in June 1991 that allowed them to avoid extradition to the United States and serve out modest sentences in the luxurious La Catedral prison that Escobar had built to his own specifications outside of Medellín. But President Bush, the cartel's old antagonist, was outraged at Gavira's "surrender," and with the help of the local DAS and the families of Escobar's victims, he eventually pressured his Colombian counterpart to rescind the deal that allowed the Extraditables to run La Catedral as a veritable Playboy Mansion with wine, women, and a concealed arsenal. Although Gavira sent an entire brigade of the Colombian Army to ensure the transfer of Escobar to a regular prison in July 1992, the world's most notorious *narcotraficante* easily escaped.

For the next 18 months until his assassination in December 1993, Escobar traded atrocities back and forth with a relentless new enemy, Los Pepes. As Mark Bowden explains in his bestselling account, Los Pepes were an elite death squad. Sponsored by the DEA and the US Special Operations Command, the group was composed of secret police officers (from the Bloque de Búsqueda) and local enemies of Escobar, including other *narcotraficantes*. Their strategy, according to Bowden, involved "killing off the secret white-collar infrastructure of Pablo's organization, targeting his money launderers, bankers, lawyers, and extended family." They were financed by the DEA, fed intelligence by the CIA, and most likely managed by the secret team of Delta Force commandos led by dirty-war veterans of Vietnam (Operation Phoenix) and Chile (overthrow of President Salvador Allende) that were sent into Colombia immediately after Escobar's escape. The operation, in-itiated by Bush, continued by Clinton, and presided over by the departed spirit of Bill Casey, put the United States back into the business of sponsoring car-bomb attacks.[17]

Disapproval of clandestine state terrorism, of course, does not imply any sympathy for the devil, and the carnage wrought by Escobar in his final days was undoubtedly his most indiscriminate and appalling. Six months after his escape, for example, one of his car bombs devastated a bookstore full of parents and children in Bogotá, killing 20 of them and injuring more than 60. "The scene," the press reported, "was one of utter destruction: broken glass stained with blood, demolished buildings, bodies strewn about, mothers screaming for their children and a six-foot hole in the ground."[18] In April 1993, Medellín henchmen again attacked an up-scale shopping center in Bogotá, detonating 440 pounds of high explosives in a stolen van near the Centro 93 mall. "'Why, why, why!' screamed a woman, [the *New York Times* reported] as she tore at the twisted and charred wreckage of a car in the hope of finding the body of her young daughter, whom she had left inside. The force of the blast hurled the remains of the vehicle into the front of a furniture shop."[19]

According to Bowden, Los Pepes, taking advantage of public anger and fear, struck back ruthlessly at Escobar's family and neighbors. "In January, one day after the terrible bookstore bombing in Bogotá, La Cristalina, a hacienda owned by Pablo's mother, Hermilda, was burned to the ground. Then two large car bombs exploded in the El Poblado section of Medellín in front of apartment buildings where Pablo's immediate and extended family members were staying. A third bomb exploded at a *finca* owned by the drug boss, injuring his mother and his aunt. Several days later, another of Pablo's country homes was torched." Soon Medellín's back alleys were full of bodies, victims of Los Pepes, many of whom were tagged with hand-lettered signs taunting Escobar ("What do you think of the exchange for the bombs in Bogotá, Pablo?") In response, Escobar sent a letter to the Colombian attorney general informing him of the address of Los Pepes' headquarters where, he claimed, "they torture trade unionists and lawyers" and rhetorically asking why the government "offers rewards for the leaders of the Medellín cartel and for the leaders of the guerrillas, but doesn't offer rewards for the leaders of the paramilitary, nor for those of the Cali cartel, authors of various car bombs in the city of Medellín."[20]

A few months later the great tiger hunt ended when the police (or was it a US Navy Seal?) shot Escobar while he was talking on the phone to his son. The major victors were the American special ops, who were able to spin a new romance about their dirty business as well as leveraging more money from Congress, and the Cali cartel, who promptly took over most of the Extraditables' business ventures and US markets. The Cali mobsters also replicated Escobar's methods, protesting the June 1995 capture of their leader, Gilberto Rodríguez Orejuela, with a huge car bomb that killed more than 30 and wounded 200 at a music festival.[21] After the eventual downfall of the Cali cartel, the Fuerzas Armadas Revolucionarias de Colombia (FARC), more committed to the coca crop than to the cause of socialism, continued to detonate car bombs in public spaces through the 1990s, with the usual appalling results.[22]

Indeed, Colombia's *danse macabre* of terror and counter-terror entered the new millennium with a particularly ghastly FARC attack in Bogotá in February 2003 which involved the unprecedented use of twin car bombs. A children's ballet performance was scheduled at the Club El Nogal, an elite sports-and-entertainment complex favored by the families of corporate leaders and foreign diplomats, when a huge explosion in the garage set the ten-story building, located near the US embassy, ablaze. At least 32 people, including 6 children, were burned to death, and more than 160 were badly injured. The bombing was rumored to be retribution for the role played by Interior Minister Fernando Londono, a prominent Club member, in increasing the presence of US Special Forces "trainers" in the country. In any event, ordinary Colombians celebrated the tenth anniversary of the slaying of their most famous billionaire criminal with little optimism that the car-bombings would ever cease. While the Colombian army and rightwing militias persist in murdering trade unionists, oppositional journalists, and leaders of the legal Left, the corrupted guerrillas of FARC defiantly maintain Escobar's war without pity on the wives and children of the oligarchy.[23]

17

Cities under Siege

The hour of dynamite, terror without limit, has arrived.

Peruvian writer Gustavo Gorriti[1]

Despite a brief flurry of interest in the early 1950s,[2] the Pentagon seems to have devoted scant attention to the destructive potential of vehicle bombs until the shockwaves of the 1983 Marine barracks bombing finally rattled windows in the Reagan White House. Sandia National Laboratories in New Mexico were invited by the National Research Council to conduct an intensive investigation into the physics of truck bombs, and researchers were soon shocked by what they discovered. In addition to the deadly air blast, the truck bombs also produced unexpectedly violent ground waves: "The lateral accelerations propagated through the ground from a truck bomb far exceed those produced during the peak magnitude of an earthquake." Sandia came to the sobering conclusion that even an offsite detonation near a nuclear power plant might "cause enough damage to lead to a deadly release of radiation or even a meltdown." These findings, however, were hidden from the public and ignored by the Nuclear Regulatory Commission, which in 1986 refused to authorize vehicle barriers to protect nuclear power installations or to alter an obsolete security plan designed to thwart a few terrorists infiltrating on foot.[3]

Indeed, after several perfunctory investigations, Washington seemed unwilling to draw any of the obvious conclusions from the Beirut catastrophes. Both the Reagan and Bush administrations appeared to regard the Hezbollah bombings as embarassing flukes, rather than as a powerful new threat that would replicate rapidly in the "blow back" of imperial misadventure. Although it was inevitable that other insurgent groups would soon emulate Hezbollah, American planners largely failed to foresee the extraordinary globalization of car-bombing in the 1990s or the rise of sophisticated new strategies of urban destabilization. However by the mid-1990s, more cities were under siege from bomb attacks than at any time since the end of World War Two, and urban guerrillas were using car and truck bombs to score direct hits on some of the world's most powerful cultural and financial institutions. Each success, moreover, emboldened new attacks and recruited additional groups to launch their own "poor man's air force."

Table 3   The 1990s Blitz

Date		Dead	Wounded
Mar. 1992	Buenos Aires	30	242
Aprl. 1992	City of London	2	44
July 1992	Lima	39	150
Feb. 1993	New York	6	1000
Mar. 1993	Bombay	257	1400
Apr. 1993	City of London	1	30
May 1993	Florence	6	—
Apr. 1994	Johannesburg	9	—
Apr. 1994	Israel	7	52
July 1994	Buenos Aires	96	200
Jan. 1995	Algiers	42	280
Feb. 1995	Zakho (Iraq)	76	—
Feb. 1995	Oklahoma City	168	800
Sept. 1995	Srinagar (Kashmir)	13	25
Nov. 1995	Ryadh	7	—
Nov. 1995	Islamabad	15	—
Jan. 1996	Colombo	55	1200
Jun. 1996	Dhahran	19	372
Jun. 1996	Manchester	0	200
Oct. 1997	Colombo	18	100
Nov. 1997	Hyderabad	23	—
Mar. 1998	Colombo	38	250
Aug. 1998	Nairobi/Dar-es-Salaam	300	5000
Aug. 1998	Omagh	29	300
Sept. 1999	Dagestan	81	—

In the early 1990s, for example, the occult Maoists of Sendero Luminoso in Peru, after a decade of almost genocidal warfare in Ayacucho province, came down from the *altiplano* to spread terror throughout Lima and Callao with increasingly more powerful *coches-bomba*.[4] "Large supplies of explosives," the Peruvian magazine *Caretas* pointed out, are "freely available in a mining nation," and the *senderistas* were generous in their gifts of dynamite: they bombed television stations and various foreign embassies as well as a dozen police stations and military camps.[5] Their Lima campaign, conceived as the literal "final conflict," eerily recapitulated the car bomb's evolution as it progressed from modest detonations to more powerful attacks on the American embassy, then to Bloody Friday-type massacres using 16 vehicles at a time.[6]

Sendero, however, added two unique entries of its own to the encyclopedia of car-bomb horrors. First, in April 1992 *senderistas* rolled a bus packed with explosives down a hill into the municipal center of Villa El Salvador, a Lima megaslum administered by the legal Left, destroying homes, schools, a community radio station, a library, and public offices as well as the police station. They also shot Villa's deputy-mayor and "Mother Courage," Maria Elena Moyano, in the face, leaving her body booby-trapped with dynamite.[7] Three months later, they used a huge ANFO car bomb – the equivalent of almost one-half ton of TNT – in an extraordinary attempt to blow up an entire neighborhood of class enemies. The elite Miraflores district was devastated, with 39 killed, another 120 injured, and almost 600 homes and businesses destroyed or badly damaged, including the newly opened, five-star Hotel las Americas. The local press described "Lima's Beverly Hills" as looking "as if an aerial bombardment had flattened the area."[8]

The Miraflores cataclysm was promptly followed by a score of other explosions in rich and poor neighborhoods alike, as well as a sustained attack on critical urban infrastructures. Whether or not it was the Maoists' actual goal, the car-bombings negatively equalized services across the city's chasm of inequality: middle-class professionals complained that their apartment buildings had become little more than "cliff dwellings," "high-rises without water, power or

Figure 5   Lima, Peru: a Peruvian policeman stands guard
at the crater left by a car bomb loaded with dynamite. The blast left
one person dead. Peruvian police said Shining Path guerrillas
planted bombs throughout the capital, exploding them just before
midnight on May 23, 1992. Twenty people were reported injured
in the explosions.

windows."[9] Sendero's crescendo was the so-called "armed strike" in late July when 16 car bombs were detonated or defused. Correspondent James Brooke described how terror was "stripping away urbanity" in the "Beirut of the Andes."

> "Keep your mouth open to avoid injuries to internal organs," one popular magazine instructed readers in a list of car-bomb survival tips. "Jump in a hole, like an empty swimming pool." In the last two weeks, the Maoist guerrillas have placed 30 car bombs in and around this city, successfully exploding half of them. A taxi that stops in front of a bank is now inevitably greeted by a chorus of shrill whistles from nervous guards. Offices are frequently emptied by alerts that send workers stampeding down sidewalks.
>
> "Let's play 'bomba,'" 4-year-old Cantu Lentz proposed to a recent visitor to her apartment. Without coaching, she threw herself under the dining room table, opened her mouth and counted to 10.[10]

Setting aside the 1993 bombing of Manhattan's World Trade Center and the 1995 Oklahoma City bombing, as well as the 1990s car-bomb campaigns by the Mafia and the IRA – those will be analyzed in later chapters – the next great city brought to its knees by explosions was Bombay on March 12, 1993. The "Black Friday" bombings were the culmination of a cycle of sectarian violence that began with the destruction by Hindu extremists of the Babri Masjid Mosque in Ayodhya in December 1992, followed by five days of rioting and lynching in the *chawls* of Bombay that left almost 1000 dead, mostly Moslems. None of this was spontaneous: the attack on the mosque was organized by militants of the Rashtriya Swayamsevak Sangh (RSS), a movement whose roots go back to the assassination of that "traitor to Hinduism, Gandhi," while the grisly burnings and decapitations of ordinary Moslems in the streets of Bombay were carried out by thugs of the Shiv Sena, the semi-fascist party that advances both Marartha and Hindu supremacy, often with the collusion of the police. Revenge in the name of dead Moslems, in turn, was plotted by the Pakistani ISI – proving once again that it was the world's most proficient terrorist organization – using local gangsters controlled by Bombay's Al Capone, the legendary Dawood Ibrahim.

Dawood Ibrahim: one recent biographer deems him, not Osama bin Laden, truly the "most dangerous man in the world," but "unlike bin Laden, he lives like a king in his mansion in Karachi, Pakistan, while bin Laden moves from cave to cave in the dark of night. And while bin Laden sleeps on dusty, insect-ridden floors . . . Dawood sleeps until noon, often waking up with Karachi's youngest and most beautiful just-deflowered virgins by his side."[11] Master smuggler, financier, and the dark power behind many Bollywood extravaganzas, Dawood spent the late 1980s running the Bombay underworld from his "White House" in friendly Dubai across the Indian Ocean. Writer Gilbert King claims that the Dawood empire (originally known as "D Company") also tithed nearly $1 billion each year to the ISI and its jihadist franchises.[12]

In early 1993, Dawood is alleged to have sent three boats from Dubai to Karachi, where they were loaded with 1500 kilograms of military high explosives; meanwhile 19 members of D Company, led by Dawood's henchman Tiger Menon, had taken an ISI crash course outside Karachi in car-bomb manufacture and urban sabotage. Indian customs officials were bribed to look the other way as the deadly "black soup" was smuggled into Bombay via small fishing ports north of the city. The top-of-the-line RDX explosive was then apportioned amongst a car-bombing fleet that consisted of a limousine, two vans, three small cars, a jeep, a motorcycle, and four scooters, in addition to three suitcase bombs to be left in the lobbies of luxury hotels.[13]

Like Sendero's "city-busting" campaign the year before, Dawood's deadly armada was launched with the dual intention of inflicting as much human and economic damage upon Bombay as possible. The professionalism of the attack was grimly manifest in the fact that 13 of the 17 devices were successfully detonated over a 2-hour time-span. The first blast, just before 1:30 p.m., erupted from the basement garage of the Bombay Stock Exchange (BSE), severely damaging the 28-story skyscraper and killing at least 50 office workers and street vendors. Local journalist Hussain Zaidi wrote:

> To the people milling around outside, eating lunch, the scene before them transformed suddenly from the familiar to the unimaginable . . . Inside the BSE, the scene was chaotic. Most of the people in the basement and mezzanine had been killed. The roof of the underground car park had caved in, flattening vehicles and trapping men . . . Outside the BSE, the street was covered in a macabre mosaic of blood, limbs, glass and share-application forms. The mounds of food, so attractive just minutes ago, were now splattered with the remains of people's bodies.[14]

The Stock Exchange was just the prelude. At 2:15, two cabs exploded side-by-side, killing five people in a wholesale market for grain and spice. Ten minutes later, a powerful bomb in the portico of the Air India skyscraper wrecked the Bank of Oman branch on the ground floor and left more than 100 casualties (20 dead) strewn on the pavement. As smoke columns rose from bomb sites and radio programs were interrupted by emergency appeals, Bombay began to be gripped by panic. At 2:30 p.m., the petrol station next to the headquarters of Shiv Sena exploded; 25 minutes later, a double-decker bus disappeared in a fireball: "there were no survivors on board; not even the bodies could be identified." More than 100 people were burnt to death. Other explosions followed in the Zaveri Bazaar, the Plaza Cinema and near the airport. The ultimate toll was 257 dead and almost 1400 injured: sectarian riots (the ISI's ultimate goal?) were only narrowly averted.[15]

While Sendero Luminoso's apocalyptic campaign in Lima was terminated by the unexpected arrest of its leader and demi-god, "Presidente Gonzalo" [Abimael Guzmán], in September 1992, Dawood Ibrahim was merely forced to relocate from his old palace in Dubai to a new mansion in Karachi where, protected by elite ISI bodyguards, he continued his underworld activities while simultaneously promoting Lashkar-e-Toiba, the jihadist group also known as the "Sword of the ISI."[16] Meanwhile, Dawood's "Bloody

Friday" entrenched car-bombings as chronic atrocities in Indian city life: a variety of domestic political groups, including rival movie producers and Sikh separatists, as well as the ISI and its fronts, began almost casually to use public massacres (like the double car-bombing in Bombay in August 2003 that killed 50 people) to settle scores or advance their sectarian agendas.[17]

No agenda, however, was more obsolete or purely evil than the vain attempts by the neo-Nazi right in South Africa to disrupt the election of Nelson Mandela in 1995 with a series of car-bombings in Johannesburg, Pretoria, and other urban centers. The attacks followed Inkatha leader Mangosuthu Buthelezi's termination of his boycott of the electoral process, a concession that effectively signaled the defeat of the white government's attempt to derail an African National Congress (ANC) victory through the promotion of Zulu separatism and the instigation of inter-ethnic violence inside the Black townships. The bombings, like the savage massacres perpetrated by the OAS in Algeria in 1962, were last-ditch attempts to foment a race war in the face of the liberation movement's remarkable discipline and strategic focus.

The ANC, to be sure, had experimented with car-bombing apartheid in the 1980s, but the tactic divided the movement's leadership and produced an unprecedented debate about the morality of attacking "soft targets."[18] Despite tremendous rank-and-file pressure for more aggressive retaliation against white atrocities, Nelson Mandela wrote from his prison cell to criticize guerrilla actions that risked death or injury to innocent civilians. Likewise Oliver Tambo, the exiled ANC president, publicly denounced his own guerrillas of Umkhonto we Sizwe for being "inexcusably careless" in a 1984 Durban car-bombing that killed four people.[19]

The April 1994 attacks by the Afrikaner Resistance Movement, in contrast, were designed to slaughter as many innocents as possible. The first bomb on election eve detonated in the street between the regional and national offices of the ANC, killing Susan Keane, an ANC candidate for the provincial legislature, and eight other people. Two white men in security uniforms were seen running from the booby-trapped car.[20]

The next day, April 25, as Black voters lined up in front of polls or waited for rides at taxi terminals, they had to run a gauntlet of car bombs. The worst attack – "a horrific morning blast that killed 10 and sprayed human body parts and mangled minivans across a taxi park" – took place in the Johannesburg suburb of Germiston, where whites had been outraged by a proposal to merge their municipality with neighboring Black townships. In any event, African voters were not intimidated, and their President-elect, Nelson Mandela, excoriated the old "government of weaklings" who had been "unable to rise to the challenge that is posed by madmen now slaughtering innocent people because they fear democracy."[21]

The slaughter continued in summer 1994 in another great Southern Hemisphere city, Buenos Aires. With the largest Jewish and Arab communities in Latin America, the Argentine metropolis was a surrogate battlefield for the ongoing uprisings against Israeli occupations of the West Bank and southern Lebanon. Two years previously (March 17, 1992), a Ford Fairlane with 220 pounds of *plastique* in the trunk had exploded in front of the Israeli embassy, demolishing the five-story structure as well as a Catholic church and its adjoining elementary school across the street; it took nearly a week to exhume all 30 bodies from the ruins, including the wife of the Israeli ambassador. Hospital emergency rooms struggled to cope with the 252 injured, including 41 schoolkids. "Never has there been at attack of such a magnitude on an Israeli Embassy," said a local rabbi. "There just is no parallel. We've never had an embassy literally shoved down into the ground. The only thing we can compare it to is the bombing of the American Embassy in Lebanon."[22]

Another Lebanon comparison was perhaps more relevant: the Israeli assassination the previous month (February 16, 1992) of Hezbollah Secretary General Al-Sayyed Abbas al-Moussawi, together with his wife and young child. The embassy bombing was almost certainly a retaliation, and having struck once in the Western Hemisphere, there was no reason to suppose that Hezbollah might not do it again. Certainly the July 1993 Israeli invasion of south

Lebanon, which destroyed thousands of homes and displaced the residents of 120 villages, created a new grievance to be redressed by car bombs.[23] So, just as the bombing of the US embassy in Beirut in 1983 had been followed by the even larger explosion at the Marine barracks, the destruction of the Buenos Aires embassy was soon overshadowed by the carnage of July 18, 1994, an atrocity that erased any distinction between "Israelis" and "Jews" as Hezbollah targets.

. The Asociación Mutual Israelita Argentina (AMIA) was the traditional hub of Jewish communal life in the entire country and, in addition to offices and social services, it housed a priceless library and historical archive. It was also the headquarters of a research team ("Project Witness") charged with excavating the history of Nazi émigrés and their local supporters from secret records recently turned over to AMIA by the Argentine government. The seven-story building was destroyed on July 18 by an ANFO explosion so powerful that almost no one was left alive to be dug out of the leveled debris – the death toll was 85 with several hundred injured, many of them maimed or crippled for life. Israel's Prime Minister Yitzhak Rabin called it the "most serious attack against a Jewish community since the end of World War II," while others described it as the "worst massacre of Jews in the Americas since the colonial era."[24]

Although local reporters immediately suspected neo-Nazis who wanted Project Witness put out of action, forensic investigation revealed that the attack was probably a classical Beirut-style suicide bombing. Both Washington and Tel Aviv quickly blamed Hezbollah (already the prime suspect in the earlier embassy bombing) and, indeed, "Islamic Jihad" – Hezbollah's usual *nom de guerre* – in Beirut promptly issued a statement taking credit for the attack. (Later, Hezbollah would erect a plaque in South Lebanon to Ibrahim Hussein Berro, the 29-year-old bomber).[25] The AMIA massacre, moreover, was immediately preceded by a car-bomb attack on the Israeli embassy in Ankara (1 dead) and soon followed by a car-bomb explosion in front of the Israeli embassy in London (20 injured), both of which were also attributed by Tel Aviv to Hezbollah.[26]

To the rage of Israelis and ordinary Argentinians alike, however, the administration of President Carlos Menem seemed to deliberately and systematically bungle the bombing investigation, prompting suspicions of official collusion that were confirmed in 2002 with the publication of testimony from a high-ranking defector from Iran's intelligence agency who claimed that Tehran paid Menem $10 million to cover up its role in the atrocity. The attack, according to the defector, had been planned by the Iranian embassy's cultural attaché working with Hezbollah members and corrupt Argentine police. Argentina's former deputy interior minister, moreover, told the *New York Times* that "state intelligence and the federal police are clearly involved, but there is also evidence pointing to the involvement of agencies ranging from Immigration to the Foreign Ministry."[27] An attempt to prosecute some of the accused police officials (perhaps to divert attention from Menem and other higher-ups) misfired, and the trial judge himself ended up under indictment. An official arrest warrant for Imad Fayez Mugniyah, Hezbollah's master bomber, struck most people as little more than a sick joke (were the Argentine police going to raid the Bekaa Valley?). A dozen years afterwards, justice for the families of the AMIA victims remains elusive (as it does for the tens of thousands of victims of the "Condor years" of military dictatorship) and Argentinians still debate the mysteries *à la* le Carré of who covered up what and who framed whom.[28]

A similar fog of conspiracy enshrouds the ultimate responsibility for the so-called "third battle of Algiers" in 1995–96. If the first battle was the FLN's uprising in the Casbah in 1957 and the second was the OAS's frenzy of destruction in 1962, the third involved car-bombings and assassinations allegedly carried out by a fundamentalist underground whose most notorious component was the Armed Islamic Groups (GIA). Just one phase of a protracted civil war commencing in 1992 that claimed more than 150,000 victims, many of them massacred in the most grisly and unspeakable fashions, the car-bombings have been interpreted as the work of fanatical "Afghans" (as Algerian alumni of the ISI training schools and Afghan War are known) emboldened by their connections to the international Salafist network. However recent evidence – including, most sensationally, the revelations of Mohammed Samraoui, a former colonel in Algerian military intelligence (Sécurité militaire) – suggests that some of the atrocities attributed to the GIA may, in fact, have been committed by the military with the aim of silencing enemies and increasing its power. Indeed, Samraoui insinuates that by the mid-1990s GIA had become little more than a front for the Sécurité militaire's campaign to eliminate secular and Islamist opponents alike.[29] The Algerian Army, moreover, was now receiving high-tech aid from Paris as well as counter-insurgency advice from such sinister experts as retired General Jacques Massu, the commander of the *paras* during the siege of the Casbah in 1957.[30]

The Army's atrocities, like the December 1994 massacre of some 3000 Islamists near Ain Defla, eerily recapitulated those perpetrated by the French 40 years earlier. This bloodbath – the Army gave no quarter to either GIA combatants or their families – was in turn one of the pretexts for the car-bomb blitz against Algiers. The deadliest attack occurred at the end of January, the busy week before Ramadan, when a suicide driver in a stolen white Fiat veered into a crowd across from the central police station, killing 42 and wounding almost 300; an illegal Islamist newspaper celebrated the "brilliant victory against apostates and their henchmen." Six weeks later (March 10), another car bomb exploded near police housing in the Kouba district of southern Algiers, wounding 63; it was followed in mid-May by the car-bombing of a police station in the eastern suburb of Khemis el-Khechna. Simultaneously, assassins stalked and killed a number of leading writers, actors, journalists, and university officials, accelerating the flight of the Algerian intelligentsia to safer havens outside the country.[31] Car-bombings resumed after the presidential elections in November and continued for more than a year, with an infamous double-header on February 11, 1996 in the popular districts of Belcourt and Bab el-Oued (the former OAS citadel, now the "hardest of all 'Islamist' strongholds") which claimed more than 100 casualties. For older residents who remembered the mad bombs of the *pieds noirs*, this post-revolutionary carnage, with so little rhyme or reason beyond the sheer propagation of terror, must have evoked a chilling sense of déjà vu.[32]

A cold déjà vu was also felt in Colombo in January 1996 when Black Tigers – undoubtedly inspired by recent car–bomb attacks on Manhattan's World Trade Center and the City of London – drove a truck carrying 440 pounds of military high–explosives into the Central Bank building. The ruins burned through the night; at least 90 were left dead and nearly 1400 injured. Twenty months later (October 15, 1997), the Tigers used another truck bomb to attack the showpiece of Sri Lanka's modernization: the twin towers of the new World Trade Center with its adjacent five–star hotel. There were more than 130 casualties and the American correspondent John Burns reported the gloomy mood as Sri Lankan President Gunawardene toured "the acres of rubble and twisted steel." "'This is an endless war,' he said, muffling his voice so as not to disturb the cathedral–like stillness among crowds of people who had gathered in vigil near the blackened crater where half a ton of high explosives detonated beneath rice bags in the back of the truck."[33]

Tiger leader Pirabhakaran, as we saw earlier, strategically used indiscriminate bombings to excavate an abyss between Tamils and Sinhalese that could neither be bridged by negotiation nor ulti- mately crossed except by recognition of his dictatorship over the Tamils. (The Sri Lankan government and military, to be sure, also have done their share of excavation: their human–rights abuses against both Tamils and the Sinhalese Left have been appalling.) Until the late 1990s, however, there was not much of a religious dimension to the growing ethnic conflict between Tamils (Hindus and some Moslems) and Sinhalese (largely Buddhist). In January 1998, Pirabhakaran decided to rectify this by sending a squad of suicide Black Tigers in a bomb–laden truck to attack the Temple of the Tooth, the holiest of Buddhist shrines on the island. Although Buddha's tooth was unharmed, the bombing which killed eight pilgrims and monks as well as the three instigators had the desired effect of setting off ethnic riots and adding a new bitterness to the conflict. "You terrorists," one 90–year–old Sinhalese man implored, "kill us, eat us, but don't attack our shrines where Buddha lives."[34]

Having patented a creative new atrocity, Pirabhakaran returned to a tried-and-true soft target six weeks later (March 5, 1998), when Black Tigers reenacted their April 1987 attack on Colombo's transit hub. This time two shrapnel-packed bombs were affixed to the sideboards of a Nissan mini-bus and detonated by the suicide driver just outside the main train station, in the midst of congested traffic and huge pedestrian crowds. More than 300 vehicles were destroyed or damaged, including a primary-school bus that was reportedly blown to bits. "School books, a plastic lunch box and children's shoes were scattered around the site, littered among the twisted hulks of cars and trucks." Altogether there were 38 dead and more than 250 injured.[35] Colombo, like Beirut, Bogotá, Lima, and Algiers, had become a city bombed out of its wits.

18

Form Follows Fear

The car bomb is the nuclear weapon of guerrilla warfare.

Charles Krauthammer[1]

The 1990s blitz was a Darwinian process that sped up the evolution of the car bomb as an engine of urban terror. The principle was simple: bomb promiscuously, probing the city's soft targets, and you will eventually discover areas of unexpected vulnerability. Nihilism, if systematic, works. Thus, for the relentless Black Tigers, bombing their enemies' faith – as in the Temple of the Tooth attack – revealed attractive shortcuts to ethnocide and civil war that have since been replicated on a grotesque scale by mosque bombings in Iraq and, on a lesser scale, in Pakistan. But the 1990s also opened two other Pandora's boxes. The first was the decision of the Sicilian Cosa Nostra, hammered by unprecedented mass arrests and so-called "maxi-trials," to retaliate against the anti–Mafia movement by vandalizing Italy's cultural treasures – literally to car-bomb Art. The second was the IRA's employment of huge ANFO bombs to devastate the City of London. Both campaigns focused on critical and insecure nodes of globalization: a world-class art heritage and the glass–and–steel sanctums of high finance (shades of Buda's original wagon).

The Mafia war on culture was an enraged response to the arrest of the fugitive Godfather, Salvatore "Totò" Riina, in January 1993. In the 1980s, Riina and his ruthless gang from the hilltop town of

Corleone had abandoned any pretension of adhering to a traditional Cosa Nostra code of honor when they started massacring the extended families, women and children included, of their opponents. (The toll was quite staggering: the Palermo magistrate Roberto Scarpinato, who prosecuted former Premier Giulio Andreotti for his Mafia ties, has estimated that organized crime, including the Neapolitan Camorra as well as the Sicilian Mafia, was responsible for nearly 10,000 deaths in Italy between 1983 and 1993).[2] With utter contempt for the power or legitimacy of the Italian state, Riina also renewed the bombing campaign against the reformist magistracy. In 1992 his henchmen killed the two heroes of the Palermo "maxi-trial": Judge Giovanni Falcone (blown up with his wife and three bodyguards by a huge mine planted under the *autostrada* from the Palermo airport) and Judge Paolo Borsellino (killed along with five bodyguards, by a powerful car bomb in front of his mother's apartment building).

At a secret summit during the summer of 1992, Riina, according to Mafia historian David Lane, pressed his fellow chieftains for "an outright attack on Italian society itself" – especially cultural institutions and public spaces – to create so much fear and havoc that the government would be forced to end its prosecutions or at least deal more leniently with convicted *mafiosi*. When "one of those present expressed concern that innocent bystanders might be hurt," the boss of bosses evoked the contemporary example of Yugoslavia. "Many children had died in Sarajevo, said Riina, who saw no problem in killing indiscriminately in Italy. Whatever the consequences, he was determined to push ahead with what he thought would further the interests of Cosa Nostra."[3]

With Riina's capture the following January, Italy braced for a wave of *cadaveri eccellenti* and indeed in May a booby-trapped Fiat Uno blew up in a posh Roman neighborhood across from the home of a popular television talk-show host who had recently applauded the arrest of Riina, injuring 23 people and forcing the evacuation of 100 damaged apartments. The explosion was described as "a rare strike by the crime organization outside its native Sicily" and police seemed to have little apprehension of where

Riina's bombers, led by Bernardo "The Tractor" Provenzano and Filippo Graviano, would attack next.[4]

In fact, the Corleonesi had decided to strike at what they characterized with rural Sicilian contempt as the "old shit": art treasures and baroque churches, the magnets that brought millions of foreign tourists to Italy every year. Their first target was the magnificent Uffizi Gallery in Florence, which housed the world's greatest collection of Renaissance art. As always, the chosen vehicle was a stolen Fiat, but this time it was a Fiorino van loaded with an unprecedented charge of almost one-quarter ton of a sophisticated cocktail of *plastique* and TNT. The detonation early on the morning of May 27 cratered the side-street behind the Uffizi and shook Florence from its sleep like a great earthquake. The interior of a medieval tower house behind the Uffizi, the Torre delle Pulci, collapsed, killing the sleeping family inside; several other people were burnt beyond recognition and 26 were injured by the fireball or flying glass, many them late-night strollers in the adjacent Piazza della Signoria.[5]

The blast, meanwhile, "shook the entire west wing of the gallery, on the banks of the Arno near the Ponte Vecchio. An exit staircase collapsed, a glass skylight was shattered and broken glass carpeted 20 of the gallery's 45 rooms and the Vasari Corridor, over the Arno."[6] Journalists were initially barred from the scene, and officials only reluctantly conceded the true scale of destruction: 135 paintings suffered significant damage, including masterpieces by Giotto, Titian, Rubens, and van Dyck, and one of the museum's most famous Roman statues, the Niobe, was shattered. The $20 million of structural damage took almost two years to repair. "Not since World War II, perhaps," fretted an art critic, "has art seemed so susceptible a target."[7] "The novelty of these attacks," added Florence's chief prosecutor, Pierluigi Vigna, "was that for the first time in its history, [the Cosa Nostra] chose monuments as its targets."[8]

A trio of bombings in July was equally "monumental." One Fiat car bomb exploded near La Scala in Milan, killing four young firemen and a Moroccan immigrant. The bomb also ruptured a gas line that caught fire and destroyed the Pavilion of Contemporary Art (which, ironically, had been built on a World War Two bomb site). Almost simultaneously another bomb-laden Fiat Uno damaged the famed Basilica of St John Lateran, the See of the Bishop of Rome (the pope). "By exploding their car-bomb in the square outside the Lateran Palace," writes Lane, "the Mafia had gone for an important religious, historical, political and artistic symbol. The blast caused considerable damage to buildings that were part of the pope's own cathedral. Frescoes crumbled and marble floors and carved wooden ceilings were badly affected. Several people were injured and only a lucky combination of circumstances prevented mass murder."[9]

Finally, a third car bomb went off across from San Giorgio in Velabro, an ancient church near the Forum. More than a dozen people were injured in the two Roman bombings. Although a papal spokesman immediately dismissed the idea that the "Mafia would want to strike against the Pope," this seems to have been precisely the objective. In 1998 Riina's lieutenants were convicted of organizing the bombings, although his successor, "Tractor" Provenzano, was still underground and could only be sentenced in absentia.[10] It was later revealed that the Provenzano and his wild bunch had wanted to blow up the Leaning Tower of Pisa and had considered leaving HIV-infected syringes on the beach at Rimini or poisoning food in supermarkets.[11]

The Mafia's war on art may have been short-lived but it created an ominous precedent for countries whose cultural wealth is concentrated in a few great museums, cathedrals or temples. If a car bomb could damage the Uffizi, why not the Louvre, Hermitage, Escorial, or Guggenheim? (Or, if you prefer, Disneyworld or Las Vegas's Bellagio?) Indeed as a consequence of the Uffizi attack, museum design increasingly has had to incorporate the functions of a cultural bunker, balancing public access and a central location with the needs of physical security in a new era of high-tech cultural terrorism. Even greater challenges, however, are faced by the managers of the world's financial flows and digital capital.

A "two-billion-pound explosion"? One meaning, of course, is the TNT yield of 50 Hiroshima-size atomic weapons (which is to

say, only half of the explosive power of a single H-bomb). Alternately, £2 billion ($3 billion) is what the IRA probably cost the
City of London in April 1993 when a blue dump truck containing a
ton of ANFO exploded on Bishopsgate Road across from the Nat
West Tower in the heart of world's second major financial center.
Explosives experts and insurance adjusters were equally stunned by
the colossal damage: "Over a million and half square feet of office
space was affected. Structures hundreds of yards apart had their
windows blown out and their interiors damaged." Although one
bystander was killed and more than 30 injured by the immense
explosion – which also demolished a medieval church and wrecked
the Liverpool Street train station – the human toll was incidental to
the economic damage that was the true goal.[12]

Whereas the other truck-bomb campaigns of the 1990s – Lima,
Bombay, Colombo, and so forth – had followed Hezbollah's
playbook almost to the letter, the Bishopsgate bomb, which
IRA historian Ed Moloney describes as "the most successful military
tactic since the start of the Troubles," was part of a novel IRA
campaign that waged war on financial centers in order to extract
British concessions during the difficult peace negotiations that lasted
through most of the 1990s.[13] Although some insurance experts
scoffed at initial estimates of £1.5 million worth of damage,
journalist Tim Pat Coogan claims that "as the days passed, and
the full nature of the damage became known, it became evident that
the final bill could well exceed the £2 billion mark."[14]

Bishopsgate, in fact, was the second and most costly of three
blockbuster explosions carried out by the elite (and more or less
autonomous) South Armagh IRA under the leadership of the
legendary "Slab" Murphy. Almost exactly a year earlier, the group
had set off a truck bomb at the Baltic Exchange in St Mary Axe that
rained a million pounds of glass and debris on surrounding streets,
killing three and wounding almost 100 people.[15] The destruction,
although less than that inflicted at Bishopsgate, was still astonishing:
about £800 million, or more than the total damage inflicted over
22 years of bombing in Northern Ireland (approximately £600
million).[16] Then in 1996, with peace talks stalled and the IRA

Figure 6   Damage in the City caused by a huge IRA bomb left in
a vehicle parked near the Natwest Tower, 1993. All that is left standing
is a window display in a men's clothes shop.

Army Council in revolt against the latest ceasefire, the South Armagh Brigade smuggled into England a third huge car bomb that they set off in the underground garage of one of the post-modern office buildings near Canary Wharf Tower in the gentrified London Docklands, killing two and causing nearly $150 million dollars in damage.[17]

Total IRA damage to English real estate most likely exceeded $5 billion if the devastation (an estimated $744 million of insured loss) to Manchester's Arndale Centre, blown up by a van bomb in June 1996, is included in the calculation.[18] The Manchester attack differed from the London explosions in its apparent disregard for civilian casualties: more than 200 shoppers were injured in an unconscionable throwback to the indiscriminate IRA bombings of the early 1970s. In the City of London, however, the IRA was only after the bottom line. As Jon Coaffee points out in his study of the bombings, if the Provisionals – like the Tamil Tigers or Al Qaeda – had simply wanted to sow terror or bring life in London to a halt, they would have set off the explosions at rush hour on a business day (instead they "were detonated at a time when the City was virtually deserted") and/or attacked the heart of the transport infrastructure, as did the Islamist suicide bombers who blew up buses and subways in July 2005.[19]

Instead, Slab Murphy and his comrades concentrated on what they perceived to be the financial weak link: the faltering British and European insurance industry. To the horror of their enemies they were spectacularly successful: "The huge payouts by insurance companies," commented the BBC shortly after Bishopsgate, "contributed to a crisis in the industry, including the near-collapse of the world's leading [re]insurance market, Lloyd's of London."[20] German and Japanese investors threatened to boycott the City unless physical security was improved and the government agreed to subsidize insurance costs.[21]

Despite a long history of London bombings by the Irish going back to the Fenians and Queen Victoria, neither Downing Street nor the City of London Police had foreseen the scale of accurately targeted physical and financial damage. Even Murphy was probably astonished by the success of his super-bombs. In response, the banking and insurance industries clamored for a "ring of steel" – concrete barriers, high iron fences, and impregnable gates – like the system that had been built to protect Belfast's city center after the first IRA car-bombings in 1972. "The City," according to financial leaders interviewed by *The Times,* "should be turned into a medieval-style walled enclave to prevent terrorist attacks."[22] What was actually implemented in the City (and later in Docklands) was a technologically more advanced network of traffic restrictions and cordons, closed-circuit television (CCTV) cameras, including "24–hour Automated Number Plate Recording (ANPR) cameras, linked to police databases," and intensified public and private policing. "In the space of a decade," writes Coaffee," the City of London was transformed into the most surveilled space in the UK and perhaps the world, with over 1500 surveillance cameras operating, many of which are linked to the ANPR system."[23]

Since 9/11, this anti-terrorist surveillance system has been extended throughout London's core in the benign guise of Mayor Ken Livingstone's celebrated "congestion pricing" scheme to liberate the city from gridlock. According to one of Britain's major Sunday papers:

> *The Observer* has discovered that MI5, Special Branch and the Metropolitan Police began secretly developing the system in the wake of the 11 September attacks. In effect, the controversial charging scheme will create one of the most daunting defence systems protecting a major world city when it goes live a week tomorrow. It is understood that the system also utilizes facial recognition software which automatically identifies suspects or known criminals who enter the eight-square-mile zone. Their precise movements will be tracked by camera from the point of entry . . . However, civil liberty campaigners yesterday claimed that millions had been misled over the dual function of the scheme, promoted primarily as a means of reducing congestion in central London.[24]

The addition in 2003 of this new panoptican traffic scan to London's already extensive system of video surveillance ensures that the average citizen is "caught on CCTV cameras 300 times a day." While it may make it easier for the police to apprehend non-suicidal terrorists, this network of thousands of cameras does little to protect the larger metropolis from well-planned and competently disguised vehicle-bomb attacks.[25] Blair's "Third Way" has been a fast lane for the adoption of Orwellian surveillance and the usurpation of civil liberties, but until some miracle technology emerges (and none is in sight) that allows authorities to "sniff" from a distance a molecule or two of explosive in a stream of rush-hour traffic, the car bombers will continue to commute to work.

19

Killing Bush, Bombing Oklahoma

> As calmly as any delivery-truck driver making a routine drop-off,
> McVeigh parked right below the tinted windows of the
> America's Kids Day Care Center on the second floor.
>
> Lou Michel and Dan Herbeck, *American Terrorist*[1]

It was billed as Washington's "largest victory celebration since the
end of World War II." The triumphal strains of John Philips Souza
echoed through the streets on June 8, 1991 as 8000 bronzed victors
of Desert Storm marched down Constitution Avenue behind their
battle flags while Stealth fighters streaked the sky above the Mall.
Like a Roman emperor welcoming his legions back from Gaul,
President George H. Bush dramatically descended from his reviewing stand to take the salute in the street from General Norman
Schwarzkopf and his victorious commanders.[2] For a moment, it was
August 1945 again and the United States seemed almost omnipo-
tent. The Soviet Union was in its final death agony and Pentagon
technology had just crushed one of the world's major military
powers. Thanks to American airpower and heavy armor, thousands
of Iraqi soldiers were now just carbonized husks on the road back to
Baghdad.

This aura of invincibility was soon dispelled by nightmare scenes
in American cities and embassies as the sordid consequences of
several decades of American covert operations and "ghost wars" in
the Middle East blew back in the face of Bush's successor, Bill

Clinton. Rented vans packed with tons of fertilizer inflicted far more death and suffering on Americans in the 1990s than had all of Saddam's supposedly fearsome Republican Guard divisions and Scud missiles. If one of the virtues of an air force is the ability to reach halfway around the world to surprise enemies in their beds, then car bombs truly began to grow wings in this period; yet the most deadly attack was mounted by fanatics from New York and Michigan (even if their brains had been originally addled in the Saudi desert). Regardless of provenance, however, the deep para-doxical meaning of "asymmetry" was revealed in a succession of colossal vehicle-bombings: each of them a rung in the ladder climbing toward the ultimate carnage of September 11, 2001.

While the first American cruise missiles were falling on Baghdad, a young Kuwait-born Pakistani, named Ramzi Yousef was hun-kered down in his studies at what Steve Coll has characterized as a "graduate-level camp for bomb makers" in Afghanistan. "He learned the bombing techniques originally developed in the bor-der-straddling guerrilla sabotage camps of Pakistani intelligence, which had been supplied with timing devices and plastic explosives by the CIA. He carried out a few attacks in Afghanistan, not because he sought to participate in the Afghan civil war, he said later, but mainly to experiment."[3] Yousef, who had also studied electrical engineering at Swansea, had remarkable technical talents as well as a driving ambition to become the world's greatest bomber. Simon Reeve believes he may have conceived the idea of car-bombing a major American monument while he was tutoring foreign jihadis at the "University of Dawa and Jihad" in Peshawar (Pakistan) in the summer of 1992. His political motivations are less clear, although his uncle, Khalid Sheikh Mohammed (the future mastermind of 9/11) was a Muslim Brotherhood member and acquaintance of Osama bin Laden who worked for Saudi-supported causes in Afghanistan.[4]

When Yousef and his comrade Ahmed Ajaj (a former pizza delivery man from Texas) arrived in New York on fake passports in September 1992, their luggage bulging with bomb-making man-uals, they were probably freelancers in search of an opportunity to create a "Hiroshima" in America. They quickly hooked up with immigrant members of the radical Egyptian Islamist group Gama'a al-Islamiyya headed by Sheik Omar Abdul Rahman (whose US visa reputedly had been arranged by the CIA), as well as a sympathetic Kuwaiti chemical engineer named Nidal Ayyad.[5] After a reconnaissance of the city, they settled on the World Trade Center (WTC) as an overweening symbol of American arrogance: their extraordinary ambition was to kill more than 100,000 New Yorkers by toppling one tower of the WTC over against its twin.[6] Although Yousef and his fellow conspirators didn't know it, the Port Authority Police had just completed a prescient security analysis – reportedly ignored by the WTC management – that emphasized the vulnerability of the towers' basement parking levels to car bombers.[7]

Yousef's chosen doomsday device was a Ryder van packed with an ingenious upgrade of the classic IRA ANFO explosive. "The bomb itself," writes Peter Lance, "consisted of four cardboard boxes filled with a slurry of urea nitrate and fuel oil, with waste paper as a binder. The boxes were surrounded by four-foot tanks of compressed hydrogen. They were connected by four 20–foot-long slow-burning fuses of smokeless powder wrapped in fabric. Yousef balanced on his lap four vials of nitroglycerine."[8] The conspirators had no difficulty parking the van on Level B-2, right next to the load-bearing south wall of the North Tower, then fled in another car.

The 1000-pound charge excavated an enormous seven-story-deep crater, but was too small to bring the tower itself down (although as horrified experts later discovered, it came close to breaching the "bathtub" retaining wall that protected the site from the Hudson River). "Our calculations were not very accurate this time," apologized Yousef in a draft of a letter to the authorities later found by investigators. "However we promise you that next time it will be very precise and the Trade Center will be one of our targets."[9] Still, the explosion killed six workers in the parking basement and filled the tower with toxic smoke that threatened to asphyxiate hundreds of others. Thousands stumbled, choking and blinded, down emergency stairs, while the NYPD helicopters evacuated others from the roof of the North Tower. By the end of the day, hospitals and aid stations had treated almost 1100 people: "more hospital casualties," claims Simon Reeve, "than any other [manmade] event in domestic American history apart from the Civil War."[10]

While the FBI squabbled with the CIA and both followed false leads that linked the WTC bombing to Iraq or Iran, the Brooklyn al-Gama'a al-Islamiyya group, led by blind Sheik Rahman, was allegedly plotting a sequel "Day of Terror" in New York, but they were arrested in July 1993 after tips from an Egyptian-American FBI informer. According to the evidence introduced by the prosecution in their 1995 trial, they were planning a vastly ambitious (and implausible) program of synchronized attacks, including the car-bombings of the United Nations and the New York FBI headquarters as well as the George Washington Bridge and the Holland and Lincoln tunnels during rush hour. A dramatic FBI videotape showed four of the ten defendants mixing ammonium nitrate and fuel oil in a garage in Queens. (Several of the defendants claimed that they were training to go to fight in Bosnia, and one testified that the car bomb was actually being prepared for an attack on a warehouse storing arms for shipment to Serbia.) Sheik Rahman was convicted, along with the others, of the rare, Civil War-era charge of "seditious conspiracy" and was sentenced to life in prison.[11]

But the "Day of Terror" case (pushed off the front page by the national obsession with the O.J. Simpson trial) left many unanswered questions: most disturbingly, the possibility that the sheik was one of Bill Casey's loose cannons, a mutinous CIA asset. The prosecution, for instance, never explained how Rahman, wanted by Egyptian authorities, managed to obtain a legal visa to enter the United States, or whether or not it was true, as President Hosni Mubarak alleged in an extraordinary interview in May 1993, that the sheik was still working for the Agency. "The sheik," claimed the Egyptian leader, "has been an agent of the American intelligence apparatus since the days of Afghanistan. He went to Peshawar and spoke about holy war. He gets a continuing salary and the visa which he obtained was not issued by mistake; it was because he had performed specific services. There is a dispute between American intelligence and the internal security apparatus."[12]

Ramzi Yousef, meanwhile, was in Pakistan. Like Mario Buda almost 70 years before, he had bombed lower Manhattan, then quietly slipped out of the country. An instant celebrity at bin Laden's compound in Peshawar, he was rewarded with funds from "wealthy Pakistani or Gulf businessmen."[13] After scheming unsuccessfully to assassinate Premier Benazir Bhutto on their behalf, he moved to Bangkok in 1994, where he built another super-bomb – one ton of ANFO turbocharged with *plastique* loaded in a stolen delivery truck – which he planned to detonate next to the Israeli embassy. However the confederate driving the truck was disoriented by Bangkok's infamous traffic and, after a collision with a motorcycle and automobile, he panicked and fled on foot. Police subsequently towed the truck and were incredulous when the owner opened the back to expose the huge bomb along with the strangled and decomposing corpse of the vehicle's original driver.[14]

Undeterred, Yousef – always the apocalyptic dreamer – relocated to the Philippines where together with his uncle, Khalid Mohammed, he organized an extraordinary and nearly successful conspiracy (Operation "Bojinka") to simultaneously blow up 12 US-bound airliners in flight. According to the police in Manila who first uncovered the airliner plot, he also tinkered with plans to kill the pope and President Clinton as well as fly a suicide plane into the CIA headquarters. A few weeks earlier French commandos had foiled an attempt by the Algerian Armed Islamic Groups (GIA) to crash a hijacked plane into a Parisian monument, perhaps the Eiffel Tower. Car-bombers like Yousef and the GIA were obviously "scaling-up" to airplanes, even if some people (like the directors of the FBI and CIA) were oblivious to the threat.[15]

But back to 1992. On April 14, well before the WTC case had been broken and while investigators were still searching for the elusive Baghdad connection, Kuwaiti authorities made a stunning announcement: they had arrested a team of Iraqi saboteurs planning to car-bomb ex-President George Bush as he arrived that day for an anniversary celebration of Kuwait's liberation. CIA and FBI officials were shown 80 kilograms of plastic explosive concealed in a Toyota Land Cruiser and were allowed to interview a suspect who confessed that "he was recruited for the specific purpose of assassinating President Bush."[16] As the editorial page of the *Wall Street Journal* loudly beat the war drums, the FBI and CIA jointly reported to President Clinton that a painstaking analysis of the car bomb revealed the indelible "signature" of the Iraqi Intelligence Service. "Certain aspects of these devices have been found only in devices linked to Iraq." On June 26, 23 Tomahawk cruise missiles launched from U.S. ships slammed into the center of Baghdad, wiping out a few maintenance workers at the heavily fortified headquarters of Iraqi Intelligence, as well as shattering some nearby homes and killing a famous local artist. President Clinton, his poll ratings soaring, defiantly invoked the United States' right to self-defense.[17]

In a November story in *The New Yorker*, however, investigative reporter Seymour Hersh dismantled much of the administration's case against Iraq: the experts he interviewed scoffed at the idea of any distinctive "signature" in the off-the-shelf circuitry used as a bomb detonator while others questioned Saddam's motives for such an adventurous action while he was in the midst of desperately begging for relief from embargoes. The confessions from the Iraqi "agents" (most likely smugglers) were almost certainly extracted under torture – and perhaps most tellingly, a secret study by the CIA's Counter-Terrorism Center "suggested that Kuwait might have 'cooked the books' on the alleged plot in an effort to play up the 'continuing Iraqi threat' to Western interests in the Persian Gulf." Clinton, indeed, had himself been skeptical of the evidence and was wary of the Kuwaitis until he was double-teamed by Attorney General Janet Reno and CIA Director James Woolsey. Their self-righteousness, as one jaded CIA official explained to Hersh, was simply self-serving: "The President asks the intelligence analysts for the bottom line: Is this real or not? You can't really lose by saying yes."[18]

But the oracles in Langley had almost nothing to say when terror went non-linear in Oklahoma City two years later. This was a different and unexpected species of blowback: two angry Army veterans – one a Gulf War hero who believed that the Pentagon had implanted a computer chip in his brain – using the 1993 Waco debacle as a pretext to massacre 168 fellow citizens, including 19 preschool children and 3 babies in the womb. Although conspiracy theorists have made much of a strange coincidence that put Terry Nichols and Ramzi Yousef near each other in Cebu City, Philippines, in November 1994, the design of the attack on the skyscraper housing federal agencies seems to have been largely inspired by Timothy McVeigh's longtime fascination with that devil's cookbook, *The Turner Diaries*.[19]

Written in 1978, after Bloody Friday but before Beirut, William Pierce's neo-Nazi novel describes with pornographic relish how white supremacists destroy the FBI headquarters in Washington D.C. with an ANFO truck bomb, then later crash a plane carrying a hijacked nuke into the Pentagon. Like Pierce's neo-Nazi hero, McVeigh used ordinary ammonium nitrate fertilizer rather than Yousef's more sophisticated mixture of industrial urea and other ingredients, but following advice he apparently picked up on the gun-show circuit, he substituted nitro racing fuel and diesel oil for ordinary heating oil. Aficionados of homemade detonations, such as the sinister "Uncle Fester" (Steve Preisler), the author of *Home Workshop Explosives*, have long extolled the "amazing wallop" contained in US Patent 3,419,444: "This mixture is mainly ammonium nitrate and nitromethane, along with a few other easily obtained ingredients. The result is an explosive which detonates at a rate comparable to the highest-quality military explosives."[20]

Indeed, the explosion that devastated the Alfred R. Murrah Federal Building on April 19, 1995 was three times more powerful than any of the truck-bomb detonations that the ATF and other federal agencies had been studying at their test range in New Mexico. Experts were flabbergasted at the radius of destruction: "equivalent to 4100 pounds of dynamite, the blast damaged 312 buildings, cracked glass as far as two miles away and inflicted 80 percent of its injuries on people outside the building up to a half-mile away." Distant seismographs recorded it as a 6.0 earthquake on the Richter scale.[21]

Figure 7 The blast that destroyed the Alfred R. Murrah
Federal Building in Oklahoma City was recorded as a
6.0 earthquake on the Richter scale.

As McVeigh undoubtedly had hoped, the horror of Oklahoma City was an immediate inspiration to other Aryan warriors, notably the so-called Viper Militia in Arizona. These dozen fans of McVeigh, who had pledged holy war against the federal government and the "New World Order," were arrested in July 1996 for conspiring to blow up federal buildings in downtown Phoenix. The Vipers had already stockpiled one ton of ammonium nitrate and 55 gallons of nitromethane; in addition they had made a video enthusiastically rehearsing the details of their planned attack on the FBI and ATF headquarters.

On the tape, Mr. Pleasant, 27, identifies the location of the building's supports and describes how the building would collapse if the supports were destroyed – as happened when the truck bomb exploded outside the Federal Building in Oklahoma City. The narrator of the videotape also advises that the destruction of an electric power transformer near the building would cut off power to it, and that employees moving in and out of the building could be harassed by the placement of "anti-personnel" explosives in nearby mailboxes.[22]

But these good ole boy bombs, with their diabolical demonstrations of Heartland DIY ingenuity, were scarcely the last word in destructive power; indeed, it was probably inevitable that the dark Olympics of urban carnage would be won by a home team from the Middle East. A new cycle of attacks on the American military presence in the region began in November 1995 with a van bomb that demolished the three-story complex in Riyadh where a US military mission trained members of the Saudi National Guard. Five Americans were killed, along with 2 Indian civilians, and 60 Americans were wounded. Although the Kuwaitis instantly tried to link the bombing to the alleged plot against Bush, it was soon clear that this was a homegrown operation mounted by Saudi dissidents belonging to the so-called Islamic Movement for Change. In 1996 four members of the group, guerrilla veterans of Afghanistan and Bosnia, were tried for the bombing and then beheaded. Although they have been retrospectively described as Al Qaeda members, their only "connection to bin Laden," according to journalist Jason Burke, "comprised reading his writings after being faxed them from London."[23]

Saudi Arabia, according to US Ambassador Raymond Mabus, had always been considered by the State Department to be "one of the safest places in the world," but after the Riyadh attack, some began to wonder if it really wasn't a volcano of ethnic and class inequality on the verge of eruption.[24] Security at American installations was dramatically upgraded following the November 1995 bombing, but it didn't prevent the Khobar Towers in Dhahran – an immense skyscraper dormitory housing the 3000 American Air Force personnel who enforced the no-fly zone over Iraq – from being shattered by a Godzilla truck bomb on June 25, 1996. The blast, which shook Bahrain 20 miles away, was caused by an estimated 4000 pounds of plastic explosive (equivalent to as much as 20,000 pounds of TNT); it left a huge meteor-like crater, 85 feet wide and 35 feet deep. The payload was so large that a suicide driver wasn't required: the heavily armed attackers simply left the explosive-laden fuel truck in the parking lot and fled in a pair of getaway cars. Although alert Air Force guards began an evacuation shortly before the explosion and thereby prevented a death toll that easily might have exceeded the slaughter at the Marine barracks in Beirut in 1983, 19 Americans and a Saudi guard were killed, and 372 people were wounded.

To intelligence experts everywhere, the Khobar Towers attack – like the 1983 Beirut bombings and the 1994 AMIA massacre in Buenos Aires – was classic Hezbollah in neon lights, and neither Al Qaeda nor Saddam Hussein were serious suspects. Evidence soon emerged that the fuel truck had been purchased in Lebanon, loaded with explosives, and smuggled into Saudi Arabia, where Hezbollah recruited support from the local Shiite minority, the alienated victims of notorious discrimination. The big question was not Hezbollah's role but Iran's involvement, yet neither Riyadh nor Washington seemed anxious to press the investigation to a logical conclusion. In Saudi Arabia's case, Iran was seen as a lesser enemy than resurgent Iraq, and there was little motive, apart from dead American airmen, for provoking a confrontation. (Prince Bandar bin Sultan, the Saudi ambassador in Washington, would later be accused by Clinton national security aides of deliberately misleading US investigators.)[25] Meanwhile, according to the *New York Times*'s James Risen, Clinton and his National Security Council deliberately downplayed Tehran's involvement (much to the disgust of FBI director Louis Freeh) in order to keep channels open to Iranian reformers and advocates of détente. The incoming Bush administration in 2001 finally indicted some Hezbollah members and unidentified Iranian officials, but as Risen points out, the Khobar investigation was soon overshadowed by Iran's tacit support for the American invasion of Afghanistan and a mutual interest in deposing the Taliban.[26]

By the mid-1990s – all memoirs and journalistic accounts agree – the Clinton administration was agonizingly divided over how to wage the "war on terrorism" it had inherited from the Reagan and Bush administrations. In contrast to the old, unitary menace of the Soviet Union and its allies, Washington now faced a chaotic spectrum of enemies, spontaneously generated by the contradictions of globalization as well as by the blowback of past policies: rogue assets like Sheik Rahman, megalomaniac bomb-school graduates like Yousef, hometown militiamen like McVeigh, self-organized Islamists like the Riyadh bombers, super-Capones like Escobar, and remnant Maoists like Sendero Luminoso – and then there was the enduring spectre of Hezbollah's Imad Mugniyah, the General Giap of urban guerrilla warfare. Calling them all "terrorists" – a playground epithet in the serious business of geopolitics – hardly advanced anyone's understanding of the post-Cold War world. What they had in common was access to vast reservoirs of anti-Americanism (incubated by cluster bombs, refugee camps, and oil corporations) and the brutal skills diffused by the CIA's and ISI's car-bomb academies (although correspondence courses were increasingly available via the Internet). They were also learning to publicize their grievances and celebrate their attacks through the World Wide Web, creating virtual networks of fellow-travelers and imitators.

Al Qaeda was merely one node – albeit very well funded and spectacularly gifted at self-publicity – within the Sunni branch of what is less an organized International in the old Marxist sense than a diffuse ecology of terror and resistance. The fundamental illusion of the Clinton administration, raised to blood-soaked farce by Bush and Rumsfeld, was the belief that such conspiracies could be decapitated by a few well-placed Tomahawk missiles or a clean shot by a Seal sniper. Such *coups de grâce* only exist in Tom Clancy novels. Even classical, hierarchical underground groups such as the Viet Cong, or for that matter, the OAS, were not easily beheaded; much less the collaborations that now arise in the ether of the Internet and depend only upon a few like-minded teenagers or angry immigrants with access to fertilizer and a stolen van.

This is not to say, however, that state patronage and friends in high places don't confer immense advantages: Al Qaeda (at least in its glory days, 1998–2002) was a black fruit carefully nurtured by Saudi wealth, but benefiting especially from the protection and intelligence offered by its friends in the Pakistani ISI. Whether, like Sheik Rahman of the "Day of Terror" plot, bin Laden was also once a valued asset of Bill Casey – or just a de facto ally in the anti-Soviet *jihad* in Afghanistan – remains the subject of considerable speculation. Simon Reeve, who interviewed various anonymous CIA veterans for his 1999 book *The New Jackals*, cites one high-level source who claims that "US emissaries met directly with bin Laden, and that it was bin Laden, acting on advice from his friends in Saudi intelligence, who first suggested the *mujahedin* should be given Stingers [the high-tech US missiles that proved so deadly against Soviet helicopters and jets]."[27]

What is indisputable is that bin Laden retained the support of the ISI long after he had become a public enemy of Washington. When Sudanese President Hasan al-Turabi, under tremendous pressure from the Americans, finally expelled bin Laden from Khartoum in 1996, the ISI arranged with its protégés, the Taliban, to provide the Al Qaeda leader not merely with sanctuary, but with a full-fledged military base. According to Lawrence Wright, "the Pakistani intelligence service had persuaded the Taliban to return the al-Qaeda camps in Host and elsewhere to bin Laden's control in order to train militants to fight in Kashmir. With ISI subsidizing the cost, the training camps had become an important source of revenue [for bin Laden]."[28] When, if ever, the ISI definitively cut its ties to Al Qaeda is a question, of course, that vexes every discussion of the regional role of Washington's reluctant ally, Pakistan's military dictatorship.

One of the characteristics, moreover, of all the groups nurtured by the ISI has been their extraordinary ruthlessness. During the later stages of the Afghan struggle when Kabul was being pounded into rubble by indiscriminate rocket attacks, the Pakistan-backed *mujahedin*, especially the fierce Pashtun brigades led by Gulbuddin Hekmatyar, were notorious for their indifference to horrific civilian casualties. This sublime disregard for collateral carnage also became one of the hallmarks of Al Qaeda's theology of violence. Like his forerunners Hermann Goering and Curtis LeMay, Osama bin Laden seems to exult in the sheer statistics of bomb damage – the competitive race to ever greater explosive yields and killing ranges, regardless of the dead children and scattered body parts. "The concept of innocence," observes Lawrence Wright in his history of the "road to 9/11," "was subtracted from al-Qaeda's calculations."[29] (By contrast, the 1980s Hezbollah, as even the Israelis admit, was exacting in its targeting and avoidance of unintended casualties: one rationale for its use of suicide drivers rather than remote-controlled detonations.)

Al Qaeda's truck-bombings of the US embassies in Nairobi and Dar-es-Salaam on August 7, 1998 were cases in point: the blasts killed relatively few Americans but inflicted horrendous casualties – hundreds dead and 5000 injured – on ordinary East Africans, some on their way to the mosque, hardly the lackeys of modern-day Crusaders. Despite a series of explicit warnings that car-bomb attacks were imminent, as well as bin Laden's histrionic announcement the previous February that he was declaring *jihad* against "Crusaders and Jews," the two embassies were sitting ducks. Located near two of the busiest streets in the city and without adequate setback or protective *glacis*, its perimeter protected by unarmed and poorly paid guards, the Nairobi embassy was especially vulnerable, as Ambassador Prudence Bushnell had repeatedly warned the State Department to no avail.[30]

Al Qaeda had spent several years carefully building local support cells, smuggling explosives and detonators into the two countries, and conducting regular survelliance of the embassies. In both cities, the attackers used medium trucks carrying a powerful mixture of TNT, ammonium nitrate, and aluminum power known as tritonal, notorious for its "exceptional thermal blast effect." The Dar-es-Salaam bomb was assembled by Khalfan Khamis Mohamed, a skilled graduate of advanced explosives training in Afghanistan. He used industrial grinders to concoct the tritonal and cleverly modified a Nissan refrigerator truck with concealed racks to hold oxygen cylinders that would amplify the explosion. Mohammed

Odeh, another Afghan alumnus, similarly customized a Toyota truck in Nairobi. Abdel Rahman, an Egyptian who was considered one of Al Qaeda's top technical experts, arrived to personally inspect the final wiring of the bomb and detonation device.[31]

In Nairobi, the two bombers in the Toyota truck arrived at the gated car park in the rear of the US embassy around 10:30 a.m. Confronted by security guards, one of the Al Qaeda commandos jumped out of the truck and threw a stun grenade at them; hearing the noise, office workers in the embassy and an adjacent business school rushed to look out of windows where they died a few moments later as the 1500 pounds of tritonal in the truck was detonated. According to one report, "Haile Selassie Avenue was a shambles. There were bits of concrete and twisted metal, broken glass and papers everywhere. Acrid smoke filled the air . . . Several buses lay burning with corpses hanging from the windows."[32] It was a massacre that left 224 dead, only 12 of them were Americans. Nearby emergency rooms were immediately overwhelmed by 1800 maimed and burned victims; thousands less seriously injured sought aid at home or at local clinics.[33]

In Dar-es-Salaam, nine minutes later, a fair-haired *kamikaze* known to his colleagues as "Ahmed the German," crashed his Nissan truck into parking lot of the US embassy. "The blast was so powerful that the body of the suicide-bomber driving the van was cut in two, and the top half of his torso hit the embassy building still clutching the steering wheel in both hands." According to later investigation, enough of the explosion's force was absorbed by a water truck parked in front of the embassy to prevent carnage on a Nairobi scale, but the toll – 12 dead, 100 injured, all Tanzanians – was still horrific.[34]

The attacks caught President Clinton with his pants off, in the midst of his public confession that he had enjoyed oral sex in the Oval Office with Monica Lewinsky. His retaliatory attack on Al Qaeda on August 20 was a spectacular fireworks display of the latest Pentagon technology: 75 Tomahawk cruise missiles blasted a training camp in Afghanistan, while another 13 demolished a chemical factory in Khartoum. But critics denounced "Operation

Infinite Reach" as a desperate attempt to deflect attention from the Lewinsky situation, and a Hollywood film, *Wag the Dog*, made delirious satire of the incident. Although several dozen jihadists were killed by the American missiles, Steve Coll argues that it only enhanced bin Laden's prestige in the Moslem world: "Without seeming to work very hard at it, bin Laden had crafted one of the era's most successful terrorist media strategies. The missile strikes were his biggest publicity payoff to date."[35]

Meanwhile, the international press was tearing apart Clinton's justification for blowing up the "terrorist" chemical plant in Khartoum, which, it turned out, was an innocuous facility that produced most of the drugs used in the Sudan to treat TB and malaria. Finally, to give "asymmetry" a monetary value, researchers at the University of Pittsburgh calculated that while Al Qaeda had spent about $50,000 to carry out the embassy attacks, the Clinton administration's cruise missiles and new overseas embassy security had cost US taxpayers almost $2 billion: "The United States [in other words] spent $38,420 for every dollar spent by al Qaeda."[36]

Bin Laden's stunning success in destroying the embassies and then side-stepping Washington's wrath may have emboldened him to endorse the scheme that Ramzi Yousef's uncle, Khalid Sheikh Mohammed, had been pitching to him for several years. Mohammed, whose nephew was now buried alive in a "super-max" federal prison in Colorado, wanted to hijack ten airliners and fly them into such major symbols of American power as the Capitol, the Pentagon, and especially the twin towers that Yousef had failed to topple. According to the investigation by the National 9/11 Commission (presumably based on the CIA's interrogation of Mohammed after his capture in 2002), bin Laden met with Mohammed in Kandahar in early 1999 and gave the go-ahead for the operation to proceed.[37]

The one unimpeachable victory over terrorism during the second Clinton administration owed nothing to the tens of billions spent annually by the CIA, NSA, and FBI on intelligence-gathering, but was instead the result of ordinary vigilance by a rank-and-file customs officer at her obscure post in Port Angeles, Washington. Suspicious at the nervousness displayed by the driver of a rented Chrysler disembarking from a Canadian ferry, she ordered him to pop the trunk and quickly discovered the ingredients – urea, nitroglycerin, timing circuitry – for a powerful car bomb. Ahmed Ressam, an Algerian immigrant to Montreal, later confessed that he was on his way to Southern California to blow up one of the terminals at LAX. The year before, he had attended an advanced bomb-making school near Jalalabad (Afghanistan), originally founded by the ISI-supported Hizb-e-Islami movement; during the six weeks he spent with jihadists from Algeria, Chechnya, Yemen, Palestinen and Saudi Arabia, they conceived a bold plan to celebrate the Christian calendar's new millennium. Ressam's Los Angeles explosion was intended to coincide with other New Year's detonations in Jordan (preempted by police raids) and Yemen (foiled when the speedboat sank).[38]

This so-called "Millennium plot," although a self-declared part of Al Qaeda's global *jihad* against "Crusaders and Jews," was very different from the East African bombings that had been directly organized by bin Laden's aides. In case of the Millennium conspiracy, as Jason Burke explains, there was no need for Mohammed to go to the mountain, since it eagerly came to him.

> . . . the Millennium attacks in Jordan and California reveal a different, and far more dangerous, pattern of operation . . . Those involved with the plot were acting on their own initiative. They were not even part of established and known local Islamic militant groups. Most importantly, they had initiated the contact with the "al-Qaeda hardcore," deciding to approach them for help with training, funding and, as their plans moved towards completion, to ask permission to claim the bombings in bin Laden's name. Indeed, it appears unlikely that any of the plotters in the American or Jordanian cells ever met bin Laden. They were not acting on the orders of bin Laden or his associates, they were merely using the facilities he was able to provide to execute the plans and projects they themselves had conceived.[39]

It is more helpful, perhaps, to think of spores, germinating wherever veterans of Afghanistan were available to pass on urban sabotage techniques, rather than "sleeper cells" implanted by a single, diabolical hand. In this emergent planetary *jihad*, the key "terrorist" infrastructure, to the extent that the Internet or the gun-show circuit didn't suffice, was not so much Al Qaeda (the phantom emirate hiding in caves), but rather the continuing collusion of wealthy Saudis and Pakistani intelligence with car bombers and hijackers. The ISI, in fact, comes closer than the now largely fragmented or defunct Al Qaeda network to the stereotype of a monstrous, centralized terrorist organization. And even in the late 1990s, according to Steve Coll, the ISI continued to nurture bin Laden, "contracting" him to train fighters for its state-sponsored *jihad* in Kashmir.[40] The ISI also provided some of the expertise that was soon blowing up Russian apartment buildings and subway stations.

20

Planet *Jihad*

A swift survey of popular newspapers in the Islamic world (and beyond) or of Friday sermons in the Middle East's mosques or a few hours spent in a bazaar or a souk or a coffee shop or kebab restaurant in Damascus, Kabul, Karachi, Cairo or Casablanca, or indeed in London or New York, shows clearly whose efforts are meeting with greater success. Bin Laden is winning.

Jason Burke[1]

Shamil Basayev died as he lived, by a massive truck-bomb explosion. The Chechen guerrilla leader – infamous as the planner of mass hostage-takings at a Moscow theater in 2002 (170 dead) and a school in Beslan in 2004 (340 dead) – was convoying a huge truck bomb for an attack in Ingushetia, the Russian republic on the western border of Chechnya, when the bomb prematurely detonated. Russian security forces claimed they had planted a remote-controlled detonator in the payload, while Basayev's followers said that the truck had simply hit a pothole.[2] In any event, Basayev had been one of the world's master car bombers (as well as kidnappers): under his orders, suicide squads had twice driven bomb-rigged trucks into Chechen government buildings (December 2002 and May 2003), killing 150 and injuring more than 200. Although Washington made much of Basayev's connections to shadowy Al Qaeda networks, his original sponsors were in power in Islamabad.

As Paul Murphy explains in *The Wolves of Islam*, the ISI had established clandestine relations with the Chechens from their earliest rebellion against Moscow in 1994. "It was through these channels that Basayev and 20 of his best men went to train in the Amir Muawia training camp in Afghanistan – the same camp that was struck by U.S. cruise missiles in August 1998 in an attempt to kill Osama bin Laden. After Muawia, Basayev's group would receive advanced training in the Markaz-i-Dawar camp in Pakistan. The ISI made all the arrangements." Basayev indeed was personally taken in hand by the Pakistani minister of intelligence and encouraged to join Tablighi Jamaat, an anti-modernist Islamist movement, heavily funded by Saudis and headed by Javed Nasir, the former director-general of the ISI. The secretive group has long functioned in Pakistani life much like Opus Dei did during the Latin American dictatorships of the 1970s: linking reactionary religious figures to top military and secret police leaders.[3] Basayev, in turn, recruited a group of Tablighis, led by the wealthy young Saudi, Amir Khattab, to return with him to Chechnya in late 1994. In crucial respects, the Chechen conflict became the continuation of the "ghost war" against the Soviet Union launched by Bill Casey, the Saudis, and the ISI in the early 1980s.

Chechen ferocity, already legendary, was raised to apocalyptic fury by Russian atrocities. After his wife and children were killed by Russian bombing in 1995, Basayev decided to take the war into Russia. His warriors invaded the town of Budennovsk and held 1600 residents hostage in a hospital; nearly 200 perished in a shootout between the Chechens and security forces. In the period of this First Chechen War, Basayev and the "international volunteers" commanded by Khattab made brilliant use of improvised mines (IEDs) to knock out Russian armor and destroy troop convoys in the style of the Afghan *mujahedin*. Vehicle bombs only came into their own in the second phase of conflict which followed Basayev's invasion of neighboring Dagestan in August 1999: a utopian or "mad" (as the Russian saw it) attempt to establish the pure Islamic Republic that had been frustrated by factional fights inside Chechnya. (Even after his conversion to Tablighi Jamaat, Basayev – like the famed Northern Alliance leader Ahmed Shah Massoud – remained a passionate fan of

Che Guevara and his romantic strategy of the revolutionary *foco*.) After ordinary bombing and strafing failed, the Russians used nightmarish fuel-oil (thermobaric) bombs to wipe out entire villages in the so-called "liberated" zone.[4]

Basayev, with the technical expertise of master bombmaker Achimez Gochiyayev (the Chechen counterpart to the Tamils' Yogaratnam, or the Provo's "Slab" Murphy), retaliated by blowing up residential towers in Moscow, killing almost 300 people, and sending car bombers to blast military housing in Buinaksk (64 dead) and an apartment bloc in Volgodonsk (18 killed).[5] Russian rockets and bombs, in turn, destroyed a street market and maternity hospital in Grozny, the Chechen capital, killing or wounding more than 500 people. In February the Russians wiped out the Chechen village of Katyr Yurt which was located "safely" behind their own lines. John Sweeney of the *Guardian* found the site "littered with the remains of Russian 'vacuum' bombs – fuel-air explosives that can suck your lungs inside out, their use against civilians banned by the Geneva Convention." Corpses, an estimated 363 of all ages and sexes, were "piled two or three high in the street."[6]

Basayev, himself maddened by inconsolable loss, now had plenty of "black widows" as the Russians called bereaved Chechen women, to bolster the suicide car bombers he sent after his enemies. In June 2000, two teenage girls, Khava Barayev and Luiza Magomadova, after recording a video that exhorted Chechen men to *jihad*, drove a truckload of explosives into the Russian post at Alkhan-Yurt, killing as many 25 police; four days later a man and woman blew their car up at another checkpoint, as did a deserter from the Russian Army, now a devout Moslem, the next day. Such bombings, many of them by women, continued on an almost daily basis through the summer, then into the fall, killing scores of Russian (and sometimes Chechen) soldiers, police and civilians. In contrast to the cool, carefully planned Hezbollah operations during the 1980s with their high body counts, the incessant Chechen *kamikaze* attacks were often poorly organized, resulting in only a few Russian casualties. Like his jihadist colleague Abu Musab al-Zarqawi in occupied Iraq a few years later, Basayev seemingly had inherited an embarrassment of riches in the form of bitter people impatient to throw themselves at their enemies.

This is not to say that the Chechens were incapable of delivering truly staggering blows. In addition to the horrific drama of the Dubrovka theater siege in October 2002, Basayev also orchestrated the destruction that December of the most heavily protected site in Chechnya, the government administrative complex in Grozny. Three guerrillas managed to maneuver a truck and jeep crammed with an estimated 4 tons of explosives "through a maze of checkpoints . . . then rammed through a fence when guards at the last stop tried to inspect the vehicles." More than 80 officials and government workers were killed, and the press was stunned when Basayev revealed that the suicide team was actually a family: father, 43; son, 17; and daughter, 15. (He claimed to have actually pushed the button himself that detonated the remote-controlled explosives.)[7] No one had ever imagined whole families of *kamikaze* car bombers.

For his part, Basayev told a reporter: "I swear to Allah, if the Russians or Americans will give us cruise missiles or intercontinental ballistic missiles, then we will not be using suicide attackers or trucks loaded with explosives."[8] His warriors (two men and a woman) replicated the Grozny attack in the village of Znamenskoye six months later. Bribing their way past Russian troops, they drove a potent truckload of ammonium nitrate, cement, and aluminum powder into the local government building, leaving little but death (60 residents) and a 16-foot-deep crater. Not long afterwards, on August 1, 2003, another huge truck blew up a military hospital in North Ossetia, killing at least 60 patients and nurses. In other attacks, "black widows" with suicide belts blew up a busload of Russian pilots and, separately, killed 16 people at an Islamic festival.[9]

Although Vladimir Putin's sledgehammer blows, including an indiscriminate air war and the routine execution of prisoners, shattered the main force of Chechen Islamist resistance, the shards reorganized as a loose network of cells scattered through the

Caucasian republics. Although not present at the scene, Basayev claimed responsibility for the school siege at Beslan in September 2004: the single most heinous act in the decade-long exchange of atrocities between Russians and Chechens. His death in 2006, whether the result of an accidental explosion or some surprising new level of competence amongst the Russian secret services, put an end to the "Tablighi" dynasty of Chechen leaders trained by the Pakistani ISI, but there is little hope that it ended an insurgency that now sees itself as an integral part of the same *jihad* being waged in Iraq and Afghanistan.

Table 4   Chechen Fury

(1) Major Car/Truck Bombings

Date	Location	Dead	Wounded
Sept. 1999	Buinaksk	64	174
	Volgodonsk	18	288
June 2000	Vladikavkaz	9	—
July 2000	Argun	25	81
Dec. 2000	Pyatigorsk	7	44
	Alkhan-Yurt	25	—
May 2002	Kaspiisk	45	100+
Dec. 2002	Grozny	83	150
May 2003	Znamenskoye	60	200
May 2006	Nazran	7	—

(2) Other Public Attacks

June 1995	Budennovsk (hospital)	203	457
Jan. 1996	Kizlyar (hospital)	78	—
Aug. 1999	Moscow (mall)	—	20
Sept. 1999	3 cities (apartments)	300	—
Mar. 2001	Stavropol	21	150
May 2001	Kaspiisk (parade)	45	90
Nov. 2002	Moscow (theater)	170	—
July 2003	Moscow (concert)	15	60
Aug. 2003	Mozdok (hospital)	50+	—
Dec. 2003	Stavropol (train)	36	150+
Feb. 2004	Moscow (train)	41	70
May 2004	Grozny (stadium)	7	50+
Aug. 2004	2 passenger trains	89	—
	Moscow (station)	10	51
	Beslan (school)	340+	—

While this Second Chechen War (from 1999) was spiraling into unimaginable horror, another ISI subsidiary was bringing the world closer to nuclear confrontation than at any time since the Cuban Missile Crisis in 1962. Just before noon on December 13, 2001, five Moslem commandos were killed in a shootout with security guards as they attempted to detonate a huge ammonium–nitrate car bomb in the portico of the Parliament House in New Delhi. Rightwing Indian Prime Minister Atal Vajpayee, convinced by his intelligence experts that the attackers were Kashmiri jihadists acting on behalf of the ISI, ordered his military to mobilize for war (Operation "Parakram"). Through the tense spring of 2002, Delhi and Islamabad were eyeball-to-eyeball with huge Indian armored forces poised to roll into the Punjab while the Pakistanis warned that any invasion would bring nuclear retaliation against Indian cities.[10]

As Steve Coll learned from frank conversations with generals on both sides, it was truly a hair-trigger situation. "Western deterrence theory," one of the fathers of the Pakistani bomb told him, "had never encountered the wild cards of the *jihadis* and the Hindu fundamentalists." Moreover, authorities on both sides worried that the tail might wag the dog: a terrorist group with state ties might deliberately incite nuclear Armageddon on its own account through car-bomb attacks or other mass atrocities.[11] (The July 2006 bombings of commuter trains in Bombay which killed 186 people were a further instigation, with Indian police charging that the ISI had planned the attacks.)

In the meantime, while Pakistan and India were dancing on the brink, the twin towers had fallen in Manhattan and Washington was launching its invasion of Afghanistan. From his cave in Tora Bora, bin Laden redoubled the call for *jihad* against "Crusaders and Jews." Like-minded groups across the world answered his appeal with more than a dozen major attacks between 2002 and 2006, most of them involving car or truck bombs. In contrast to the East African bombings and the 9/11 cataclysm, however, most of these attacks on Western tourists, European commuters, and Jewish institutions did not involve the direct participation of cadre from bin Laden's inner circle (most of whom, anyway, were now either dead or in deep hiding). With the possible exception of some of the incidents in Pakistan, these bombings were Al Qaedist by emulation: they were paradigms of the kind of "network war," conducted by enemies of a "protoplasmic nature and loosely franchised structure," which Cold War-era intelligence and military establishments were conceptually ill-equipped to fight.[12]

Table 5   *Jihad* Against "Crusaders and Jews"

(1) Al Qaeda-related Car-Bombings (outside Iraq)

Date	Target	Dead
Apr. 2002	Djerba (Tunisia)	21
May 2002	Karachi	14
June 2002	Karachi	12
Oct. 2002	Bali	202
Nov. 2002	Mombasa (Kenya)	13
May 2003	Riyadh	34
May 2003	Casablanca	31
June 2003	Kabul	4
Nov. 2003	Riyadh	17
Nov. 2003	Istanbul (x2)	56
Dec. 2003	Pakistan	14
Oct. 2004	Sinai	34
July 2005	Sharm el-Sheik	64

(2) Attacks by Other Means

Sept. 2001	USA (planes)	3000
Nov. 2004	Madrid (trains)	191
July 2005	London (trains & buses)	50

Although anarchist violence in the 1890s and early 1900s had also traveled by imitation across the world, the classical "propagandists of the deed" were usually restrained by their scruples or their primitive explosives from achieving the kind of large-scale terrorization of the bourgeoisie that their tracts so often advertised. In contrast, at the beginning of the twenty-first century, Al Qaedist "replicants" possessed potent weapons to attack the feast of soft targets represented by the international tourist industry: globalization's weakest link. Blowing up tourists may have been publically justified by the desire to match Israeli or American massacres with

Islamist massacres, body for body, but an even more compelling motive was the economic and political damage that such attacks inflicted on "apostate" regimes addicted to the earnings from hotels, casinos, and beaches. As Egypt, Kenya, and Indonesia have discovered at different times, a single bombing can instantly plunge a tourism-dependent country into socio-economic turmoil.

Local jihadist groups, moreover, tend to follow the path of least resistance. Since 9/11, the extra security around major hard targets – such as financial centers and capitals – has deflected them to softer, less well-protected targets. For example, Jemaah Islamiyah (JI), the Indonesian jihadist group that also has affiliates in Malaysia and the Philippines, originally planned a monster truck-bombing of the Israeli, American, and British embassies in Singapore in December 2001 using a fleet of six or seven vehicles, each loaded with 3 tons of ammonium nitrate; such massive explosions – equivalent to a half dozen Oklahoma City or Beirut barracks blasts going off simultaneously – would undoubtedly have killed hundreds, if not thousands of ordinary Singaporeans in adjacent streets and buildings. But Singaporean police, thanks to fortuitous evidence turned up during a raid in Kabul, arrested many of the plotters in December, forcing the survivors to fall back on an alternate plan to truck-bomb the US and Israeli embassies in Manila.[13]

When Philippine police, in turn, made new arrests and confiscated most of the group's explosives, the JI leader Hambali, an "Afghan" trained in sabotage at ISI schools, decided on a radical switch of targets. At a secret meeting of JI and Al Qaedist allies in Bangkok, Hambali (according to later FBI interrogation of one of his comrades) urged a shift from embassies to easy targets like "bars, cafes or nightclubs frequented by westerners in Thailand, Singapore, the Philippines and Indonesia."[14]

Bali, the Hindu isle that was the favorite playground of Australians and other young Western tourists in mainly Moslem Indonesia, was an obvious choice. Imam Samudra, the JI cadre who masterminded the details, focused on the popular Legian Road strip in the town of Kuta, where hundreds of young foreigners frolicked every evening at Paddy's Bar and the trendy Sari Club.

(Locals were reportedly barred from the Club except in the company of Westerners.) On October 12, 2002, the JI team blocked the one-way street outside the bars with a Mitsubishi minivan containing a payload of slightly more than 1 ton of potassium chlorate, sulphur, and powered aluminum, souped up with TNT and RDX, attached to multiple detonation devices. ("Don't ever say that Indonesians can't make sophisticated bombs," one of the JI attackers later boasted at his trial.) Inside Paddy's Bar, a *jihadi* detonated his suicide vest; hysterical customers, some already wounded or ablaze, fled into the street, straight into the explosion of the minivan.[15]

The huge fireball left Legian Road a charcoal alley of incinerated cars and screaming, grotesquely injured people. A hysterical English tourist told a reporter, "Like you look at their face and you can't make anything out; there's nothing left. People were missing ears, people were missing limbs, their skin was peeling off."[16] The 202 dead included 89 Australians and 38 Balinese plus victims from at least 20 other countries. Tourism, Indonesia's only growth industry, virtually collapsed: economists later calculated that the deadly minivan had immediately cost the country 10 percent of the value of the Jakarta stock market and at least 1 percent of its GDP.[17]

Although the Indonesian authorities eventually arrested scores of Jemaah Islamiyah activists – including its alleged "emir," Abu Bakar Bashir – suspicions remained, especially in the Australian press, that the group had received help from the Indonesian military. Since the massacre of several hundred thousand "Communists" during the 1965 coup, the military had routinely depended upon Islamic gangs to do the dirty work of political and sectarian murder. More recently, the Indonesian Army's figurative fingerprints – or rather, those of two members of Kopassus, its elite special forces – were found on the car bomb that rocked the Jakarta Stock Exchange (15 dead) in September 2000. President Abdurrahman Wahid himself hinted that this bombing and several others were part of a campaign of destabilization waged by a military determined to preserve its unaccountable power and immunity from prosecution for past crimes.[18] With such precedents, it was not beyond reason to believe that the Indonesian military intelligence, like its counterpart in Pakistan, still maintained contact (or more) with Jemaah Islamiyah and other Al Qaeda-oriented groups.[19]

Whatever the case, the mass arrests of JI members failed to end the car-bomb *jihad* against Western tourists. In August 2003, Jemaah Islamiyah claimed credit for the *kamikaze* who blew up an SUV in front of the Sailandra Restaurant in Jakarta's Marriott Hotel, a favorite dining spot for tourists and expatriates as well as a regular venue for US Embassy banquets. The bomber's Toyota reportedly struggled under such a heavy load of explosives (potassium chloride, black powder, and TNT) that it was barely able to climb the inclined driveway. "Police said that after his vehicle exploded, the head of the [Jemaah Islamiyah] recruit, Asmar Latin Sani, landed on the fifth floor of the hotel." A dozen people were killed and 152 wounded, but the two former US ambassadors staying at the hotel escaped injury.[20] Several of the Bali bombing defendants heard news of the Marriott bombing just before they were sentenced to death: "Amrozi [bin Nurhasyim] reacted with joy . . . He grinned and yelled out. 'Bomb!' The alleged mastermind of the Bali blasts, Imam Samudra, shouted, 'I am happy, especially if the perpetrators were Muslims.'"[21]

Over the next two years, Jemaah Islamiyah kept its martyrs happy with further explosions, including the September 2004 car-bombing of the Australian embassy in Jakarta (9 dead, 140 wounded), and another suicide attack on Bali resorts (19 dead). An Islamist car bomb, perhaps carried out with JI assistance, also made its first appearance in Thailand in 2005: killing five in a sex-tourism hotel in the far south. Meanwhile, other car-bombings were rocking embassies, frightening away tourists, and depressing economies across much of the Moslem world, from Karachi to Casablanca. They also were adding a new dimension of horror to attacks on Israeli civilians.

Pakistan's metropolis, not surprisingly, was a strategic magnet for wrathful holy warriors from all over the region. Karachi hosted a variety of Kashmiri revanchists and Islamist grouplets, and everyone, not just Al Qaeda, wanted a piece of the Americans bunkered down in their huge consulate. Amongst the first to die in a post-9/11 car-bombing, however, were a dozen French naval engineers whose bus was rammed by a *kamikaze* in a beat-up Toyota Corolla just outside the Karachi Sheraton hotel in May 2002. (The bomber narrowly missed killing the New Zealand and Pakistani national cricket squads boarding buses across the road.)[22] A month later – despite a government roundup of some 2000 suspected militants – another Corolla blew up in front of the walled and heavily guarded US consulate, killing a dozen police and pedestrians. An American reporter who visited the scene shortly afterwards was disconcerted by the flocks of hungry crows hovering over a rubble composed of car parts, shredded clothing, and dismembered bodies.[23]

Almost exactly a year later, a busload of Chinese engineers on their way to work in the Karachi port district was car-bombed. Three weeks after this attack, two car bombs in succession damaged the home of the US consul-general, killing 2 and wounding almost 40 others. In the fall of 2005, jihadists attacked the Crusader leader Colonel Sanders: 3 security guards died and 20 customers, including several tourists, were injured when a remote-controlled car bomb detonated in front of a Kentucky Fried Chicken outlet. Then, on the eve of a visit by President Bush in March 2006, a suicide car bomber struck at the Karachi Marriott, killing David Foy, a senior American diplomat, and three others. Although all of these attacks were blamed on "Al Qaeda," and indeed cadre acting under the direct instructions of bin Laden may have been involved, the sheer number of jihadist groups in the city, including well-armed cells of the ISI-subsidized Kashmiri liberation groups, makes authorship almost a moot question.[24]

While the American consulate in Karachi was under siege, Israelis and overseas Jewish institutions were facing the most lethal car-bomb attacks since the destruction of the AMIA in Buenos Aires in 1994. In April 2002 more than a dozen German tourists were killed and 100 people wounded in a suicide car-bombing of Africa's oldest synagogue in Djerba, Tunisia.[25] In June and again in October,

Islamic Jihad unveiled a deadly new tactic: using *kamikaze* cars to blow up buses along Route 65 in northern Israel. The first attack burned to death 16 passengers, and the second killed 14. "Survivors," wrote the *New York Times* of the October bombing, "described leaping through shattered windows as the fire spread . . . Debris and body parts were blasted over an area larger than a football field; the engine and transmission of the vehicle carrying the explosives lay some 50 yards from the bus, by a left leg severed below the knee."[26]

Israelis were also being attacked on vacation: in late November 2002 a suicide bomber devastated a popular Israeli retreat, the Paradise Hotel on the beach in Mombasa, Kenya. "The car bomb that rammed the gate and exploded at the steps of the lobby obliterated windows, burned shrubbery and hurled trees hundreds of feet. In some spots, the blast tore the hotel roof completely off its moorings, and burned hot enough to melt steel." Three Israelis and ten Kenyans were killed. Almost simultaneously, shoulder-fired anti-aircraft missiles narrowly missed an Israeli charter jet carrying 261 passengers as it was taking off from the Mombasa airport. Most experts attributed the meticulously planned attacks (designed to kill hundreds) to an Al Qaeda affiliate or clone rather than a Palestinian group.[27]

This eclectic war against Jews, foreign tourists, and Crusader governments continued in 2003 with a bloody attack in May upon a foreign residential compound in Riyadh (26 dead), followed a few days later by suicide satchel-bomb attacks on tourist cafés and hotels in Casablanca (45 dead), and then in November by a deadly sequence of car-bombings in Istanbul. The Istanbul attackers were apparently affiliated with a group known as "Turkish Hezbollah" (unrelated to the Lebanese movement) and several had received training in Pakistan and Afghanistan. In mid-November they used suicide truck bombs to destroy two synagogues crowded with families celebrating bar mitzvahs, killing 25 and injuring more than 300. Five days later, while President Bush was meeting with Tony Blair in London, a pair of *kamikaze* trucks in Istanbul were unleashed against the British consulate and the 18-story headquarters of the UK-based HSBC bank. The resulting explosions sheared off the façade of the bank tower and collapsed the consulate into a brick pile. The nearly 500 casualties (27 dead) included the British consul-general and his assistant, whose bodies were excavated from the ruins of their office.[28]

In contrast to the attacks mounted by Al Qaeda *sensu stricto,* with its corps of middle-class Saudis, these bombings were largely the work of an Islamist underclass. The Casablanca attackers (members of Salafia Jihadia), for example, came from the forgotten slum of Sidi Moumen, while the Istanbul *kamikazes* were from the dire, impoverished Kurdish city of Bingol (with its 80 percent male unemployment) in eastern Turkey.[29] A similar sociology of marginalization seems to have underlaid the anger of the largely Bedouin group that car-bombed the Sinai tourist resorts of Taba in 2004 (34 dead) and Sharm el-Sheikh in 2005 (83 dead).

Excluded from the beach-and-gambling boom on the Red Sea which followed the Camp David accords, or employed only in the most menial, erratic and ill-paid jobs, the Sinai Bedouin bristled at Israeli tourists, foreign workers, and police roadblocks. "Bit by bit," explained a tribal leader, "more people are becoming religious extremists." The massive arrests (more than 3000) in the southern Sinai that followed the Taba bombing, together with the rampant use of torture, only recruited more support for the homegrown group known as Tawhid and Jihad (the same name as the original al-Zarqawi group in Iraq). As a result, "local young men scoured the desert for explosives left from previous wars, and fashioned crude but deadly bombs in small workshops." The resulting car-bomb attack on Sharm el-Sheikh was especially shocking to Egyptians as they recognized that they themselves – and not just Israeli and foreign tourists – were the intended targets.[30]

As a Bedouin taxi driver told *Al-Ahram*'s Serene Assir, "Rest assured whoever staged these attacks knew exactly what they were doing. They targeted three strategic areas, seeking to cause as much destruction, death and panic as possible." "Indeed," continues Assir: "the targets were people, not institutions."

The attackers did not pick out the wealthiest, most luxurious hotel. Rather they picked the one linking Peace Road with Naema Bay – one of the busiest spots in the city. Secondly, the attack in the bay itself came on a parking lot – not on a hotel or a similar institution. The only targets there are drivers – and therefore locals – and passengers, both local and foreign . . . Thirdly, and perhaps most significantly, the attack on the Sharm market area – inhabited mostly by Egyptian workers who serve the airport, hotels, shops and tourism services – was the worst hit, and the explosion here was heard throughout an entire one-kilometer radius. In other words, the target was the very core of Sharm, and not just what it stands for within the context of a globalized economy.[31]

21

The King of Iraq

The life of the Iraqi citizen is going to dramatically improve.

President Bush, March 10, 2003[1]

The indiscriminate horror of Sharm el-Sheikh, of course, was just another day's work in occupied Iraq. Indeed vehicle bombs now terrorize Iraq like no other country in history. In a June 2005 paper titled "Why the Car Bomb Is King in Iraq," military analyst James Dunnigan warned that the car bomb was supplanting roadside bombs (which "are more frequently discovered, or defeated with electronic devices") as the "most effective weapon" of Sunni insurgents as well as of Al Qaeda-linked sectarian terrorists, and thus "[they] are building as many as they can." The recent "explosive growth" in car ownership in Iraq, he added, had made it "easier for the car bombs to just get lost in traffic." At the time of writing, he estimated that some 500 car bombs had killed or wounded more than 9000 people, with 143 car-bomb attacks in May 2005 alone.[2]

Using the database of the respected 'Iraq Body Count Project' which monitors civilian deaths, I offer a more conservative calculation (Table 6) of the number of lethal car-bomb attacks since July 2003.[3] Adding bombs that resulted in civilian injuries only, as well as duds and bombs intercepted by police, however, would almost certainly raise the total number of attempted car-bombings to around 1000. Since the full-scale outbreak of resistance to the Occupation in August 2003, deadly car-bombings have increased from approximately one every 10 days to one every 36 hours. Suicide attacks increased dramatically in 2005, but have fallen off sharply in the first half of 2006 despite the descent into sectarian civil war; whether this is due to a change in tactics, the depletion of martyrs, or some other factor, is unclear. (One explanation is that foreign martyrs have been diverted to Afghanistan where the number of suicide car-bombings has soared since early 2006.)

Table 6   Deadly Car Bombs in Iraq

Semester	Non-Suicide	Suicide	Total
June–Oct. 2003	12	7	19
Jan.–June. 2004	22	14	36
July–Dec. 2004	40	46	86
Jan.–June. 2005	63	100	163
July–Dec. 2005	49	88	137
Jan.–June. 2006	115	22	137
Total	301	277	578

The car bomb, however, is a foreign monarch. Until the fall of 2003, Iraqis had only infrequent acquaintance with the weapon that had so shattered Beirut and Damascus in the early 1980s. As we have seen, Saddam, who was held responsible by Syria's President Assad for some quotient of the terrorism unleashed by the Moslem Brotherhood, was punished with the car-bombing of the Iraqi embassy in Beirut in 1982. Likewise, in the course of their terrible war, Iran sponsored the underground Shiite movement, Al Dawa, which detonated a few car bombs in Baghdad, while the Baathists reciprocated by helping the Peoples' Mujahedin blow up several hundred citizens of Tehran (one car-bomb near Khomeini's house narrowly missed the ayatollah).[4] After the invasion of Kuwait in 1990, the Iraqi occupiers were reportedly the victims of at least one major suicide car-bombing by resistance forces aided by Al Dawa members previously imprisoned for attacking the American embassy in 1983.[5] Whether or not Saddam then organized the supposed plot against ex-President

Bush in Kuwait City in 1993, he was certainly a chief suspect (along with the rival Kurdish Democratic Party) in the February 1995 car-bombing of a market street in Zakho, a city in the American-protected "exclusion zone" governed by the Patriotic Union of Kurdistan. The huge explosion killed as many as 60 people and injured almost 100 more.[6]

But the real authors of the car bomb as a barbarous tool of Iraqi domestic politics, long before Abu Musab al-Zarqawi cast his dark shadow over Baghdad, were the CIA and its favorite son, Dr Iyad Allawi, head of the Iraqi National Accord. As the *New York Times* revealed in June 2004, the CIA apparently reprised the same tactics it had used against the Russians in Kabul:

> Iyad Allawi, now the designated prime minister of Iraq, ran an exile organization intent on deposing Saddam Hussein that sent agents into Baghdad in the early 1990s to plant bombs and sabotage government facilities under the direction of the CIA, several former intelligence officials say. Dr. Allawi's group, the Iraqi National Accord, used car bombs and other explosive devices smuggled into Baghdad from northern Iraq . . . One former Central Intelligence Agency officer who was based in the region, Robert Baer, recalled that a bombing during that period "blew up a school bus; schoolchildren were killed."[7]

According to one of the *Times*'s informants, the bombing campaign – dead schoolkids and all – "was a test more than anything else, to demonstrate capability"; it allowed the CIA to portray Allawi and his suspect group of ex-Baathists as a serious opposition to Saddam and an alternative to the coterie (so favored by Washington neo-conservatives) around Ahmed Chalabi. "No one had any problem with sabotage in Baghdad back then," another CIA veteran reflected. "I don't think anyone could have known how things would turn out today."[8]

Indeed, the hurricane of resistance in Iraq since August 2003 has exposed how little the Pentagon, despite Rumsfeld's obsession with military novelty, understands – or, conversely, how much it has

forgotten – about classical guerrilla warfare (even when practiced by
the CIA). The landmines and hidden bombs (or IEDs in contemporary parlance) that have turned so many hundreds of Humvees and Bradley Fighting Vehicles into flaming coffins were, after
all, ancient mainstays of Colonel Grivas's campaign against British
armored cars in Cyprus in the 1950s. They also paved Vietnam's
"street without joy" (to use Bernard Fall's piquant phrase) with
burnt-out trucks and half-tracks, and they littered the back roads of
Afghanistan with the hulks of devastated Soviet convoys. The
American failure, moreover, to confiscate or destroy the vast
stockpiles of regular munitions left behind in Iraq has been a
cornucopia to local insurgents, who, unlike their peers elsewhere,
don't have to steal dynamite from quarries or bootleg bombs from
bags of fertilizer.

Figure 8   Baghdad. A suicide bomb killed 30 people at the
entrance to the CPA (Coalition Provisional Authority)
Green Zone, January 2004.

More profoundly, the American occupation, despite the bitter lessons of Beirut, radically underestimated the menace of the car bomb and the hundreds of unspeakable massacres it has wrought between the Tigris and Euphrates in less than four years. It is the one weapon of mass destruction that the Bush administration totally ignored, despite the fact that before American tanks had even entered Baghdad, a suicide car bomber had already killed four US soldiers in Najaf.[9] Indeed, the very factors that made the invasion of Iraq such a pushover for American airpower and heavy armor – that is to say, a largely desert geography of heavily urbanized oases and petrochemical complexes joined together by a modern highway system – also make it a paradise for car bombers. Despite the 50,000 American and Iraqi troops concentrated in Baghdad by the end of summer 2006, the city was rocked by several *kamikaze* or remote-detonated car-bomb explosions almost every day.

By the most conservative estimates, 50,000 Iraqi civilians have died violently since the White House boasted "Mission accomplished!" in May 2003 (at least 6600 civilians were killed during the US invasion).[10] In the face of so many daily explosions, murders, and armed skirmishes, it is difficult to make much sense out of the mere chronology of violence. Yet, taking a step back and focusing just on the largest bombings (deaths in the dozens or more – see Table 7), a strategic pattern – at least in the utilization of car bombs – becomes evident.

In the first phase (August 2003 through February 2004) car bombs targeting the United Nations missions, the embassies of Moslem powers, and troop contingents from allied countries countered American attempts to give the occupation a broader legitimacy than the invasion. In the second phase (especially in 2004–05) after the Americans had retreated into their fortified "Green Zone," car bombers focused on police recruiting stations and military training camps, obviously seeking to prevent the interim government from acquiring any means of self-defense. In the third phase (reaching a crescendo in winter 2005–06), car-bombings were used to incite civil war between Sunnis and Shiites, with the repeated attacks on Shia shrines as well as crowds

Table 7   The Logic of Carnage

PHASE 1: PREEMPTIVE STRIKES

		Dead
Aug. 2003	Jordanian embassy	17
	UN hdq.	22
	Najaf	95–125
Sept. 2003	Baghdad ceremony	42
Oct. 2003	Iraq Gov. Council	6
	Turkish embassy	0
Nov. 2003	Italian compound	13
Jan. 2004	Coalition hdq.	31
Feb. 2004	Kurd hdq. (Arbil)	117

PHASE 2: KILLING THE POLICE
(40+ dead)

Feb. 2004	Baghdad	47
	Iskandariyah	55
Apr. 2004	Basra	74
*June 2004	Mosul	62
July 2004	Baqouba	70
Sept. 2004	Baghdad	47
*July 2005	Rabia	48
	Baghdad	48
*Dec. 2005	Baghdad	40
*Jan. 2006	Ramadi	60

PHASE 3: FOMENTING CIVIL WAR
(Attacks on Shiites: 40+ dead)

*Mar. 2004	Karbala	60
June 2004	Mosul etc.	100
Feb. 2005	Hilla	136
July 2005	Musayyib	98
Sept. 2005	Baghdad	114
Nov. 2005	Baghdad, etc.	80
Jan. 2006	Karbala	60
Mar. 2006	Baghdad	58
*Apr. 2006	Baghdad	90
July 2006	Kufa	53
Aug. 2006	Baghdad	64
Nov. 2006	Baghdad	200+

* non-vehicular bombs

congregated in markets and mosques. (They were also deployed more frequently against the occupiers, especially with the adoption of the tactic of sending suicide bombers to cruise the streets in search of targets of opportunity.) The fourth phase, following the destruction of the Golden Mosque in Samarra in February 2006, has been low-intensity civil war, with a dramatic upsurge in Shiite shootings (although seldom car-bombings) of ordinary Sunnis.

"The real war in Iraq – the one to determine the future of the country," claims the *Washington Post*'s Thomas Ricks, "began on Aug. 7, 2003, when a car bomb exploded outside the Jordanian Embassy, killing 11 and wounding more than 50."[11] According to eyewitnesses, "the blackened dead lay about at odd points on the embassy grounds, while burned and bleeding survivors crawled from the wreckage on their hands and knees."[12] Presumably the bombing was a warning to Jordan, which during the invasion had allowed several thousand US Special Operations troops to use the kingdom as a base for attacking Iraq. Most Western analysts have attributed the operation to the Jordanian *jihadi*, Abu Musab al-Zarqawi, who operating in the name of Al Qaeda but without "the managerial oversight of bin Laden," rallied Sunni and foreign fighters against the Occupation.[13] (Journalist Mary Anne Weaver has claimed, however, that al-Zarqawi's ultimate goal always remained the overthrow of the Jordanian monarchy and that he plotted unsuccessfully in 2004 to attack Amman with a mega-truck bomb "packed with enough chemicals and explosives to kill some 80,000 people.")[14]

Twelve days later in a carefully planned attack (again allegedly masterminded by al-Zarqawi), a *kamikaze* drove a "gleaming new" cement truck, packed with between 1000 and 1500 pounds of military munitions, into the side of the former Canal Hotel, now the headquarters of the United Nations special envoy, Sergio Vieira de Mello. Although the UN staff had received warning of an imminent car-bombing, they had failed to block off the streets in front of the building.[15] The giant explosion ironically coincided with a news conference to discuss UN plans for defusing the myriad of landmines strewn across Iraq. De Mello, his legs crushed but still conscious and able to talk, was trapped under the rubble and slowly bled to death before rescuers could excavate him from the debris. Twenty others were also killed, including UN experts working on food relief, restoration of the electric grid, and housing for displaced people. As a result of this cataclysm (and a subsequent car-bombing a month later), the UN abandoned Baghdad and cut back most of its programs: this was a decisive blow to American efforts to legitimize their occupation with a blue veneer.[16]

Ten days later (August 29), the Americans lost their key Shiite ally, Ayatollah Mohammed Baqir al-Hakim, in an even larger car-bomb holocaust in holy city of Najaf. The suicide driver was none other than al-Zarqawi's father-in-law, Yassin Jarrad. "The bomb was detonated," explains journalist Anthony Shadid, "soon after the end of the Friday prayers that Hakim led; it was a moment when the narrow streets and ocher markets of the holy city were teaming with pilgrims, worshippers, and shoppers." The blast killed at least 90 people (some accounts say 125), and "the body of Hakim was never found, save perhaps for a few shreds of flesh that a cleric brought in a bag to Najaf's hospital." As Shadid emphasizes, Hakim was "seen as crucial in U.S. attempts to court religious Shiites. Without him U.S. officials lost perhaps their most important link with the community at a time that they acknowledged as delicate. [Muqtada] Sadr was implacably opposed to the occupation, in any incarnation, and [Grand Ayatollah Ali] Sistani, as he would continue to do, was refusing to meet U.S. officials."[17]

In the *New York Times*, reporter Dexter Filkins sourly observed the "political vacuum" and "confusion" among US and Iraqi officials in the aftermath of Hakim's assassination: "There were no speeches calling for calm and few public appearances by anyone in charge. L. Paul Bremer III, the chief American administrator, was on vacation. Nobody seemed to know when exactly he would return. The American military command here said nothing." American military authorities and journalists – yet unaware of al-Zarqawi's superintending role – did debate whether the bombers were Baathist guerrillas, foreign *jihadis*, Al Qaeda or some combination of all three, but this only highlighted the official cluelessness that reigned in both Baghdad and Washington.[18]

In the meantime, the resistance continued to strike shrewd, highly effective blows against the Occupation's pretense that it could guarantee law and order. The Najaf cataclysm was followed in the fall by car-bombings of the Turkish embassy, the International Red Cross, the UN carpark, the Italian Carabinieri training center in Nassiriyah, a hotel occupied by members of the Iraqi Governing Council, and the Kurdish headquarters in Arbil, as well as a rocket attack that almost nailed one of the invasion's primary architects, visiting Deputy Defense Secretary Paul Wolfowitz.

For American "liberators," Baghdad was suddenly as insecure as Saigon in 1965, or maybe more to the point, as dangerous as Kabul in 1985. One of the godfathers of the CIA's *jihad* in Afghanistan, the legendary Milt Bearden, made the analogy official in an op-ed piece in November, entitled "Iraqi Insurgents Take a Page from the Afghan 'Freedom Fighters.'" He provided a sobering balance-sheet of what the car bombers had accomplished since August, and sounded a remarkable warning about the likely outcome of the struggle.

> Since the focused attacks began, most Arab League missions in Baghdad have distanced themselves from the coalition; the United Nations secretary general, Kofi Annan, has withdrawn his international staff from Baghdad; the Red Cross followed suit, prompting other international aid organizations to pare down in Baghdad as well. The Turkish government, for a number of complex political reasons, has now reconsidered sending troops. Even Spain, part of the original coalition, has decided to withdraw the bulk of its diplomatic staff from Baghdad. It appears that after disrupting the American strategy, the insurgents have made progress in undermining its alliances.
>
> . . .
>
> The Soviet Union tried to denigrate the Afghan mujahadeen by calling them bandits. This did not help the Russian cause. Americans are confronting a foe that is playing down and dirty – but remarkably effectively – on his own turf. Yes, there are criminals and foreign terrorists among them, but the Pentagon

seems to understand little about the identity of its enemy beyond that.

. . .

There were two stark lessons in the history of the 20th century: no nation that launched a war against another sovereign nation ever won. And every nationalist-based insurgency against a foreign occupation ultimately succeeded.[19]

By the end of the autumn, even the Americans were evacuating most of Baghdad, if only to barricade themselves in considerable luxury within Saddam's old forbidden city, now known as the "Green Zone." Indeed, the stark division of Baghdad into "green" and "red" zones, with the Americans unable to live in or even enter many parts of the city except in heavily armed patrols or convoys, was the real strategic victory that the insurgents won in this first phase of urban guerrilla warfare. By withdrawing into the Green Zone – a medievalized enclave surrounded by concrete walls and defended by M1 Abrams tanks and helicopter gunships as well as an exotic corps of corporate mercenaries – the Americans were conceding the de facto hopelessness of the security situation. They were also demonstrating the cultural arrogance that has diseased every aspect of the Occupation. Once the Xanadu of the Baathist ruling class, the 10-square-kilometer Green Zone, with its palaces, tennis courts, and underground bunkers, quickly became, like Long Binh in 1967, a surreal theme park of the suburban American way of life.

As *Newsweek* described the bizarre ambience:

Women in shorts and T-shirts jog down broad avenues and the Pizza Inn does a brisk business from the parking lot of the heavily fortified U.S. Embassy. Near the Green Zone Bazaar, Iraqi kids hawk pornographic DVDs to soldiers. Sheik Fuad Rashid, the U.S.-appointed imam of the local mosque, dresses like a nun, dyes his hair platinum blond and claims that Mary Mother of Jesus appeared to him in a vision (hence the getup). On any given night, residents can listen to karaoke, play badminton or frequent one of several rowdy bars, including an invitation-only speakeasy run by the CIA.[20]

Not surprisingly, wealthy Iraqis and employees of the new government have clamored for admission into the security of the Green Zone, but US officials have rebuffed such requests with the blunt declaration that only high Iraqi officials were welcome and "plans to move the Americans out are 'fantasy.'"[21] Billions have been invested in the Green Zone, a huge enbunkered US embassy, and a dozen other American enclaves officially known as "Enduring Camps" to make them as invulnerable as possible to car-bomb and rocket attacks, while ordinary Iraqis have to navigate the helter-skelter of crime, insurgency, and sectarian murder.

Recruits to the new Iraqi police and army, in particular, have become sitting ducks for the bombers in search of softer targets. On July 5, 2003, a month before the Jordanian embassy explosion, seven police recruits were blown up at their graduate ceremony in Ramadi. Since then, car bombers and infiltrators wearing suicide vests have massacred hundreds, perhaps even thousands of luckless police trainees, traffic guards, and military recruits – Sunni as well as Shiite – as they have waited in application lines or paraded in squares. (Economic desperation in Iraq is so great that when recruits are killed, others will step over the bodies to take their place. This is exactly what happened in Ramadi in early January 2006 when a suicide car bomber killed 60 men in a throng of applicants; the survivors, afraid of losing their places, quickly crowded back into line to continue the screening process for police jobs.)[22]

Although ruthless in the extreme, such attacks do serve a rational strategy of resistance to the American occupation, as well as preventing the consolidation of a national government dominated by Shiites and Kurds. But what (and whose) purpose has been served by the escalating mass murder of ordinary Shiites? For the forces that call themselves "Al Qaeda in Mesopotamia," secular Iraqi nationalism – whether of the Baathist, Communist, or neo-liberal variety – seems almost as much an enemy of God as the Crusaders. "[I]n his correspondence with bin Laden," claims journalist Loretta Napoleoni, "al Zarqawi relentlessly stressed the need to prevent Iraqi Shi'ites and Sunnis from uniting around a genuine nationalism. If this were to happen, he concluded, the jihadists would be cut out because they were foreigners and the insurgency would become secular."[23]

Almost daily for four years, car bombs driven or left by sectarian *jihadis* have slaughtered Iraqi Shiites in front of their homes, mosques, police stations, and markets. Twelve years after their US-instigated rebellion was abandoned to the vengeance of the Republican Guards by the Bush Sr administration, the Shia again found American promises of protection to be worthless. In a ghastly and rapidly growing catalogue of atrocity, with several thousand Shiites (at least) slain in public spaces in broad daylight, the car-bombings in Hilla and Musayyib (in February and July 2005, respectively) stand out as landmarks in sectarian horror.

The recent history of Hilla, a city of 400,000 built from the rubble of ancient Babylon, summarizes Shiite oppression. In March 1991, after a brief rebellion against Saddam, the Republican Guards executed several hundred residents, dragging their bodies in the streets and hanging them from power pylons as a warning. Twelve years later the city was cluster-bombed by US jets, which killed 61 people and injured more than 450, many of them children. Reuters and AP photographers caught the carnage on film – "babies cut in half, amputated limbs, kids with their faces a web of deep cuts caused by American shellfire and cluster bombs" – but only censored versions were shown in the West.[24] Then, on February 28, a market Monday when lines of people, some of them National Guard recruits, waited outside a health clinic, and hundreds more, mainly women and children, shopped amongst the fruit and vegetable stalls, a white Mitsubishi sedan exploded in a huge fireball, killing 136 people and injuring 150 more. (Such high mortality ratios, according to an earlier study of terrorist bombings, are not unusual in open-air car-bomb explosions involving so much shrapnel and flying glass.)[25]

All that remained of the suicide bomber was a charred forearm handcuffed to a steering wheel; the fingerprints identified Raed al-

Banna, a middle-class Jordanian with a law degree who previously had lived in Rancho Cucamonga, California, and who, according to interviews conducted by the *Los Angeles Times*, was warmly recalled by his former friends and co-workers as a "really nice guy . . . into partying . . . sex, drugs and rock 'n roll." In the aftermath of the 9/11 attacks and amidst rising hostility toward Moslems, the previously secular al-Banna joined a mosque, then quit his job after accusing a co-worker of defaming Islam. After returning to Jordan he was unable to find employment, so he renewed his US visa and flew to Chicago, where he was denied entry by a suspicious customs official, "even though his name was not on a terrorist watch list." Consumed by frustration and rage (so the *Times*'s account suggests), he was recruited to one of the cells led by fellow Jordanian al-Zarqawi. Telling his parents that he had found a job as a "truck driver," he eventually became the angel of death in Hilla.[26]

On the same day that Hilla's health clinic was blown up, a second car bomb killed policemen at a checkpoint in the nearby Shiite town of Musayyib, 20 miles to the north. The killers returned in July with a diabolical new tactic to bypass the roadblocks and other security measures desperately put in place to protect against car bombers. A *kamikaze* wearing an explosive belt sat drinking coffee in a café as he awaited the arrival of a gasoline tanker at a gas station near a vegetable market in front of a Shiite mosque. (Worried municipal authorities had banned trucks from the center of the city, but had made exceptions for fuel deliveries.) When the tanker arrived, after having been carefully inspected at a checkpoint, the suicide bomber ran up to the truck and detonated his charge (some witnesses claim that the driver, probably an accomplice, had already escaped). Burning fuel instantly engulfed the market and nearby homes: "Many described being caught in an inferno that shot flames 40 feet into the sky, towering over the minaret of a downtown mosque." "It was just like hell itself," said a policeman. "I saw how the flames swallowed the panicked people as they ran away," another survivor told a Western journalist. "The fire chased the people down and ate them alive." Almost 100 were burned alive in the street, in their homes, or on the steps of the mosque.[27]

From May through October 2005, suicide car-bombings (at least 126 fatal incidents, with 15 in Baghdad alone in one 48-hour-period) reached an extraordinary crescendo, forcing Shiites to trust only their own militias for self-defense, not the Americans or the reborn Iraqi military. (Some of the suicide attacks were beyond horrific, such as the July 2005 blast that killed several dozen children in the Shiite neighborhood of al-Jedidah in eastern Baghdad.)[28] The bomb blitz and the inevitable counter-terror by Shiite gunmen also accelerated the exodus of the Iraqi middle class that began in 2004. "In the last 10 months," reported the *New York Times* in May 2006, "[Baghdad] has issued new passports to 1.85 million Iraqis, 7 percent of the population and a quarter of the country's estimated middle class." The *Times* also estimated that the Iraqi diaspora in Jordan alone already constituted almost one million people.[29] These statistics, of course, were staggering blows to the prestige of the Occupation on the eve of national elections, and as US officials conceded to the press, "They have yet to find a way to control the insurgents' most effective weapon [the car bomb]." The only consolation, according to an American military spokesman, was that "it's a spike." The bombers, he explained, "are expending a lot of resources right now. We don't know how long they'll be capable of sustaining it."[30]

What, in fact, are the logistics of car-bombing on such an epic scale, and how have the insurgents provisioned themselves with sufficient cars and willing martyrs? (The supply of explosives, thanks to the mountain of cached munitions left behind by the Baathist regime, has thus far not been a constraint on the incidence of attacks.) In October 2005, an FBI counter-terrorism unit acknowledged that they were investigating a new international industry: SUVs stolen from suburban driveways in California and Texas were being exported to the Middle East for new careers as car bombs. "The inquiry began," reported the *Boston Globe*, "after coalition troops raided a bomb-making factory in Fallujah last November and found a sport utility vehicle registered in Texas that was being prepared for a bombing mission . . . Iraqi insurgents prefer American stolen cars because they tend to be larger, blend in more easily with the convoys of U.S. government and private contractors, and are harder to identify as stolen."[31]

The supply side of suicide bombers is an even more disconcerting subject. In spring 2006, Ayman al-Zawahiri, the purported military leader of Al Qaeda, boasted that fraternal forces (such as the group led by al-Zarqawi) had carried out more than 800 suicide attacks in Iraq, most of them involving vehicle bombs.[32] Although the propensity of Iraqi Sunnis to deliberately blow themselves up is a hotly debated topic, there is no question about the eagerness of foreign volunteers, especially large numbers of Saudis and Jordanians, to martyr themselves in flame and molten metal for the sake of killing a few Shiite schoolkids or street vendors.

In May 2005 alone, the Syrians claimed to have detained 137 Saudi *jihadis* en route to Iraq. Interrogation revealed mindsets closer to zombies than to classical *kamikazes*. "The [Syrian] commander who interviewed them," writes journalist Loretta Napoleoni, "said that their ideology was non-negotiable. In mind and spirit they were already martyred; what they needed was someone to co-ordinate the attack, someone to tell them which target to hit, where to go, and how to complete their mission. Al-Zarqawi and his network of jihadists provide such information." Napoleoni adds that "their handlers look at them not as people or jihadists, but as weapons" and waste no time or money on their training. "To guard against being shot before reaching their target . . . suicide bombers are strapped to the steering wheel and have their foot taped to the accelerator."[33]

Indeed — at least in 2005 — the supply of *madrasa* graduates seeking to use car bombs as stairways to paradise seemed to considerably exceed what the logic of suicide bombing (as perfected by Hezbollah and the Tamil Tigers) actually demanded: many of the explosions could just as easily have been detonated by remote control (as increasingly they were in early 2006). The Chechens, too, have squandered martyrs with tactical extravagance, but in their case, the irresistible logic of revenge, in the face of Russian ruthlessness, commands an urgency of sacrifice. The *jihadis* in Iraq might claim a similar mandate if they were blowing up Crusaders to avenge the larger wrongs of the Middle East, but the strategic thrust of the car-bombing campaign mounted by the Al Qaedist elements organized or inspired by al-Zarqawi (killed by an American airstrike in June 2006) has been the instigation of intra-Moslem violence, not the strengthening of resistance to imperialism.

As Sunni ultras have aligned themselves with al-Zarqawi and his successors, it is hard to see what advantage would accrue to the Sunni community from the destruction of Iraq's precarious national fabric, so largely woven on their own looms. Even Al Qaeda has recoiled from the sectarian violence of its erstwhile allies: in July 2005, al-Zawahiri wrote a letter to al-Zarqawi that reportedly complained, "why were there attacks on ordinary Shia?" "In bin Laden's view," argues Lawrence Wright, the al-Zarqawi forces are "leading the Sunnis in Iraq to hell, and he [bin Laden] doesn't know what to do."[34] One can speculate on whether there are other dark forces, including state security agencies, with an interest in fomenting a Sunni-versus-Shiite Armageddon, but the collapse of Sunni supremacy may have simply unleashed a wild and uncontrollable rage that exceeds even Al Qaeda's requirements. Rational-actor presumptions, after all, don't always apply in real history: just think of the self-immolation by atrocity of the OAS in Algeria in 1962. In any event, the Zarqawian obsession with destroying the "internal enemy" finally provoked in 2006 a symmetrical backlash of indiscriminate Shiite fury.

After the destruction of the Golden Mosque, the Askariya shrine in Samarra on February 22 by a team of Al Qaedist commandos led by Haitham al-Badri, dozens of Sunni mosques were attacked and hundreds of Sunnis were dragged from their homes, workplaces, even prison cells, and murdered, sometimes after being grotesquely tortured with power tools. In Baghdad, where 47 Sunni factory workers were ambushed and killed in the immediate aftermath of the mosque bombing, the situation was almost insurrectionary, and the government was forced to declare a daytime curfew for the first time, while American troops – blamed for failing to protect the Shiite shrine – were recalled to their barracks for safety.[35]

Table 8   Descent into Civil War – Violent Civilian Deaths in Iraq[36]

Date	Total	Per day
May 2003	422	14
December 2003	412	13
May 2004	688	22
December 2004	839	27
February 2005	992	35
(Samarra mosque bombing)		
January 2006	1778	59
March 2006	2378	79
June 2006	3149	105
July 2006	3590	120
August 2006	3009	97
September 2006	3345	112
October 2006	3709	120

Despite ecumenical demonstrations and joint Sunni–Shia calls for unity, tit-for-tat violence increased almost exponentially through the spring as Shiite gunmen, often in police uniforms, stalked Sunnis in mixed neighborhoods while Saddamists and *jihadis* escalated their car-bomb attacks on Shiite mosques and neighborhoods. The spiral of vengeance was implacable.

Following the murder of a Sunni iman in Basra at the beginning of June, for example, a suicide car bomber devastated a market, killing at least 27. A month later a Shiite mosque was car-bombed in the poor but mixed Baghdad neighborhood of Jihad; within hours, the police were finding dozens of dead Sunnis; Sunni gunmen then mowed down 42 people in the Shiite town of Mahmoudiya, and this atrocity soon produced another three dozen tortured Sunni corpses in Baghdad. The chessboard response was a suicide car bomb in the Shiite shrine town of Kufa, a stronghold of Muqtada al-Sadr's movement, which killed a group of Iranian pilgrims and provoked ex-prime minister Iyad Allawi to tell the *Sunday Times* that "we are practically in stage one of a civil war as we speak."[37]

Confirmation came on July 18 when a driver approached a large group of day laborers near the shrine in the center of Kufa. As he beckoned to them to come closer, the job-hungry workers crowded around his van or minibus – at least 53 of them were killed in the ensuing blast. When police arrived at the scene of the massacre, they were stoned by crowds demanding that al-Sadr's Mahdi Army be allowed to take charge of security.[38] Meanwhile, as impotent Sunni and Shiite political leaders meeting in the Green Zone bickered with one another, the undeclared civil war ratcheted up another notch with car-bombings of outdoor markets in Baghdad's Sadr City (42 killed) and Kirkuk (21 dead). In return, dozens more dead Sunnis – disfigured by torturers wielding Black-and-Decker power-tools – appeared in alleys and drainage ditches. Soon afterwards, a car bomb devastated a shopping street in the middle-class Shiite neighborhood of Karada in Baghdad, killing 32 and turning "several buildings into mangled heaps of twisted steel girders, rubble and dust."[39]

The July violence in Baghdad accelerated the transformation of the metropolis into an medieval archipelago of warring Sunni and Shiite neighborhoods where residents, especially those too poor to emigrate, increasingly put their faith in local confessional militias and the culture of vendetta rather than the false promises of security offered by the internally divided government of Prime Minister Nouri al-Maliki and his American patrons. Indeed the Occupation often receives as much blame for the car-bomb blitz as the actual instigators. Bitter Shiites in eastern Baghdad especially criticized the US military for systematically dismantling the Mahdi Army road-blocks that protect markets and mosques from car bombs. "When the Americans come through and break up the checkpoints," complained a resident of Sadr City after the July 23 bombing, "that's when we get hit by suicide bombs, like today. I support the Mahdi Army because they know us here, and we know them. Their checkpoints protect us. They know all the families, and who has business here. It's clear the Americans don't want to provide us with security. They've had three years."[40]

22

The Gates of Hell

Four centuries after Galileo, a science of disorder has asserted itself alongside a science of order.

Daniel Bensaid[1]

Any history of technology risks self-absorption and exaggeration. It is too easy to believe that the modern world is simply the addition of its inventions and their automatic social consequences: steam engines and socialists, trains and tourists, radios and dictators, computer chips and geeks, and so on. But as Marx long ago cautioned us, the future of any innovation depends upon existent social structures (or "relations of production") capable of developing its potentials and harvesting its effects. The Alexandrian Greeks, for example, delighted themselves with steam-powered toys but in an age of abundant slave labor they had no use for labor-saving technology. Likewise, the car bomb existed in principle, as a potent template for future terrorism, for a generation or more before the Stern Gang first used it to plow the fertile fields of hatred in Palestine; its subsequent development in the Cold War era, like the rise of "terrorism" in general, was to some extent held in check by the authority of the superpowers and their networks of alliance. After Beirut and Kabul, however, and thanks especially to Bill Casey and his Pakistani counterparts, the car bomb proliferated across the planet like a kudzu vine of destruction, taking root in the thousand fissures of ethnic and religious enmity that globalization has paradoxically revealed. It also flourishes in the badlands of extreme inequality, on the edges of poor cities, and even in the embittered recesses of the American heartland.

Having opened Pandora's Box, can it ever be closed? The Pentagon has launched a crash program, an anti-terrorist "Manhattan Project," to counter the threat of roadside bombs and other improvised explosives, including car bombs. The formidably titled "Joint Improvised Explosive Device Defeat Task Force" originated as an ad hoc working group of a dozen people in October 2003, then, as insurgent IEDs decimated Humvees on the highways outside Baghdad in winter and spring 2004, it was transformed into one of the Pentagon's most urgent and high-priority projects. US military planners had not only been blindsided by the widespread use of IEDs, but they had also failed to anticipate the insurgents' ingenuity in keeping pace with defensive responses: as Americans, for example, added heavier armor to their vehicles, the insurgents increased bomb yields, utilized more deadly shaped charges, and changed their cell-phone detonators to less detectable systems using garage-door openers. (As a colonel in the Combat Engineers told participants in an "IED Defeat Seminar" in 2005: "The folks building these things are very sophisticated. They need to die, but they are very sophisticated.")[2] Despite frenetic US countermeasures, the number of makeshift bomb attacks (both IEDs and car bombs) almost doubled from 5,607 in 2004 to 10,593 in 2005; the number increased again by 30 percent in the first half of 2006.[3]

In response, the Pentagon keeps pouring more money into counter-IED research. By summer 2006, the budget for the Task Force, now headed by retired four-star general Montgomery Meigs, had increased to $3.5 billion, although "senior officials say they essentially have a blank check." Mobilizing the expertise of hundreds of top military engineers, forensic scientists, physicists, and intelligence experts, the Task Force, according to the *New York Times*, also funds "some 100 technology initiatives" through 80 private contractors to combat "the rising number of increasingly powerful and sophisticated homemade bombs that are the No. 1

killer of American troops in Iraq."[4] Altogether, according to the Associated Press, "from 2004 to 2006, some $6.1 billion will have been spent on the U.S. effort – comparable, in equivalent dollars, to the cost of the Manhattan Project installation that produced plutonium for World War II's atom bombs."[5] NATO, now under attack from IEDs and suicide car bombs in southern Afghanistan, as well as being bombed in its own capital cities, is mounting a parallel technology campaign and recently appointed a Counter-Terrorism Technology Coordinator to oversee the development of "cutting-edge technologies to detect, disrupt and pursue terrorists."[6]

It remains an open question, however, whether these ambitious technology initiatives will yield authentic magic bullets or just temporary palliatives that will eventually be foiled by insurgents' own innovations. (As I write, Hezbollah is again rewriting the rules of warfare in the Middle East, using Katyushas, IEDs, and sophisticated shoulder-launched anti-tank missiles with unprecedented success against Israeli heavy armor.) But as daunting as are the problems of protecting military patrols from hidden IEDs, passenger airlines from hijackers, and public-transit systems from suitcase bombs, they are dwarfed by the extraordinary challenge of protecting sprawling cities, rich and poor, from roving car bombers.

In August 2004, after a federal alert that closed roads, bridges and banks in Washington, D.C., and New York City in face of rumors of an imminent truck-bomb attack on a major financial institution, the *Washington Post* surveyed experts about the country's preparedness to deal with the threat. Reporters Spencer Hsu and Sari Horwitz quickly learned that there are 2.6 million heavy-duty trucks and another 90 million smaller trucks, ranging from delivery vans to pickups, on the nation's highways, and that 5 million tons of ammonium-nitrate fertilizer are sold over the counter every year without any national system to report or track the sales. Although Washington had spent more than $1 billion enhancing physical security at federal buildings and embassies with concrete barriers and setbacks, this undoubtedly will only redirect terrorists to softer targets. The reporters also found that "truck bombs have been very far down the list" of Bush priorities, as Homeland Security spending was initially focused upon airline security and bioterrorism. Indeed, "eleven years after Muslim extremists used an explosives-laden van to attack the World Trade Center and nearly three years after the September 11, 2001 terrorist attacks, senior federal agents acknowledge that the country has virtually no defense against a terrorist barreling down the street with a truck bomb."[7]

To be fair, since this *Washington Post* report some additional federal money – if only a smidgen of that devoted to IEDs – supports advanced research on the detection of vehicle bombs as well as the protection of structures against their blast effects. Unfortunately, the technologies under development, such as robotic arms that use "fast" neutrons to scan car bodies to detect explosives, or cutting-edge systems of vanadium steel/concrete-composite wall construction, are only really applicable to protecting government buildings, international border crossings, and elite "ring of steel" districts like the Green Zone, where vehicles are stopped and inspected at security points.[8] "Stand-off detection," supersensitive systems that can "smell" ammonium nitrate or TNT molecules at a distance of several hundred feet, are still "at least a decade away," according to experts at Sandia National Laboratories.[9] Although science writers like to fantasize about "vast networks of imaging or trace sensors deployed throughout cities," such Orwellian systems, if they actually become available, will probably be too expensive to find widespread use, especially in poorer countries.[10]

A future "technological fix" for the car-bomb threat, in other words, will only be relevant to certain privileged residential zones, transport hubs, and decision-making centers. Bomb-detection portals and robotic inspection systems, for the most part, will remain luxury goods. Bomb-sensors under current development for use in garages or military checkpoints, for example, will cost at least $165,000 and have a range of only a few feet.[11] "Pre-bomb cordons" using concrete obstacles and traffic barriers may seem a cheaper and more feasible alternative, but, according to City of London Police Superintendent Timothy Hillier (a world authority), adequate protection against large vehicle bombs "require[s] a minimum cordon of 400 meters (437 yards), or more than the length of four football fields. An explosion can cause injuries and damage even beyond this distance, so everyone should exercise caution near the perimeter. Considering this scale in the center of any city, the enormous difficulties encountered with pre-bomb cordons become apparent."[12]

The almost insuperable problem of security for the urban masses is brutally illustrated by the immense, ongoing security mobilization in Baghdad that has largely failed to deter car-bombings and mass murder. By July 2006, according to the *New York Times*, there were an estimated *6000* checkpoints in Baghdad, manned by 51,000 soldiers and police – an astonishing mobilization – yet car bombers were still setting off deadly explosions on an almost daily basis.[13] If the Green Zone was effectively off limits to bombers in stolen American cars, they had no problem finding their way to tempting soft targets in poor Shiite neighborhoods and suburbs; and when the dramatic introduction of thousands more US troops in August temporarily reduced the carnage in Beirut, the *jihadis* simply moved on to less secure cities, such as Kirkuk with its volatile population mix of Sunnis, Kurds, and Turkomans. In Baghdad itself, attackers circumvented roadblocks and traffic curfews with bicycle bombs – *circa* Saigon 1952.

When American military spokesmen claimed a dramatic reduction in killings in August, their figures were immediately disputed by hundreds of uncounted, hideously tortured bodies warehoused in the Baghdad morgue. Moreover, sectarian violence spiked dramatically again in September with car-bombings in eastern Baghdad, which were immediately repaid with more disfigured Sunni corpses. (In Kirkuk, meanwhile, jihadists choreographed five suicide car-bombings within minutes of each other, a terrifying warning that the "martyrs" had returned in force.) In sheer desperation, the Pentagon announced that American and Iraqi forces would attempt to seal off Baghdad with a "ring of reinforced checkpoints, berms, trenches, barriers, and fences." "The enemy is changing tactics," President Bush explained at a later press conference, "and we're adapting. The enemy moves and we will help the Iraqis move. And so they've building a berm around the city to make it harder for people to come with explosive devices . . . They got a clear build–and–hold strategy."[14]

The obvious model is Fallujah, which since its reconquest by US Marines in November 2004 had been converted into an urban prison along the lines of Gaza under the Israelis. "The American forces," explains the *New York Times*, "have run the city as a mini police state, with people who want to enter required to show identification cards at checkpoints."[15] But Baghdad is vastly larger than Fallujah and critics immediately assailed the Bush administration's folly of trying to build an anti–terrorist dike or moat around its sprawling 60-mile-long perimeter. Unlike Fallujah, moreover, the residents of Iraq's megalopolis do not carry obligatory identity cards, the pre–requisite to any effective system of checkpoints. The proposed ring around Baghdad, in other words, has more to do with sustaining the American occupation's flagging PR campaign than with defeating a "terrorism" that has become so deeply and terrifyingly entrenched within the city's neighborhoods.

In any event, sectarian car bombers reclaimed ownership of Baghdad on November 23, 2006 with a horrific and carefully choreographed attack on Sadr City. Beginning at 3 pm and continuing at 15-minute-intervals, Sunni suicide bombers set off five enormous half-ton explosions in the Jamila and al–Hay markets, and al–Shahidein Square. Iraq's Health Minister Ali al–Shemari estimated the death toll at 200, although "many of the dead have been reduced to scattered body parts and are not counted yet." The next day, while furious Shiites in Baghdad were burning Sunnis alive and shelling their mosques, another suicide car bomber killed 22 people in the northern, largely Turkmen city of Tal Afar. A week later, two car bombs were exploded outside hospital morgues in Baghdad in an attempt to kill relatives of earlier victims or perhaps just blow up the dead a second time.[16]

In truth, cities as large as Baghdad, London or Los Angeles, with their vast seas of cars, trucks, and buses, and their thousands of vulnerable institutions and infrastructural nodes, will never enjoy universal security. Like drug dealers, car bombers will always find a place to do business. Writer Martin Amis, who frets that in the future "riding a city bus will be like flying El Al," has no need to worry: El Al has a level of professional security far beyond what most sprawling and cash-strapped municipalities will ever be able to afford.[17] The vast majority of us will continue to live in the "Red Zone," vulnerable to sinister Fiats and Ryder vans. As Rhiannon Talbot points out in a reflection on the IRA's Bishopsgate bombing, "No matter how many police officers are on duty, or how many special constables and auxiliary police officers are drafted we cannot guard every building of significance in the country nor every street where hundreds could die if a devastating bomb were to be detonated."[18] Such common sense, of course, must be pounded into the heads of politicians and police officials besotted with fantasies of "beating the terrorists" with panoptical surveillance, ion detection technology, roadblocks, and, that *sine qua non*, the permanent suspension of civil liberties.

A deeply revealing conversation in this regard, reported by Irish journalist Tim Pat Coogan, occurred in the course of the secret meetings between Irish and British security officials in 1996, where it was debated whether or not the current IRA ceasefire was "genuine," and whether the peace process could go forward without the complete "decommissioning" of the Provisional IRA's arsenal. As Coogan explains, the issue of the IRA arsenal, so fetishized by Loyalist and British politicians, "was actively de-bunked, not by an Irish spokesperson as one might have imagined, but by a senior RUC [Royal Ulster Constabulary] officer," who also offered a remarkable assessment of the role of car bombs in the "Troubles."

This is not a military issue, it is a political issue. The major portion of the damage and death caused over the entire period of the troubles did not come from hand guns and rifles, from home-made mortars, or even from Semtex explosive. It was caused by the fertilizer bombs which can be made up by anyone with a schoolboy knowledge of chemistry. Two men with shovels can make up a thousand pound bomb in a Fermanagh cowshed and,

if for some reason the operation has to be aborted, they can
decommission it again, all within twelve hours. You can't
decommission shovels. It's minds which have to be decommis-
sioned.[19]

Since there is little likelihood of any of the socio–economic reforms
or concessions to self-determination that might lead to the large-
scale "decommissioning of minds" (indeed the trends are quite the
opposite), the car bomb probably has a brilliant future. The recent
car–bombings of critical oil hubs in the Niger Delta and Saudi
Arabia preview a global assault on the vulnerable petroleum
industry, just as the arrest of a group in Canada in summer 2006
who were stockpiling tons of ammonium nitrate for a doomsday
truck bomb is reminder that no country is immune to the con-
tagion.[20] The 50 or so suicide car–bombings in Afghanistan in the
first ten months of 2006, moreover, are proof that in *madrasas*
somewhere (probably in neighboring Pakistan) the future *mujahedin*
are chanting: "One, two, three, many Iraqs!"[21] All sides, moreover,
now play by Old Testament rules and every laser-guided missile
falling on an apartment house in southern Beirut or a mud–walled
compound in Kandahar is a future suicide truck bomb headed for
the center of Tel Aviv or perhaps downtown Los Angeles. Buda's
wagon truly has become the hot rod of the apocalypse.

Notes

1. WALL STREET 1920

1. Paul Avrich, *Sacco and Vanzetti: The Anarchist Background*, Princeton 1991, p. 137. Avrich, who died in 2006, was the foremost historian of American anarchism. Thanks to the twilight reminiscences of Buda's anarchist contemporaries, he succeeded, where J. Edgar Hoover and the FBI had earlier failed, in establishing Buda's identity as the Wall Street bomber. My account is based on Avrich as well as the *New York Times* and *Chicago Tribune*, September 17–21, 1920. See also Charles McCormick, *Hopeless Cases: The Hunt for the Red Scare Terrorist Bombers*, Lanham 2005. McCormick demurs from assigning responsibility for the bombing.

2. POOR MAN'S AIR FORCE

1. George Orwell, "You and the Atomic Bomb" (*Tribune*, October 19, 1945) reprinted in Sonia Orwell and Ian Angus (eds), *In Front of Your Nose, 1945–1950: The Collected Essays, Journalism and Letters of George Orwell*, volume IV, New York 1968, p. 7.
2. The first consul was asleep in his carriage, on the way to the opera for the premiere of Haydn's *Die Schöpfung,* when Breton *chouans* exploded a huge cask of gunpowder mixed with iron scrap. Although the conspirators were Royalists, Napoleon took most of his rage out upon jailed Jacobins, whom he guillotined.
3. Lawrence Wright, *The Looming Tower: Al-Qaeda and the Road to 9/11*, New York 2006, p. 303.
4. See table 3, p. 117.
5. "Currently active" (late 2006) includes Iraq, Afghanistan, Chechnya/Russia, Pakistan, India, Sri Lanka, Colombia, and perhaps Corsica. "Recently active" (2004–06) includes Indonesia, Thailand, Burma/Myanmar, Philippines, Thailand, Saudi Arabia, Uzbekistan, Egypt, Jordan, Lebanon, Algeria, Turkey, Kenya, Nigeria, Serbia, and Spain. In 2005–06 major car-bomb plots were reportedly foiled in Britain, Romania, and Canada.

6. James Dunnigan, "Why the Car Bomb Is King in Iraq," June 26, 2005, www.strategypage.com.

7. Cyberpunk meets the Pentagon in the influential anthology published by Rand's National Defense Research Institute: John Arquilla and David Ronfeldt (eds), *Networks and Netwars: The Future of Terror, Crime, and Militancy,* Santa Monica 2001.

8. US withdrawal from Lebanon; formulation of "Weinberger–Powell Doctrine."

9. The Hezbollah truck bomb that destroyed the Marine barracks in Beirut in October 1983 was estimated to have used 12,000 pounds of high explosive; in contrast the Consolidated B-24 (see www.b24.net/aircraft.htm) had a long-distance bomb load of only 5000 pounds.

10. Dr Ronald Massa, written testimony to House Subcommittee on Public Buildings and Economic Development, June 4, 1998 (www.fas.org/irp/congress/1998_hr/h980604–massa.htm).

11. Wright, *The Looming Tower,* p. 308.

12. Régis Debray, "Le passage à l'infini," in Catherine Lavenir and François-Bernard Huyghe (eds), *La scène terroriste,* Les Cahiers de médiologie 13, Paris 2002, p. 11.

13. Peter Lance, *1000 Years for Revenge: International Terrorism and the FBI,* New York 2003, pp. 102 and 112; and Lou Michel and Dan Herbeck, *American Terrorist: Timothy McVeigh and the Oklahoma City Bombing,* New York 2001, p. 176. $1 billion damage figure from March 9, 1993 testimony of Police Commissioner Raymond Kelly to House Judiciary Committee.

14. US Department of Justice, *1997 Report on the Availability of Bombmaking Information,* Washington D.C. 1997, full text with bibliography of bomb manuals at www.usdoj.gov/criminal/cybercrime/bombmakinginfo.html.

15. On Irhabi, see "London Case Led to Terror Arrests in Canada," *Wall Street Journal,* June 6, 2006. On Amazon.com, see, for instance, "Uncle Fester's" *Home Workshop Explosives,* second edition, Green Bay (WI) 2002.

16. Cf. Martin Shubik, *Terrorism, Technology, and the Socioeconomics of Death,* Cowles Foundation Paper no. 952, Yale University, New Haven 1998, esp. pp. 406–07; and John Robb, "Requiem for Preventative War (and Political Big Bangs . . .)" (June 14, 2006) at http://globalguerrillas.typepad-com/globalguerrillas/.

17. Debray, "Le passage à l'infini,", pp. 11–12.

3.   PRELIMINARY DETONATIONS

1. "School Dynamiter First Slew Wife," *New York Times,* May 20, 1927.

2. Murray Bookchin, *The Spanish Anarchists: The Heroic Years, 1868–1936,* Edinburgh 1998, p. 174.

3. Note to author from Marc Viaplana (Barcelona), June 3, 2006. Viaplana is writing a fascinating history of "infernal machines."

4. Debra Pawlak, "Just Another Summer Day: The Bath School Disaster," at www.themediadrome.com. The chief contemporary account is M. Ellsworth,

The Bath School Disaster, reprinted 1981, Clinton County (Michigan) Historical Society. Thanks to Aaron Dennis and Josh Kerr for drawing my attention to this horrific incident.

5. "Maniac Blows Up School," *New York Times*, May 19, 1927. Newspaper accounts differ as to timing of the several explosions.
6. Ibid.
7. On the origin and social composition of the ABC, see Luis Aguilar, *Cuba 1933: Prologue to Revolution*, Ithaca 1972, pp. 118–20 and 125–26; Louis Perez, Jr, *Cuba Under the Platt Amendment, 1902–1934,* Pittsburgh 1986, pp. 289–90; and Russell Porter, "Amid Cuba's Gayety Stalks the Terror," *New York Times Magazine*, April 30, 1933, pp. 5 and 18.
8. R. Hart Philips, *Cuban Sideshow*, Havana 1935, p. 13.
9. "Automobile Bomb Seized in Havana," special cable to the *Chicago Tribune* (April 19), reprinted in the *New York Times*, April 20, 1933.
10. The *New York Times Index* from 1930 to 1940 lists almost 100 separate bombings.

4. ORANGES FOR JAFFA

1. "Terror," *He Khazit (The Front)*, August 2, 1943. This was LEHI's underground publication. Thanks to Dan Monk for research in Israel.
2. J. Bowyer Bell, *Terror out of Zion: Irgun Zvai Leumi, LEHI, and the Palestine Underground*, New York 1977, p. 85.
3. Ibid., pp. 42–49. The inventor of the disguised time bombs that had caused such terror in Arab markets was Gundar Yitzhaki, who accidentally blew himself up in 1939. According to Bell, when British intelligence agents found him dying, they asked his name. "My name is death," were his last words (p. 43).
4. Ibid., pp. 183–84.
5. "Haifa Blast Ends Palestine Truce," *New York Times*, January 13, 1947; and "Blast Haifa Police Station," *Chicago Daily Tribune*, January 13, 1947. The *Tribune* describes the bomb vehicle as a car rather than truck.
6. "16 Die in Palestine in Bombing Wave," *New York Times*, March 2, 1947.
7. "Five Killed in Palestine by Gang Bomb," *Los Angeles Times*, April 26, 1947; and Bell, *Terror out of Zion,* p. 202.
8. Uri Milstein, *History of the War of Independence, Volume One: A Nation Girds for War*, Lanham (MD) 1998, pp. 85–86.
9. Excerpt from *City of Oranges: Arabs and Jews in Jaffa*, London 2006, published in the *Independent*, January 25, 2006.
10. Local Haganah leaders, acting independently of Golda Me'ir and their national leadership, believed that the hotel was being used as the headquarters for Iraqi fighters; however, as Milstein notes, "Arab and British documents reveal that the commanders of the Iraqi volunteers were not at the hotel that night and that none of the dead had any connection to the fighting forces" (*History of the War of Independence,* p. 91).

11. Milstein, *History of the War of Independence,* p. 97; and Bell, *Terror out of Zion,* p. 267 (he describes the vehicle as a "police van"). The year before (September 29, 1947) clever Irgun engineers had built a ramp on top of a three-ton truck which they used to roll an enormous barrel bomb into a police headquarters in Haifa, killing 10 and wounding 54 (see Bell, p. 245).
12. Bell, *Terror out of Zion,* p. 104.
13. Ovid Demaris, *Brothers in Blood: The International Terrorist Network,* New York 1977, pp. 94–97.
14. Ibid.; and Milstein, *History of the War of Independence,* pp. 106–07.
15. Milstein, *History of the War of Independence,* p. 108.
16. Larry Collins and Dominique Lapierre, *O Jerusalem!,* New York 1972, p. 192.
17. Ibid., p.193; and Demaris, *Brothers in Blood,* pp. 94–97.
18. Milstein, *History of the War of Independence,* p. 112.
19. Ian Black and Benny Morris, *Israel's Secret Wars: A History of Israel's Intelligence Services,* New York 1991, p. 42. According to the *New York Times,* a "two-ton barrel bomb" in a truck was also sent to "blow up the Arab town of Nablus" in early March, but it was intercepted and captured by al-Husseini's men. In the course of trying to dismantle the contraption, two of the British deserters working for the sheik were killed in a gigantic explosion ("Haganah Accord on Irgun Reported," *New York Times,* March 9, 1948).
20. Milstein, *History of the War of Independence,* p. 117. Bell (*Terror out of Zion,* p. 268) claims that Kutub's "masterpiece" contained "a quarter-ton of TNT and an elaborate detonator – a mixture of mercury, nitric acid, and alcohol." The extraordinary Kutub had been trained in explosives by SS experts in Holland during World War Two – after quarreling with the Nazis, he was interned in a concentration camp with Jews.

5. OUR MAN IN SAIGON

1. Graham Greene, *The Quiet American,* London 1955, p. 154.
2. On Greene in Saigon, see Bruce Franklin's fascinating essay, "By the Bombs' Early Light," *The Nation,* February 3, 2003.
3. Sergei Blagov, *Honest Mistakes: The Life and Death of Trinh Minh Thé,* Huntington (NY) 2001, p. 48.
4. Jean Lartéguy, *Soldats perdus et fous de Dieu: Indochine 1945–1955,* Paris 1986, pp. 179–81.
5. Graham Greene, *Ways of Escape,* New York 1980, p. 171.
6. Norman Sherry, *The Life of Graham Greene, Volume II (1939–1955),* London 1994, p. 431.
7. "Saigon Blasts Laid to Non-Red Group," *New York Times,* January 25, 1952. This piece corrects the story, "Reds' Time Bombs Rip Saigon Center,' which appeared on January 10.
8. "Cao Dai General," *New York Times,* May 4, 1955.
9. Landsdale talking to reporter Keyes Beech, as quoted in Jonathan Nashel, *Edward Lansdale's Cold War,* Amherst 2005, p. 157. In his movie *JFK,* Oliver Stone depicts Lansdale as the organizer of President Kennedy's assassination.

6.   *FESTIVALS DE PLASTIQUE*

1. Quoted in *Le Monde,* August 27, 1992.
2. See Robert Holland, *Britain and the Revolt in Cyprus, 1954–1949,* Oxford 1998, esp. p. 286.
3. Philippe Bourdrel, *Le livre noir de la guerre d'Algérie,* Paris 2003, p. 55.
4. Alistair Horne, *A Savage War of Peace: Algeria, 1954–1962,* London 1977, p. 318.
5. Bourdrel, *Le livre noir,* p. 310. Malleable explosives, stable over a wide range of temperatures, were extensively used by the British Special Operations Executive during World War Two. Concocted by mixing a "plasticizer" with the high-explosive RDX, *Explosif Plastique* was air-dropped to the French Resistance and other partisan movements. The spelling is inconsistent in both French and English: *plastique* or *plastic* both being common, with *plasticage* in French to denote explosions. Semtex and C-4 are probably the most well-known varieties of *plastique* in current use.
6. Horne, *A Savage War of Peace,* pp. 515–16.
7. Ibid., pp. 497–98.
8. "L'Attentat du Ministère des Affaires Etrangers," *Le Monde,* 24 January 1962.
9. Georges Fleury, *Histoire secrète de l'OAS,* Paris 2002, p. 586; and Bourdrel, *Le livre noir,* pp. 373–74. The OAS would ultimately detonate 1190 explosions in Oran – "ville d'apocalypse" (Fleury, p. 689).
10. Ibid, p. 600; and Remi Kauffer, *OAS: Histoire d'une Guerre Franco-Française,* Paris 2002, p. 305.
11. Henry Tanner, "Algiers Rightists Slay 91 Moslems; 62 Die in a Blast," *New York Times,* May 3, 1962.
12. "L'Explosion du Camion d'Essence sur les Hauts D'Alger," *Le Monde,* May 6–7, 1962.
13. "Terrorists Try to Burn Moslems," *New York Times,* May 5, 1962.
14. "Slayings of Women in Algeria Rising," *New York Times,* May 11, 1962.
15. "Angry Moslems Slay European," *New York Times,* May 8, 1962.
16. Horne, *A Savage War of Peace,* p. 531 (his emphasis).

7.   DEMON SEEDS

1. John Dickie, *Cosa Nostra: A History of the Sicilian Mafia,* London 2004, p. 307.
2. "Italy's Senate Asks Mafia Investigation," *New York Times,* April 12, 1962.
3. Dickie, *Cosa Nostra,* pp. 312–15.
4. Ibid., p. 306.
5. "Massive Mafia Car Blast Kills Key Judge", *Los Angeles Times,* July 30, 1983; and "Sicily Car Bomb Kills 3," *New York Times,* April 3, 1985.
6. Emmanuel Farrugia and Paul Serf, *Corse: le terrorisme,* Paris 2004, pp. 42–43 and 81–82.
7. Ibid., pp. 46–47.
8. Ibid., pp. 61–66. See also the detailed chronology of *attentats* at storiacorsa.unita-naziunale.org.

9. Ibid., p 196.
10. Craig Whitney, "Corsica: Idyllic with an Edge," *New York Times Magazine*, September 1, 1996, p. 9.
11. Quoted in "Corsica's Tourism, Stunted by Strife," *New York Times*, August 16, 1996.

8. WELCOME TO BOMBSVILLE

1. "Red Campaign in Saigon," *Chicago Tribune*, November 20, 1963.
2. MAC/SOG (The Mariah Project), *A Study of the Use of Terror by the Viet Cong,* Saigon 1966 (declassified 1978), p. 15.
3. Greene, *The Quiet American,* p. 139.
4. Truong Nhu Tang, *A Viet Cong Memoir,* New York 1985, pp. 64–65.
5. "Time Bombs in Saigon Injure 13 U.S. Troops," *Los Angeles Times*, October 22, 1957; and "Vietnam Dooms 2 Reds," *New York Times*, August 19, 1960 (on 1958 explosion).
6. *A Study of the Use of Terror by the Viet Cong,* p. 15.
7. "Terrorists' Booby Traps Kill 11." *Washington Post*, June 29, 1963.
8. "Red Campaign in Saigon," *Chicago Tribune*, November 20, 1963.
9. "Christmas Eve Bomb in Saigon," *New York Herald Tribune*, December 25, 1964.
10. "Terrorists Bomb Saigon Quarters of U.S. Officers," *New York Times*, December 25, 1964; and Peer de Silva, *Sub Rosa: The CIA and the Uses of Intelligence*, New York 1978, p. 254.
11. "Vietcong Blow Up U.S. Barracks," *New York Times*, February 11, 1965.
12. "The attacks were a major influence," wrote the *New York Times* on March 30, 1965, "on President Johnson's decision to stage retaliatory bombings against North Vietnam, which Washington regards as the guerrillas' chief supporter."
13. See Edward Miguel and Gerard Roland, *The Long Run Impact of Bombing Vietnam,* Department of Economics, U.C. Berkeley, March 2005, pp. 2–3.
14. Don Moser, "The Vietcong Cadre of Terror," *Life,* January 12, 1968.
15. Ibid.
16. Ibid.
17. De Silva, *Sub Rosa,* p. 266.
18. "Bomb in Vietnam Rips U.S. Embassy," *New York Times*, March 30, 1965.
19. Seah Chiang Nee, "Reasons to Fear," January 12, 1979, posted at www.littlespeck.com.
20. Bobbi Hovis, *Station Hospital Saigon,* Annapolis 1991, pp. 65–66.
21. "Police Compound at Saigon Bombed," *New York Times*, August 16, 1965.
22. "Saigon G.I. Billet Bombed in Vietcong Terror Attack," *New York Times*, December 4, 1965.
23. Ibid.
24. "New Terror Drive is Feared in Saigon," *New York Times*, October 8, 1966.
25. "Saigon Police Foil Plot," *Los Angeles Times*, January 7, 1966.

26. "Vietcong Kill 5 at Saigon Billet" and "Attack on U.S. Billet in Saigon," *New York Times*, April 1–2, 1966.
27. "GIs and Vietcong Battle in Saigon," *New York Times*, May 10, 1966.
28. "U.S. Acts to Ease Saigon Crowding," *New York Times*, October 7, 1966. Long Binh was the template for other "Little Americas," including the four huge "contingency operating bases" that will constitute the permanent US military presence in Iraq,
29. Attacks on Americans in Saigon continued regularly through 1971, with a major car-bombing in August 1969 that killed 12 Vietnamese and wounded 23 Americans at a US school for the Vietnamese army. ("Viet Battles, Bombings Break Lull," *Washington Post*, August 8, 1969.)

9.   "THE BLACK STUFF"

1. *City on Fire*, New York 2003, p. 43. This is the definitive history of the Texas City tragedy.
2. The problem of safely manufacturing, transporting, and storing ammonium fertilizers remains unsolved. Ten days after the 9/11 attacks on Manhattan, 300 tons of ammonium nitrate in a warehouse in Toulouse exploded from an unknown cause, resulting in 2473 casualties (31 dead) and a staggering 2.3 billion in property damage. See Major Accident Hazard Bureau, European Commision's Joint Research Center, *Summary Report; Workshop on Ammonium Nitrate*, Ispra (Italy) 2002.
3. Tom Bates, *Rads: The 1970 Bombing of the Army Math Research Center at the University of Wisconsin and Its Aftermath*, New York 1992, pp. 31 and 158. Thanks to David Julyk and Robert Fassnacht for reminding me about the Madison bombing.
4. Ibid., pp. 162–65.
5. Ibid., pp. 289–90.
6. Ibid., p. 8.
7. Ed Moloney, *A Secret History of the IRA*, New York 2002, p. 115.
8. Ibid., p. 115.
9. Ibid., p. 116.
10. "Truck Bomb Blast Injures 63 in Belfast Shopping District" and "Gasoline Truck Bomb Defused in Belfast," *Chicago Tribune*, January 4 and February 4, 1972.
11. "Bomb Blast Injures 60 in Belfast," *Washington Post*, May 23, 1972.
12. M. Smith, *Fighting for Ireland? The Military Strategy of the Irish Republican Movement*, London 1995, pp. 99 and 109.
13. Gelignite, available in many commercial variants, is a combination of nitroglycerine and a collodion (partially nitrated cellulose), similar to but much more powerful than classical dynamite.
14. Moloney, *A Secret History of the IRA,* p. 116.
15. Ibid., p. 126.

10.   LAUGHING AT THE DEAD

1. Houses of the Oireachtas, Joint Committee on Justice, Equality, Defence and Women's Rights, *Interim Report on the Report of the Independent Commission of Inquiry into the Dublin and Monaghan Bombings* (henceforth, *First Interim Report*), Dublin 2003, p. 31 (counting from title page: report as published is unpaginated). This is an on-going parliamentary "report on a report," interrogating the so-called Barron Report that responded to Yorkshire Television's 1993 *Hidden Hand* documentary about the Dublin and Monaghan bombings.
2. *First Tuesday* series, Yorkshire Television, *Hidden Hand: The Forgotten Massacre*, broadcast July 6, 1993 and reproduced in Don Mullan, *The Dublin and Monaghan Bombings*, Dublin 2000, p. 167.
3. I lived in Belfast for part of 1974–75 and generalize from visits and conversations with friends in the South. Although the British embassy in Dublin had been burned down by angry crowds after the Bloody Sunday massacre in 1972, public interest in the Northern Ireland crisis had considerably waned by 1974.
4. Recollection of Bridget Fitzpatrick in Mullan, *The Dublin and Monaghan Bombings*, pp. 51–52.
5. Quoted in ibid., p. 33
6. See *First Interim Report*, p. 25.
7. Yorkshire, *Hidden Hand* in Mullan, *The Dublin and Monaghan Bombings*, p. 166.
8. *First Interim Report*, p. 28.
9. Ibid., pp. 160–61.
10. Statement of former SAS operative provided to Mullan by producers of the *Prime Time* documentary (broadcast June 8, 1995), p. 227.
11. *First Interim Report*, p. 31.
12. *Hidden Hand* in Mullan, *The Dublin and Monaghan Bombings*, pp. 163–64.
13. Houses of the Oireachtas, Joint Committee on Justice, Equality, Defence and Women's Rights, *Final Report on the Report of the Independent Commission of Inquiry in the Dublin Bombings of 1972 and 1973*, Dublin 2005, p. 41 (Dr. FitzGerald).
14. *Hidden Hand* in Mullan, *The Dublin and Monaghan Bombings*, pp. 163–64 and 167. Following the *First Tuesday* report, there were various attempts to discredit its allegations – all of which are discussed at length and rebutted by Mullan in his important book. At the end of the day, the most persuasive evidence that the SAS was *not* involved was an official declaration by the UVF in July 1993 that it was solely responsible for the bombings. But the UVF with several hundred comrades in prison or on the run certainly had obvious reason to curry favor with British authorities by absolving London of complicity.

11.   HELL'S KITCHEN

1. Rashid Khalidi, *Under Siege: PLO Decisionmaking during the 1982 War*, New York 1986, p. 88.
2. Tabitha Petran, *The Struggle over Lebanon*, New York 1975, p. 270.

3. Black and Morris, *Israel's Secret Wars*, p. 272. It is important to note that this bombing, which also killed Kanafani's teenage niece, preceded the Munich massacre in September 1972: the Mossad had been assassinating leading Palestinians long before the deaths of Israeli Olympians provided its agents with a new halo for their activities.

4. "Beirut Blast," *Chicago Tribune*, January 4, 1977; and "A Lebanese Leader Sees Communist Role in Bomb Death of 40," *New York Times*, January 6, 1977.

5. Black and Morris, *Israel's Secret Wars*, pp. 272–73 and 277; and "Death of a Terrorist," *Time*, February 5, 1979.

6. Cited in "Dozens Killed,"*Los Angeles Times*, February 24, 1982.

7. See, for example, the *Mujahedin* car bombings in Tehran in 1981 and 1982 ("Car Bomb Kills 2 . . . Near Khomeini's House," *Washington Post*, April 23, 1981; and "Iranians Kill 4 Iraqi 'Agents,'" *New York Times*, September 13, 1982) and the Al Dawa bombing of the Iraqi News Agency in central Baghdad two months later (Iraq Says Six Were Killed by Car Bomb in Baghdad," *Washington Post*, December 17, 1982). Also in March 1985, Iraq launched air attacks on 11 Iranian cities in retaliation for a huge car bomb that exploded in front of the Rafidain Bank in Baghdad. ("Iraq Says its Jets Hit 11 Iran Cities," *New York Times*, March 17, 1985.)

8. "Bomb Kills 20," *Los Angeles Times*, September 18, 1981; and "20 Die in Lebanon in Anti-Left Bomb," *New York Times*, September 18, 1981.

9. "Another Car Bomb Explodes in Beirut;" "Bomb in Beirut Theater Kills 4;" and "New Terrorist Bombings Keep Lebanon on Edge," *New York Times*, September 19, 20 and 21, 1981; and 'Car Explodes in Lebanon," *Los Angeles Times*, September 28, 1981.

10. Yezid Sayigh, *Armed Struggle and the Search for State*, Oxford 1997, p. 513.

11. "Bomb in Beirut," *New York Times*, October 2, 1981. The final toll was 83 dead, including scores of women trapped by fire in their sewing workshop, with 300 wounded (*New York Times*, October 3).

12. Sayigh, *Armed Struggle and the Search for State,* p. 513.

13. "A Car Bomb in Beirut," "2 People Die as Car Explodes," "7 Killed and 60 Hurt by 2 Car Explosions," and "Beirut Car Bomb," *New York Times*, December 20–21, 1981 and February 24 and 28, 1982.

14. Sayigh, *Armed Struggle and the Search for the State,* pp. 530–37.

15. Khalidi, *Under Siege,* pp. 88 and 202, note 39.

16. Petran, *The Struggle over Lebanon,* p. 270.

17. "Bomb in Beirut," *New York Times*, October 2, 1981. In riposte, a car bomb killed 1 person in Christian East Beirut on October 26, near a Lebanese Army base. "The Phalangists," reported the *New York Times*, "have greatly tightened security in their areas over recent months, and have introduced explosive-sniffing dogs to help them protect against car bombs." ("Bombings Widened in Beirut", October 27, 1981)

18. Sayigh, *Armed Struggle and the Search for the State,* p. 521.

19. Robert Fisk, *Pity the Nation: The Abduction of Lebanon*, London 1990, p. 261; also "3 Admitted Bomb Carriers for Israel Executed by PLO," *Los Angeles Times*, July 8, 1982. Israeli intelligence agents may still favor car bombs. Thus

Lebanese Prime Minister Fouad Siniora "indirectly blamed Israel" for the May 2006 explosion that killed senior Islamic Jihad leader Abu Hamza and his brother. (See *Los Angeles Times*, May 27, 2006.)

20. Patrick Seale, *Asad: The Struggle for the Middle East*, London 1988, p. 335.
21. Ibid., p. 336.
22. Ibid., p. 331; and "Damascus Bomb Blast," *New York Times*, September 4, 1981,
23. "Syrie," *Le Monde*, December 1, 1981; "Bomb Explosion in Syria, *New York Times*, November 30, 1981; "Death Toll Reaches 90," *Washington Post*, December 1, 1981 (death toll revised upward to more than 200 on January 23, 1982).
24. "Un Attentat" and "Liban," *Le Monde*, December 16 and 17, 1981; "Bomb razes Iraqi Embassy," *Chicago Tribune*, December 16, 1981; and "Rescue Efforts End in Beirut," *New York Times*, January 12, 1982.
25. "Bomb Hurts 6 at Iraqi Embassy in Paris," *Washington Post*, August 12, 1982.
26. Fisk, *Pity the Nation*, p. 186.
27. "Syria's Chief Says U.S. Sends Arms to Insurgents," *New York Times*, March 8, 1982.
28. "France Expels Two Syrians After Bombing," *Washington Post*, April 23, 1982.
29. "Bomb in Paris Kills 1," *New York Times*, April 23, 1982.
30. "Une voiture piègée a explosé," *Le Monde*, May 25, 1982.
31. Jacques Isnard, "Des services secrets français plus offensifs?" *Le Monde*, May 26, 1982.
32. In *Le Monde*, however, Lucian George explored the even more Machiavellian – which is to say, Levantine – possibility that the Israelis and Iraqis were really behind the bombing, which they knew would be blamed on the Syrians. (May 26, 1982)
33. Victor Ostrovsky with Claire Hoy, *By Way of Deception*, New York 1990, pp. 319–20. Robert Fisk writes: "Later, the Phalange would suggest that Bashir Gemayel was killed by the Israelis because he had refused to give way to Begin's demand for a formal peace treaty with Israel. No Lebanese was likely to dismiss such an idea." (*Pity the Nation*, p. 397).
34. "Lebanon Car-Bomb Blast Kills 14," *New York Times*, January 29, 1983.
35. "18 Die as Car Bomb Hits PLO Beirut Office," *Washington Post*, February 6, 1983.

12.   THE BEIRUT HILTON

1. Quoted in Christopher Dobson and Ronald Payne, *War Without End*, London 1986, p. 36.
2. "Death Toll Hits 90 in Tyre Explosion," *Chicago Tribune*, November 14, 1982. Shin Bet initially tried to cover up the attack by claiming it was caused by an accidental explosion of cooking-gas cylinders. The Hezbollah video, released in 1995 after Israeli Forces had evacuated Qassir's home village, definitively refuted this fairytale.

3. Naim Qassem, *Hizbullah: The Story from Within*, London 2005, p. 89.
4. Three other major Hezbollah martyrs died in famous car-bomb attacks against Israeli forces: Haitham Dbouk who killed or injured 30 Israeli troops in August 1988; Abdallah Atwi who inflicted 43 casualties in October 1988; and Sheikh Asaad Berro who killed an Israeli general and wounded 20 soldiers in August 1989. (See Qassem, pp. 102–03.)
5. On the Israeli use of cluster bombs provided by the United States against Moslems in Beirut, see George W. Ball, *Error and Betrayal in Lebanon*, 1984, p. 48.
6. Sharon, of course, was the zealot mastermind of the Israeli invasion of Lebanon, who unleashed Phalangist militia to massacre hundreds of Palestinian women and children in the Sabra and Shatilla refugee camps (September 1982). Even after the Kahan Commission in 1983 recommended his dismissal, he remained in Menachem Begin's cabinet as minister without portfolio.
7. "Car Bomb Kills Figure in 1982 Lebanese Massacre," *New York Times*, January 25, 2002.
8. Edgar O'Ballance says that Sheikh Abbas Moussawi, the secretary-general of Hezbollah, claimed credit for the invention of the suicide car bomb. (*Islamic Fundamentalist Terrorism, 1979–95*, London 1997, p. 65.) Was the proto-Hezbollah, then, the actual organization that carried out the attack on the Iraqi embassy on behalf of Damascus and/or Tehran?
9. Fisk, *Pity the Nation*, p. 479.
10. "Attack Seventh against U.S. Embassies since 1975," *Los Angeles Times*, April 19, 1983.
11. Robert Baer, *See No Evil: The True Story of a Ground Soldier in the CIA's War on Terrorism*, New York 2002, p. 67.
12. Fisk, *Pity the Nation*, pp. 478–79.
13. Ibid.
14. A year later, Hezbollah completed their massacre of the CIA in Beirut when they kidnapped and executed the replacement station chief, William Buckley.
15. Bob Woodward, *Veil: The Secret Wars of the CIA, 1981–1987*, New York 1987, p. 320.
16. David Martin and John Walcott, *Best Laid Plans: The Inside Story of America's War Against Terrorism*, New York 1988, pp. 107–09.
17. Ostrovsky, *By Way of Deception*, pp. 320–22.
18. Fisk, *Pity the Nation*, p. 505.
19. "Lebanese Army Reportedly Kills 4 Moslems," *New York Times*, October 17, 1982.
20. For portraits of the enigmatic Mugniyah, see Baer, *See No Evil*, p. 99; and Timothy Naftali, *Blind Spot: The Secret History of American Counterterrorism*, New York 2005, p. 236. Hezbollah and Islamic Amal operated under the name of "Jihad al-Islami."
21. Hexogen (cyclotrimethylenetrinitramine) is also known as RDX (Research Department Explosive) after the research department at the UK's Woolwich arsenal where it was first formulated. Mixed with plasticizers it forms one of the most popular plastic explosives.

22. Department of Defense (DOD), *Report of the Commission on Beirut International Airport Terrorist Act, October 23, 1983*, Part Six, p. 4. The largest, deliberately-detonated conventional blast in history was the 6700 tons of explosives that the British Army used to destroy German fortifications on the North Sea island of Helgoland in April 1947. (See "North Sea Isle and the Day It Blew Up," *New York Times*, May 5, 1987.) The most deadly conventional explosion – 600 tons of high explosives packed into 19 mine tunnels – was detonated under German trenches at Messines Ridge in June 1917: instantly killing 10,000 German soldiers. (See Alexander Barrie, *War Underground*, New York 1961.)

23. *Report of the Commission on Beirut*, pp. 3–4 (my emphasis).

24. Martin and Walcott, *Best Laid Plans*, p. 126. See also Eric Hammel, *The Root: The Marines in Beirut, August 1982–February 1984*, San Diego 1985, p. 303.

25. Hammel, *The Root*, pp. 342–52.

26. Quoted in Thomas Friedman, *From Beirut to Jerusalem*, New York, 1989, p. 204.

27. Fisk, *Pity the Nation*, p. 512 (his emphasis). The third major contingent of the MNF, the Italians, refused to side with the Phalange, and, according to Fisk, they won much local admiration for their lack of "swagger and arrogance," as well as their instinctive sympathy with the Moslem slum-dwellers with whom they lived. As a result, they were left alone. (See pp. 451–52.)

28. Magnus Ranstorp, *Hizb'allah in Lebanon*, New York 1997, p. 116.

29. Interview with Bob Woodward, PBS Frontline: *Target America*, October 2001, posted at www.pbs.org; and Friedman, *From Beirut to Jerusalem*, p. 206.

30. Martin and Walcott, *Best Laid Plans*, p. 158.

31. "Blast Kills Driver," *New York Times*, September 21, 1984.

32. Martin and Walcott, *Best Laid Plans*, p. 159.

33. A major Hezbollah attack on the US embassy in Rome ("the same as in Beirut") was foiled by Italian police in November 1984; two years later, Egyptian secret police claimed that they had busted up a Libyan-financed cell in the course of planning a suicide truck-bombing of the American embassy in Cairo. (See "8 Seized as Suspects in Plot to Bomb U.S. Embassy," *New York Times*, November 28, 1984; and Naftali, *Blind Spot*, pp. 167–68.)

13. CAR-BOMB UNIVERSITY

1. George Crile, *Charlie Wilson's War: The Extraordinary Story of the Largest Covert Operation in History*, New York 2003, p. 141.

2. Martin and Walcott, *Best Laid Plans*, p. 156.

3. Woodward, *Veil*, p. 412.

4. Martin and Walcott, *Best Laid Plans*, pp. 159–60; and Woodward, *Veil*, p. 450.

5. Woodward interviewed on PBS Frontline: *Target America* (October 2001).

6. The Saudis have episodically financed car-bombings for their own foreign-policy objectives. In addition to Saudi-backed bombings in Beirut and Kabul, a saboteur confessed to Yemeni authorities in 1997 that he had been paid by the Saudis to detonate car bombs in Aden and Sa'ada at the time of acute

border tensions between the two countries. The Saudi interior minister denied the allegation: "This type of thing does not happen from Saudi Arabia because we do not believe in this method and we respect the security of each country." See article by Brian Whitaker at Middle East International, December 19, 1997 (www.al-bab.com/yemen/artic/mei29.htm).

7. Woodward, *Veil*, p. 455.
8. Nora Boustany, "Beirut Bomb's Legacy," special to *Washington Post*, March 6, 1988.
9. Woodward, *Veil*, p. 455; "60 Killed by Beirut Car Bomb," *Guardian* (London), March 9, 1985; and Fisk, *Pity the Nation*, p. 581.
10. Boustany, "Beirut's Bomb's Legacy;" and Qassem, *Hizbullah*, pp. 99–100.
11. See Steve Coll, *Ghost Wars: The Secret History of the CIA, Afghanistan and bin Laden*, New York 2005, pp. 99–100.
12. Ibid., p. 126.
13. On the Reagan administration's campaign to undermine a negotiated settlement, see the account by UN envoy Diego Cordovez (with Selig Harrison): *Out of Afghanistan: The Inside Story of the Soviet Withdrawal*, Oxford 1995.
14. Coll, *Ghost Wars*, p. 165.
15. Simon Reeve, *The New Jackals: Ramzi Yousef, Osama bin Laden, and the Future of Terrorism*, Boston 1999, p. 137.
16. Coll, *Ghost Wars*, pp. 128–29
17. "Bomb Kills 27 in Afghan City," *Washington Post*, October 10, 1987.
18. Afghan Rebels," "Bomb in Kabul," and "Bomb Blast in Afghan Capital," *New York Times*, April 7, 1986, February 2, 1987, and April 28, 1988; "Mujahidin bomb mars Kabul festival," *The Times* (London), April 28, 1988: and "Jitters Start in Kabul," *Washington Post*, May 3, 1988.
19. Coll, *Ghost Wars*, p. 132.
20. "Truck Bomb Kills 6," *Washington Post*, April 28, 1988.
21. "Truck Bomb in Kabul Kills 8," *Washington Post*, May 14, 1988.
22. "Truck Bomb in Kabul," *Washington Post*, July 16, 1989; and "Afghan Minister Faults U.S. ," *New York Times*, July 17, 1989.
23. Coll, *Ghost Wars*, p. 132.
24. Zachary Abuza, *Militant Islam in Southeast Asia*, London 2003, pp. 10–11.
25. Coll, *Ghost Wars*, p. 145.
26. Jason Burke, *Al Qaeda*, London 2003, p. 20.
27. On the raids into Soviet Uzbekistan, see Coll, *Ghost Wars*, pp. 104–05 and 161–62.

14.   THE SUICIDE TIGERS

1. Jonathan Spencer, "Popular Perceptions of Violence: A Provincial View," in James Manor (ed.), *Sri Lanka in Change and Crisis*, London 1984, p. 620.
2. Richard Hallion, Air Force Historical Studies Office, *Precision Weapons, Power Projection, and the Revolution in Military Affairs*, USAF Air Armament Summit, Eglin AFB, Florida 1999, pp. 4–5.

3. Edwin Hoyt, *How They Won the War in the Pacific: Nimitz and His Admirals,* New York 2000, p. 444; and Strategic Bombing Survey quoted in Richard O'Neill, *Suicide Squads,* New York 1981, p. 144.

4. It was Colin Powell, then military aid to Caspar Weinberger, who broke the news of the Marines' catastrophe to the secretary of defense. On the shaping of the doctrine, see James Mann, *Rise of the Vulcans,* New York 2004, pp. 118–120.

5. Robert Pape, *Dying to Win: The Strategic Logic of Suicide Terrorism,* New York 2005, pp. 22–23.

6. Fisk, *Pity the Nation,* pp. 610–11; and Seale, *Asad,* pp. 49 and 469.

7. C. Christine Fair, *Urban Battle Fields of South Asia,* Santa Monica 2004, p. 38.

8. Ibid., pp. 40–41.

9. Pape, *Dying to Win,* p. 142. According to Edgar O'Ballance, the first LTTE car bombing was the 1984 attack on a police station in Chevakachcheri, killing 29. (*The Cyanide War: Tamil Insurrection in Sri Lanka,* London 1989, pp. 145–56.)

10. Fair, *Urban Battle Fields of South Asia,* p. 47.

11. "Curfew Imposed to Shield Tamils from Reprisals," *New York Times,* April 22, 1987

12. The Tigers, however, were not the only ones trying to foment sectarian war. When in November 1986 the Sri Lankan Supreme Court sent a pair of bills to Parliament, establishing regional autonomy for Tamils in line with a July peace agreement, the so-called Peoples' Liberation Front, a Sinhalese group, detonated a bus bomb that killed 32 and wounded more than 75. (See 'Bomb Blast Kills 32 in Sri Lanka," *New York Times,* November 10, 1987.)

13. Alan Bullion, *India, Sri Lanka and the Tamil Crisis, 1976–94,* London 1995, p. 98.

14. O'Ballance, *The Cyanide War,* pp. 106, 128, 145–56; and Fair, *Urban Battle Fields of South Asia,* p. 35.

15. Anita Pratap, *Island of Blood,* New Delhi 2001, pp. 98–99.

16. Ibid., p. 103.

15. SOFT TARGETS

1. "Car Bomb Kills 15 at Barcelona Store," *Washington Post,* June 20, 1987.

2. Robert Clark, *Negotiating with ETA,* Reno 1990, p. 43.

3. Ibid., pp. 66–67.

4. Robert Clark, *The Basque Insurgents: ETA, 1953–1980,* Madison 1984; and Paddy Woodworth, *Dirty War, Clean Hands,* New Haven 2001.

5. Indeed, the trademark of an ETA car bomb became 65–75 kilos of GOMA-2, the nitroglycerin-based explosive manufactured by Union Espanola de Explosivos S.A and easily purloined from Spanish quarries and mines. In 1999, however, ETA pulled off one of the greatest explosive heists in history: stealing 12,000 kilos of high-grade Titadine from its manufacturer in Plevin, France – enough for several hundred car bombs.

6. Alvaro Baeza, *ETA (1959–2003)*, Madrid 2003, pp. 334 and 336.
7. Clark, *The Basque Insurgents*, pp. 110 and 113–14; and Ludger Mees, *Nationalism, Violence and Democracy: the Basque Clash of Identities*, Basingstoke 2003, pp. 62–63. Alternately, Pertur may have been assassinated by dissident, pro-revolutionary-war members of his own organization.
8. Baeza, *ETA*, pp. 199, 386, 397 and 403; "Car bomb in Spain kills American," Chicago Tribune, September 12, 1985; and "11 Killed by Bomb" and "9 Killed by a Car Bomb," *New York Times*, December 12, 1987 and May 30, 1991.
9. Cf. Baeza, *ETA*, p. 84; "15 killed in Eta bomb attack," *The Times* (London), June 20, 1987; "Car Bomb Kills 15," *Washington Post*, June 20, 1987; "Barcelona Bomb Kills 15 Civilians" and "Spain Fears Bombing," *New York Times*, June 20 and 23, 1987.
10. Woodworth, *Dirty War, Clean Hands*, pp. 147 and 154.
11. Baeza, *ETA*, pp. 448–49.

16.   *LOS COCHES BOMBA*

1. Interviewed in "In the Capital of Cocaine," *New York Times*, June 7, 1990.
2. James Kohl and John Litt, *Urban Guerrilla Warfare in Latin America*, Cambridge (MA) 1974, p. 10. The classic texts are Abraham Guillén, *Estrategia de la guerrilla urbana* (1966), and Carlos Marighella, *Minimanual of the Urban Guerrilla* (1970).
3. "8 Killed, 20 Injured by Car Bomb" and "Car Bomb Kills Boy, Woman in El Salvador," *Los Angeles Times*, September 6, 1980 and March 28, 1981; and "Bogotá Terror Intensifies" and "Car Bomb in Haiti," *Washington Post*, March 12, 1982 and January 2, 1983; "Car Bomb in Chile," *Washington Post*, November 28, 1985.
4. David Bushnell, *The Making of Modern Colombia*, Berkeley 1993, pp. 259–68; and Mark Bowden, *Killing Pablo: The Hunt for the World's Greatest Outlaw*, New York 2001, p. 4.
5. Quoted in Bowden, *Killing Pablo*, p. 55.
6. "Latin American Drug Kingpins Besiege DEA," *Washington Post*, March 4, 1985.
7. Bowden, *Killing Pablo*, pp. 54 and 74.
8. "Car Bomb in Colombia Kills 4, Wounds 37," *Washington Post*, May 31, 1989.
9. "Colombian Governor Slain in Medellín," *Washington Post*, July 5, 1989.
10. "Bombed Bogotá Newspaper May Close" and "4 Dead in Bombing of Colombian Daily," *Washington Post*, October 5 and 17, 1989.
11. "Bomb at Police Building in Bogotá," *New York Times*, December 7, 1989 (my emphasis); and "Barco Defiant After Deaths of 52 in Blast," *Washington Post*, December 8, 1989.
12. Quoted in Bowden, *Killing Pablo*, p 85.
13. "In the Capital of Cocaine, Savagery is the Habit," *New York Times*, June 7, 1990; Bowden, p. 96 (total police dead).
14. "Car Bombs in Colombia Kill 25," *Washington Post*, May 13, 1990. The Cali cartel apparently retaliated the following February with a car bomb outside a

Medellín bullring which killed 15 and injured 125. ("19 Killed in Medellín," *New York Times,* February 17, 1991.)

15. "Bomb Kills 14 at Police Station in Medellín," *New York Times,* June 29, 1990.
16. Bowden, *Killing Pablo,* p. 95.
17. Ibid., pp. 184–86 and 194–97. Special ops in Colombia drew upon the expertise of General William Garrison, who had led Phoenix assassin teams in Vietnam, and CIA station chief William Wagner who had fought the Tupamaros in Uruguay and helped plan the overthow of Allende in Chile (pp. 177–78).
18. "3 Bombs Explode in Colombia Cities," *New York Times,* February 1, 1993.
19. "A Huge Car bomb Kills 15 in Bogota," *New York Times,* April 16, 1993.
20. Bowden, *Killing Pablo,* pp. 175–76 and 193.
21. "Bomb in Medellin Kills 30," *New York Times,* June 12 1995.
22. "Bomb Kills 5" *New York Times* December 19, 1999.
23. "Blast at Social Club," *New York Times,* February 9, 2003.

17.   CITIES UNDER SIEGE

1. Quoted in *Caretas* (Lima), June 8, 1992, p. 16.
2. In the same period that the CIA was subsidizing General Thé's bombing campaign in Saigon, vehicle bombs were being studied as likely accompaniments to a Soviet nuclear attack on the United States. Thus in a 1952 civil defense exercise in Los Angeles, imaginary Communist saboteurs used car bombs to blow up local police stations and sow panic. (See "1000 Civil Defense Aides Join Atomic Disaster Test," *Los Angeles Times,* November 24, 1952.)
3. "The Truck Bomb Problem," *Three Mile Island Alert,* tmia@tmia.com. Research on truck bombs was renewed after the first attack on the World Trade Center in 1993. "Project Dipole Might," co-sponsored by the Army Corps of Engineers, the Bureau of Alcohol, Tobacco, and Firearms (ATF), and the Defense Nuclear Agency, blew up numerous trucks and vans at the White Sands Proving Ground in order to generate a computerized database and investigative protocol for high-yield vehicle bombs.
4. See the brilliant essay by Jo-Marie Burt, "Shining Path and the 'Decisive Battle' in Lima's *Barriadas,*" in Steve Stern (ed.), *Shining and Other Paths: War and Society in Peru,* Durham: (NC) 1998.
5. *Caretas,* June 8, 1992, pp. 10–15.
6. The US embassy and adjacent ambassador's residence in Lima were first bombed by the Tupac Amaru Revolutionary Movement in April 1986. Sendero bombed the complex in January 1990 (9 killed) just before a visit by President Bush, again in February 1992 (2 dead), and a third time in July 1993.
7. "Peru's Path Still Terror-Filled," *New York Times,* April 15, 1992.
8. "Ante el horror sin limite, hay salida?" *Ideele,* August 1992, pp. 3–17; and Brook Larmer, "Any Car Could Have a Bomb," *Newsweek,* August 3, 1992 p. 40.

9. Terrorist Bombs Strip Lima of Utilities and Its Urbanity," *New York Times*, August 1, 1992.

10. Ibid.

11. Gilbert King, *The Most Dangerous Man in the World: Dawood Ibrahim*, New York 2004, pp. 3–4.

12. Ibid., p. 6.

13. Suketu Mehta, *Maximum City: Bombay Lost and Found*, New York 2004, p. 137; and S. Hussain Zaidi, *Black Friday: The True Story of the Bombay Bomb Blasts*, New Delhi 2002, pp. 26, 52, and 83.

14. Ibid., pp. 2–3.

15. Ibid., pp. 9–10 and 16.

16. For Dawood's role in the Karachi underworld, see Ghulam Hasnain, "Karachi's Gang Wars," *Newsline* (Karachi), September 2001. As of fall 2006, Pakistan was still refusing India's demands to extradite Dawood, "public enemy number one."

17. "India boost security after blasts," CNN.com., August 26, 2003. For other deadly car bombings in the wake of Bloody Friday, see "A Car Bomb Explosion Kills 23 Outside a Movie Studio in India" and "3 Killed and 62 Hurt by Blasts at a Crowded Market in Delhi," *New York Times*, November 20, and December 1, 1997.

18. In response to a South African attack on ANC offices in Maseru (Lesotho) in late 1982 that killed 42 people, the liberation movement detonated an Alfa Romeo loaded with explosives in front of offices used by the South African Air Force in May 1983, killing 16 and injuring 190. Pretoria, in turn, cluster-bombed a neighborhood in Maputo (Mozambique) that housed offices and residences of the ANC. (See "16 Killed, 190 Hurt in Pretoria Blast" and "South Africa Jets Raid Mozambique," *New York Times*, May 24–25, 1983.)

19. Steven Mufson, *Fighting years: Black Resistance and the Struggle for a New South Africa*, Boston 1990, p. 198–99; and "Rebels 'Careless' in South Africa, Leader Charges," *Washington Post*, August 11, 1984.

20. "Leading Candidates," *New York Times*, April 25, 1994.

21. "Blasts Kill 12 – Black Voters Undeterred," *New York Times*, April 26, 1994. Fear of democracy also seems to have been the motive behind the small massacre caused by a car bomb in front of a Tirana (Albania) supermarket two years later. The February 27, 1996 explosion, which killed 5 people (one of them a pregnant woman) and wounded 30, was attributed to former members of the Sigurimi, Enver Hoxha's once all-powerful secret police. (See "Bomb Kills 5 in Albania," *New York Times*, February 27, 1996)

22. "14 to 20 Are Dead in Embassy Blast," *New York Times*, March 19, 1992.

23. For a Hezbollah viewpoint, see Qassem, *Hizbullah*, pp. 107–12.

24. Quoted in "Argentines Protest Bombing," *New York Times*, July 22, 1994.

25. See, for instance, the testimony of Philip Wilcox, State Department counter-terrorism coordinator to Congress in September 1995 (reprinted in Bruce Maxwell, *Terrorism: A Documentary History*, Congressional Quarterly, Washington D.C. 2003, pp. 172–76). Some accounts, however, persist in saying that

the white Renault van was left parked outside the AMIA, rather than driven into the entrance by Berro.

26. "14 to 20 Are Dead," *New York Times*, March 19, 1992.
27. "Iran Blew up Jewish Center," *New York Times*, July 22, 2002.
28. For a revisionist view, see Roberto Caballero with Gustavo Cirelli, *AMIA: La Verdad Imposible*, Buenos Aires 2005.
29. Mohammed Samraoui, *Chronique des années de sang: Algérie, comment les services secrets ont manipulé les groupes islamistes*, Paris 2003. An earlier account of government war crimes by a former Army officer Habib Souaida (*La sale guerre*) appeared in Paris in 2001. ("I've seen colleagues burn a 15-year-old child alive.") In addition, the same claims about infiltration of the GIA and government responsibility for "the worst atrocities of the war," were repeated to Robert Fisk by a senior militant of the larger Islamic Salvation Front. See *The Great War for Civilisation*, London 2005, pp. 567–68 and 584.
30. Fisk, *The Great War for Civilisation*, p. 557.
31. "A Car Bombing in Algiers," "Bomb Wounds 63," "Car Bomb Injures 13," and "15 Are Killed," *New York Times,* January 31, March 11, May 18 and December 13, 1995. Also Fisk, *The Great War for Civilisation*, p 558.
32. "17 Are Killed" and "Car Bomb Near Algiers," *New York Times*, February 12 and November 11, 1996; and Fisk, *The Great War for Civilisation,* p. 560.
33. John Burns, "Bombing's Fallout Adds to the Gloom Hanging over Sri Lanka," *New York Times*, October 17, 1997.
34. "11 Killed in Truck Bombing," *New York Times*, January 26, 1998.
35. "32 Killed in Sri Lanka," *New York Times*, March 6, 1998.

18.   FORM FOLLOWS FEAR

1. Charles Krauthammer, "War by Car Bomb," *Washington Post*, October 31, 2003.
2. Cited in Peter Robb, *Midnight in Sicily*, New York 1998, p. 380. See also Tom Behan, *See Naples and Die: The Camorra and Organized Crime*, London 2002.
3. David Lane, *Berlusconi's Shadow*, London 2004, p. 18.
4. "Mafia Link to Rome Car Bombing," *New York Times,* May 16, 1993.
5. "Bomb outside Uffizi," "Italians Seeking to Solve Bombing Riddle," "For Florence's Glories, Bomb Repairs Go On," and "24 Guilty in Bombings," *New York Times*, May 28, July 29, and August 7, 1993, and June 7, 1988.
6. "Bomb outside Uffizi," *New York Times*, May 28, 1993.
7. Michael Kimmelman, "Ruined Works Stand as Symbols of Vulnerability," *New York Times,* May 28, 1993.
8. Quoted in "For Florence's Glories," *New York Times*, August 7, 1993.
9. Lane, *Berlusconi's Shadow*, p. 20.
10. "Bomb Attacks Kill 5 in Milan," *New York Times*, July 28, 1993. For a capsule history of the Pavilion of Contemporary Art, see also Giorgio Verzotti, "Party Lines: Art Institutions in Milan," *ArtForum*, Summer 1997.
11. Lane, *Berlusconi's Shadow*, p. 22.

12. Tim Pat Coogan, *The IRA*, London 1993, p. 587.
13. Moloney, *A Secret History of the IRA*, p. 411.
14. Coogan, *The IRA*, p. 587. "I visited the scene myself some weeks later and found that the TV and newspaper pictures had not conveyed a sense of the full extent of the devastation."
15. Timothy Hillier, "Bomb Attacks in City Centers," September 1994, www.e-mergency.com/carbomb.htm.
16. Jon Coaffee, *Terrorism, Risk and the City: The Making of a Contemporary Urban Landscape*, Aldershot 2003, p. 131.
17. Moloney, *A Secret History of the IRA*, p. 441.
18. "Is the Economy Bombproof?" *Sunday Times*, July 27, 2005.
19. Coaffee, *Terrorism, Risk and the City*, p. 87.
20. BBC, April 23, 1993.
21. Coaffee, *Terrorism, Risk and the City*, p. 138. The government ultimately agreed to become insurer of last resort against terrorist attacks.
22. "Walled City Mooted," *The Times*, April 27, 1993.
23. Jon Coaffee, "Rings of Steel, Rings of Concrete and Rings of Confidence," *International Journal of Urban and Regional Research* 28:1 (March 2004), pp. 203–05.
24. Mark Townsend and Paul Harris, "Security Role for Traffic Cameras," *Observer*, February 9, 2003.
25. Coaffee, "Rings of Steel," p. 209.

19. KILLING BUSH, BOMBING OKLAHOMA

1. Lou Michel and Dan Herbeck, *American Terrorist: Timothy McVeigh and the Oklahoma City Bombing*, New York 2001, p. 230.
2. "Parade Unfurls Symbols of Patriotism in the Capital," *New York Times*, June 9, 1991. Patriotic euphoria, however, did not reach 1940s levels. The administration had predicted a crowd of 1.4 million, but, according to the National Park Service, only 200,000 actually lined the streets.
3. Coll, *Ghost Wars*, p. 249.
4. Reeve, *The New Jackals*, p. 138.
5. O'Ballance, *Islamic Fundamentalist Terrorism*, p. 31 (on CIA connection).
6. Coll, *Ghost Wars*, pp 249–50. Reeve believes that Yousef originally hoped to make a radiological 'dirty bomb' but was unable to obtain the necessary isotopes or radioactive waste (*The New Jackals*, pp. 146–47).
7. Peter Garam, *The 1993 World Trade Center Bombing*, London 2001, p. 14. The Lebanese-American Garam was the Port Authority detective in charge of anti-terrorist intelligence.
8. Lance, *1000 Years for Revenge*, p. 116.
9. Ibid., p. 116.
10. Reeve, *The New Jackals*, pp. 15 and 25. He forgets the Texas City explosion in 1947 with its 5000 injured.
11. "Sheik and Followers Are Found Guilty," *New York Times*, October 2, 1995.

12. Quoted in "Egyptian Paper Says It Misquoted Mubarak," *New York Times*, May 31, 1993. The subsequent retraction of the interview by the semi-official newspaper *Al Gomhuriya* has little credibility and was obviously a response to complaints from Washington.
13. Burke, *Al-Qaeda*, p. 108.
14. Reeve, *The New Jackals*, pp. 64–65.
15. Naftali, *Blind Spot*, pp. 240–41; and Coll, *Ghost Wars*, pp. 274–75.
16. President Clinton, "Responds to Attack by Iraqi Government," Department of State *Dispatch*, 4:27 (July 5, 1993).
17. "U.S. Strikes Iraq for Plot to Kill Bush," *Washington Post*, June 27, 1993.
18. Seymour Hersh, "A Case Not Closed," *The New Yorker*, November 1, 1993. Whatever the ultimate truth about the Kuwait City plot, car bombs (exploded alongside processions or in public spaces) were becoming increasingly popular instruments of assassination: Eduard Shevardnadze, the President of Georgia, and Kiro Gligorov, the President of Macedonia, were both injured in separate car-bombings in 1995.
19. See Michel and Herbeck, *American Terrorist*, pp. 38–39, 59–60n and 329–30. McVeigh was also obsessed with *Star Wars* and compared himself to Luke Skywalker. "Think about the people [in the federal building] as if they were storm troopers in Star Wars," McVeigh told two reporters after his arrest. "They may be individually innocent, but they are guilty because they work for the Evil Empire" (p. 166).
20. "Uncle Fester," *Home Workshop Explosives*, Green Bay 2002, p. 135.
21. Spencer Hsu and Sari Horwitz, "Impervious Shield Elusive Against Drive-By Terrorists," *Washington Post*, August 8, 2004; "The Truck Bomb Problem," Three Mile Island Alert (tmia@tmia.com).
22. "U.S. Charges 12 in Arizona Plot" and "Official Says Militia Weighed Attacking Familes of Agents," *New York Times*, July 2 and 6, 1996. In October 1995, a militia group had sabotaged a railroad trestle southwest of Phoenix, causing a train wreck that killed a sleeping-car attendant and injured 78 passengers.
23. Burke, *Al-Qaeda*, pp. 154–55. Also "Bomb in Saudi Arabia" and "Anti-US Bomb Baffles," *New York Times*, November 16, 1995 and January 11, 1996. A week after the Riyadh bombing, a suicide truck bomb destroyed the Egyptian embassy in Islamabad.
24. "Bomb in Saudi Arabia," *New York Times*, November 16, 1995.
25. "Book by Clinton Aides Says Saudi Diplomat Misled F.B.I," *New York Times*, October 1, 2002.
26. James Risen, *State of War: The Secret History of the CIA and the Bush Administration*, New York 2006, pp. 213–15.
27. Reeve, *The New Jackals*, p. 167.
28. Wright, *The Looming Tower*, p. 251.
29. Ibid., p. 271.
30. "Security Flaws Left Embassy in Nairobi Open to Attack," *New York Times*, September 9, 1998.
31. *Anatomy of a Terrorist Attack*, Matthew Ridgway Center, University of Pittsburg, working paper nos 2005–17, pp. 12, 15, 20, 60–61n and 68–70.

Did Mossad again, as alleged in Beirut in 1983, deliberately fail to accurately share intelligence with Washington? "[A] United States informant in Kenya contacted Israel's Mossad intelligence service two weeks before August 7, 1998, warning the American government that the Nairobi embassy was to be targeted for a bombing. Upon advice from Israeli intelligence sources, however, the informant was discredited" (p. 20).

32. Burke, *Al-Qaeda*, p. 159.
33. "1800 Injured Overwhelming Kenya Hospital," *New York Times*, August 9, 1998.
34. Reeve, *The New Jackals*, p. 200.
35. Coll, *Ghost Wars*, p. 412.
36. Ridgway Center, *Anatomy of a Terrorist Attack*, p. 29.
37. Coll, *Ghost Wars*, p. 477
38. See Burke, *Al-Qaeda*, chapter 13, pp. 198–212.
39. Ibid., pp. 198–99.
40. Coll, *Ghost Wars*, p. 407.

20.   PLANET *JIHAD*

1. Burke, *Al-Qaeda*, p. 274.
2. "Blast Kills Leader of Separatists in Chechnya," *Washington Post*, July 11, 2006.
3. Paul Murphy, *The Wolves of Islam: Russia and the Faces of Chechen Terror*, Washington D.C., 2006, p 16.
4. "Chechens Flee Russian Bombs by Thousands" and "Russia Uses a Sledgehammer", *New York Times*, September 27, and December 8, 1999.
5. The Russian billionaire, Boris Berezovksy, claimed in 2002 that the Federal Security Service (the former KGB) had staged these atrocities in order to put its former director, Vladimir Putin, into the presidency and manufacture public support for a new invasion of Chechnya. Those who champion Berezovksy's charges – perhaps out of justifiable suspicion of Putin, who has truly been a butcher in Chechnya – often forget that he was Boris Yeltsin's "shadow president" and a completely sinister figure in his own right. In at least the case of the Dagestan car-bombing (one of Berezovsky's examples), moreover, Chechen guilt was convincingly established in the 2001 trial of the 6 perpetrators.
6. John Sweeney, "Revealed: Russia's worst war crime ," *Guardian*, March 5, 2000.
7. Murphy, *The Wolves of Islam*, p. 205; and "Chechnya Bomb Toll Rises Past 80," *New York Times*, December 31, 2002.
8. Quoted in Murphy, *The Wolves of Islam*, p. 198.
9. Ibid., p 208 and chronology, pp. 264–67.
10. For an Indian view of the crisis, see Lt. Gen. V.K. Sood Pravin Sawhney, *Operation Parakgram: The War Unfinished*, New Delhi 2003.
11. Steve Coll, "The Stand-Off," *The New Yorker*, February 13 and 20, 2006, pp. 126–39.

12. David Martin-Jones, "Back with a Vengeance: The Resilience of Jemaah Islamiah," *AIJAC Review*, October 2004, p. 3.
13. Zachary Abuza, *Militant Islam in Southeast Asia*, London 2003, pp. 153–54.
14. Quoted in ibid., p. 164.
15. Dewi Anggraeni, *Who Did This to Our Bali?*, Briar Hill (Australia) 2003, pp. 27–29 and 168–69.
16. "Survivors of Indonesia Blast Are Left Stunned," *New York Times*, October 14, 2002.
17. Abuza, *Militant Islam in Southeast Asia*, p. 3.
18. See "Death toll hits 15 in Jakarta stock exchange bomb," CNN.com, September 14, 2000.
19. See Gary LaMoshi, "Terrorism links in Indonesia point to military," *Asia Times* (www.atimes.com), 2004.
20. "Indonesia Bombing Kills at Least 10" and "Indonesia Identifies Hotel Bomber," *New York Times*, August 6 and 9, 2003.
21. "Terror Group Linked to Hotel Blast," CBS News, August 6, 2003.
22. "Al-Qa'eda suicide bomb kills 14," *Daily Telegraph*, 9 May 2002.
23. "Car Bomb Explodes Outside U.S. Office," *New York Times*, June 15, 2002.
24. "Car bomb hits Karachi restaurant," BBC News, November 16, 2005; and "Pakistan blasts kill U.S. diplomat," CNN.com., March 2, 2006.
25. "Plusieurs touristes tués à la synagogue de la Ghriba," *Le Monde*, April 13, 2002.
26. "14 Die as Bomb-Filled SUV Rams Israeli Bus," *New York Times*, October 22, 2002. A giant car ANFO bomb, comparable to the World Trade Center device of 1993 and capable of killing hundreds, was intercepted by Israeli police in September. ("Israel Captures and Destroys Huge Car Bomb," *New York Times*, September 6, 2002.)
27. "Kenyans Hunting Clues to Bombing," *New York Times*, November 30, 2002.
28. "20 in Istanbul Die in Bombings at Synagogues," "Blasts Hit 2 British Sites," and "Turkish Town's Despair Breeds Terrorists," *New York Times*, November 18, 21 and 27, 2003.
29. See my "The Urbanization of Empire: Megacities and the Laws of Chaos," *Social Text* 81 (Winter 2004).
30. "Out of Desert Poverty, a Caldron of Rage in the Sinai," *New York Times*, May 7, 2006; and "Militants emerge in Egypt bombings: resentments seen in Bedouin region," *Boston Globe*, July 27, 2005.
31. Serene Assir, "Shock in Sharm," *Al-Ahram Weekly*, July 23, 2005.

21. THE KING OF IRAQ

1. Quoted in Anthony Shadid, *Night Draws Near*, New York 2005, p. 339.
2. James Dunnigan, "Why the Car Bomb Is King in Iraq," June 26, 2005, www.strategypage.com.
3. My calculation based on the thousands of incidents logged at www.Iraqbodycount.org. This database distinguishes between "car bomb" and "suicide

car bomb." I have also counted the few instances of bicycle and motorcycle bombs.

4. "Iraq Says Six Were Killed by Car Bomb in Baghdad," *Washington Post*, December 17, 1982.

5. "Kuwaitis Still Fighting Invaders" and "Freed Shiite Terrorists Said to Fight Iraqis," *Washington Post*, August 20 and September 24, 1990.

6. "Car Bomb Kills at least 54 in Kurdish Iraq," *New York Times*, February 28, 1995.

7. Joel Brinkley, "Ex-CIA Aides Say Iraq Leader Helped Agency in 90's Attacks," *New York Times*, June 9, 2004.

8. Ibid. Allawi was the American choice for interim Iraqi prime minister after the departure of Paul Bremer in summer 2004. "Not long after his appointment," according to Iraqis interviewed by an Australian journalist, ". . . Dr. Allawi had executed prisoners in cold blood in the Al Amiriya security center just days before Washington handed control of the country to his interim govern-ment." *Sidney Morning Herald* paraphrased in Zaki Chehab, *Inside the Resistance*, New York 2005, p. 166.

9. Thomas Ricks, *Fiasco: The American Military Adventure in Iraq*, New York 2006, p. 124.

10. Relying only upon official press releases and published accounts, the Iraq Body Count Project tabulated a minimum of 48,829 and a maximum of 54,191 dead as of 28 November 2006. In an article published in the prestigious British medical journal *Lancet* in fall 2006, however, four public-health experts used survey data to estimate approximately 650,000 "excess" deaths since the American invasion – a staggering *2.5 per cent* of the Iraqi population. (G. Burnham et al., *Lancet* [doi:10.1016/S0140-6736(06)69491-9], 2006.).

11. Ricks, *Fiasco,* p. 215.

12. "11 Die in Baghdad," *New York Times*, August 8, 2003.

13. Lawrence Wright, "The Terrorist," *The New Yorker*, June 19, 2006, p. 30.

14. Mary Anne Weaver, "Inventing Al-Zarqawi," *The Atlantic Monthly*, July/ August 2006, p. 98.

15. George Packer, *The Assassins' Gate*, New York 2005, p. 214.

16. "Huge Suicide Blast," *New York Times*, August 20, 2003.

17. Loretta Napoleoni, *Insurgent Iraq*, New York 2005, p. 157; and Anthony Shadid, *Night Draws Near: Iraq's People in the Shadow of America's War*, New York 2005, pp. 255–57.

18. "Death and Hesitation," *New York Times*, August 30, 2003.

19. Milt Bearden, "Iraqi Insurgents," *New York Times*, November 9, 2003.

20. Scott Johnson, "Lost in the Green Zone," *Newsweek*, September 20, 2005. See also William Langewiesche, "Welcome to the Green Zone," *The Atlantic Monthly*, November 2004.

21. Johnson, "Lost in the Green Zone."

22. "Iraq suicide bomb blasts kill 120," BBC News, January 5, 2006.

23. Napoleoni, *Insurgent Iraq,* p. 160.

24. "Cluster bombs liberate Iraqi children," *Catholic New Times*, April 20, 2003.

25. Jeffrey Arnold et al., "Mass-Casualty, Terrorist Bombings" (Part One), *Prehospital and Disaster Medicine,* 18:3 (2003), pp. 220–34.
26. "Unlikely Candidate for Car Bomber," *Los Angeles Times,* April 15, 2006. "Albana' in *Times*" story.
27. "Iraqi Town Left Devastated by Attack," *Los Angeles Times,* July 18, 2005; and Neil MacDonald, "Iraq; the scourge of the bombers," *Middle East International,* July 21, 2005.
28. "Children die in Baghdad car bomb," *BBC News,* July 13, 2005.
29. "As Death Stalks Iraq, Middle-Class Exodus Begins," *New York Times,* May 19, 2006.
30. "Car Bombs, Suicide Attacks Taking Toll," *Los Angeles Times,* May 12, 2005.
31. "U.S. car theft rings probed for ties to Iraq bombings," *Boston Globe,* October 2, 2005.
32. "Al-Zawahiri praises insurgents in video," CNN.com, April 29, 2006.
33. Napoleoni, *Insurgent Iraq,* pp. 84–85.
34. Wright, "The Terrorist," p. 31. There is heated debate whether al-Zarqawi really masterminded most of the terror attributed to foreign jihadists, or whether his role was grossly inflated to serve the American need for a demonic figure to incarnate the insurgency.
35. According to Iraqi National Security Adviser Mowaffak al-Rubaie, a captured Tunisian *jihadi* revealed that the attack had been planned by al-Badri. "The sole reason behind his action," said al-Rubaie, "was to drive a wedge between the Shiites and Sunnis and to ignite and trigger a sectarian war in this country." See "Tunisian held in Samarra mosque bombing," CNN.com, June 28, 2006; also the interview with reporter Tom Lassiter, embedded in Samarra with the 101st Airborne at www.democracynow.org (February 24, 2006).
36. 2003–2005 figures (using data from Iraq Body Count Project) from BBC News, July 19, 2005; and 2006 statistics compiled by UN Assistance Mission for Iraq.
37. "Allawi: this is the start of civil war," *Sunday Times* (London), July 10, 2006; and "Sectarian violence out of control in Iraq," AP, July 18, 2006.
38. "Iraqi Death Toll Exceeds 100 Per Day," *New York Times,* July 19, 2006.
39. "32 Killed in Baghdad Blasts," *Los Angeles Times,* July 28, 2006.
40. "Seeking safety, Iraqis turn to militias," *Christian Science Monitor,* July 24, 2006.

22. THE GATES OF HELL

1. Daniel Bensaid, *Marx for Our Times,* London 2002, p. 295.
2. "Base Offers Course on Insurgents' Bombs," *Los Angeles Times,* June 16, 2005.
3. "Pentagon Widens Program to Foil Bombings in Iraq," *New York Times,* February 6, 2006; and chart in "A Platoon's Mission: Seeking and Destroying Explosives in Disguise," *New York Times,* July 12, 2006.
4. "Pentagon Widens Program," *New York Times,* February 6, 2006.
5. "U.S. spending billions to stop Iraq IEDs," AP, March 13, 2006.

6. Marshall Billingslea, "Combating terrorism through technology," *NATO Review*, Autumn 2004 (www.nato.int/docu/review/2004/issue).
7. "Impervious Shield Elusive Against Drive-By Terrorists," *Washington Post*, August 8, 2004.
8. For some examples of anti-car-bomb technology emerging from the private sector, see the websites of HiEnergy Technologies Inc. and MYY Ltd., Israel. Also see Frank Vizard, "The Boom in Bomb Detection," Scientific.American.com (May 3, 2004); and Abolhassan Astaneh-Asi, Casey Heydari, and Qiuhong Zhao, "Analysis of Car-Bomb Effects on Buildings Using MSC-Dytran Software and Protective Measures," Proceedings of the MSC Software Virtual Product Development Conference, Dearborn (MI), October 13–15, 2003.
9. Samantha Levine, "The Car Bomb Conundrum," *U.S. News and World Report*, August 16, 2004.
10. Gary Stix, "Better than a Dog," *Scientific American*, p. 74. See also National Research Council, *Existing and Potential Standoff Explosives Detection Techniques*, Washington D.C. 2004.
11. Vizard, "The Boom in Bomb Detection".
12. Timothy Hiller, "Bomb Attacks in City Centers," September 1994, www.e-mergency.com/carbomb.htm.
13. "Battle for Baghdad," and "Baghdad's Chaos Undercuts Tack Pursued by U.S.," *New York Times*, July 26 and August 6, 2006.
14. "Security Ring for Baghdad Underway," *Washington Post*, September 16, 2006.
15. "Iraqis Planning Network of Trenches Around Baghdad," *New York Times*, September 16, 2006.
16. "Shiites torch Sunni people, mosques, houses," CNN, November 25, 2006.
17. Martin Amis, "The Age of Horrorism," *Observer*, September 10, 2006.
18. Rhiannon Talbot, *The Devil Within*, Working Paper 2001/07, Newcastle Law School, November 2001, p. 1.
19. Coogan, *The IRA*, p. 675.
20. "Delta militants' car bomb kills two," Reuters, April 20, 2006; "5 Men Are Arrested in Attack on Saudi Oil Plant,"*New York Times*, April 19, 2006; and "Truck Bombs Part of Canada Plot," CNN.com June 8, 2006.
21. Former Afghan president Sibghatullah Mujaddedi, leader of the upper house of parliament, accused the Pakistani ISI of engineering the suicide car-bombing in Kabul on March 12, 2006 that left him with burn injuries and killed 2 civilians. (See "Kabul Bombing Could Set Back Talks with Taliban," *Washington Post,* March 13, 2006.)

Index